Surviving Indonesia's Gulag

A Western woman tells her story

Carmel Budiardjo

CASSELL

Cassell
Wellington House
125 Strand
London WC2R 0BB

215 Park Avenue South
New York
NY 10003

First published 1996

British Library Cataloguing-in-Publication Data
A catalogue record for this book is available from the British Library.

ISBN   0-304-33561-4 (hardback)
       0-304-33562-2 (paperback)

Printed and bound in Great Britain by Biddles Ltd, Guildford and King's Lynn

Contents

Foreword

In the six months following the coup attempt of 1 October 1965, perhaps three-quarters of a million people were slaughtered in an anti-communist bloodbath, and hundreds of thousands more were arrested and thrown into prison because of their suspected connection with the Communist Party of Indonesia (PKI). The Americans aided and abetted the massacre, and Britain seems to have known about the plans to overthrow the Sukarno regime. The cold war made the West turn a blind eye to the atrocities committed by many right-wing dictators against their left-wing opponents, but the complicity of the 'free world' in the Indonesian purge of 1965 and its aftermath may have been on a different level. Probably we shall never know for certain.

Carmel Budiardjo may have been the only British citizen to have suffered imprisonment without trial, among the tens of thousands arbitrarily detained after the coup, and this partly accounts for the collective amnesia we display over the events she describes. But also, under Sukarno, Indonesia was seen as a threat to regional peace, with its policy of *konfrontasi* against Malaysia, and with Australian fears of an invasion from the north. The overthrow of the Sukarno regime, and the ruthless extermination of communists, were seen as a necessary price to pay for the installation of a dictator who would be more friendly to the West. Thirty years later, we may still find it uncomfortable to be reminded of what that meant to the victims of the colossal purge that followed the massacre.

The record of physical and psychological brutality in the prisons of Indonesia is not well documented. Mrs Budiardjo's vivid and intensely personal account is therefore all the more valuable, not only as a piece of history, but also for its testimony about the nature of the rulers of present day Indonesia. For it was Suharto, the dictator of the last 30 years, who organized and implemented the violent changes of 1965. The blood of those victims lies on his hands, even if today he is courted as a valuable purchaser of British military aircraft, as a large recipient of British aid, and as the leader of a country which offers enticing prospects to British oil companies and engineering contractors.

Carmel Budiardjo's dreadful experience in the Indonesian gulag did not quell her indomitable spirit. In the Postscript she mentions briefly that after her release and her return to Britain, she established TAPOL, the Indonesian human rights organization, which became her life work. She campaigns incessantly and effectively on behalf of the people of East Timr, of Aceh and of West Papua, and for the rights of all the subjects of the Javanese empire to freedom of expression and association. The quality of her research and the keen and analytical mind she applies to the political background, have made her respected and honoured throughout the world. The Parliamentary Human Rights Group has relied on her for information and advice, and the results can be seen in a steady increase in the number of references to Indonesia in the Hansards of both Houses.

Three people who played an important part in the campaign for Carmel Budiardjo's release were Stefanie Grant, Sarah Leigh, and Anthony Lester. Like Carmel herself, they are all still heavily involved in human rights work, and their example demonstrates that we can influence even the most impervious dictatorships. It is worth trying, and the brave resistance of one woman to an ordeal challenges us all to continue.

LORD AVEBURY,
Chairman, Parliamentary Human Rights Group

Introduction

Nearly 27 years have elapsed since the story I relate in this book began, and it is now 30 years since General Suharto, who still rules over Indonesia, seized power in a brutal and bloody coup. Why has it taken me so long and why are there so few books that chronicle those days of massacres and mass imprisonment?

I started writing these memoirs not long after I returned to London in November 1971 from Indonesia, where I had just spent more than three years in detention without trial. As I became more involved in a campaign to defend human rights in Indonesia, the memoirs got pushed aside, almost forgotten, until my grand-daughter Claire came across a pile of letters I had written to her mother from Jakarta. She wanted to know if I had written anything else, so I dug out the chapters and gave them to her to read. It seemed to me at the time that I had more important things to do, but she was so keen that she urged me to complete them and get them published. It was her enthusiasm that led me to reread what I had written and realize that it was a story worth publishing. As I passed them round to others in the family and to friends, the idea of publishing them became an obsession.

In Indonesia itself, the only memoirs published by a former Indonesian political prisoner are *Nyanyian Sunyi Seorang Bisu*, 'The Silent Song of a Mute', by the country's foremost writer and novelist, Pramoedya Ananta Toer, and an autobiography by Oei Tju Tat. Pramoedya spent fourteen years in prison without trial, ten of them at the Buru Island forced labour camp. Oei Tju Tat, a minister in President Sukarno's last cabinet, was arrested after that cabinet fell in March 1966 and was later sentenced to thirteen years.

A few others have produced articles or short stories about their experiences, but most have opted to keep their memories to themselves. Some literary works have been published dealing with the lives of children who were left alone at home when their parents were swept up by the mass arrests that followed General Suharto's seizure of power in October 1965. One or two former prisoners have told their stories in interviews for publication in academic journals, but these have usually appeared under an assumed name. To my knowledge, apart from some chapters written by another former Buru prisoner, S. Hersri, and published by Index on Censorship, none of the former prisoners now living abroad has published anything.

Nor is there much written about the massacres instigated by the army that left up to a million people dead in the wake of General Suharto's seizure of power. The history of the events that plunged Indonesia into a deep political and social crisis in the early years of Suharto's New Order is in danger of being lost as the men and women who lived through those dark days begin to die of old age.

One reason for the reluctance to write or even speak about these experiences is fear. With Suharto still in power, anyone suspected of being a communist, an 'ex-PKI', has to endure discrimination in a variety of forms. Nearly 1½ million people have had the initials 'ET' for 'ex-tapol' (a contraction of *tahanan politik* or political prisoner) stamped on their identity cards for years, marking them out for special treatment. They are excluded from many kinds of employment which might enable them to 'exert an influence' on public opinion. Many are required to report regularly to the local military command and need special permission when they want to travel or move elsewhere. Occasionally, they are summoned to attend indoctrination courses. Tens of thousands of ex-tapols are prohibited from voting in general elections; all are prohibited from standing for election or playing an active role in any of the parties and organizations permitted to exist by the regime.

In 1986, the regime introduced a new set of regulations requiring people to produce evidence that they come from a 'clean environment', meaning that there are no ex-PKI among their siblings, parents, grandparents and in-laws. This so-called *litsus* test is used when people apply for jobs in designated sectors and even when school-leavers wish to enrol to enter state universities. The fear of being publicly identified as a former communist is still very much a part of life in Indonesia 30 years after Suharto installed his New Order.

Still worse are the traumatic experiences of many millions of people during the massacres of 1965/66. These have not yet been – perhaps never will be – expunged from people's memories. No one today takes seriously the regime's frequent warnings that the country faces the threat of a 'communist comeback'. Yet deep down in the national psyche, especially in Central and East Java and in Bali – the most heavily populated regions of the country – where the massacres left no families unscathed, is the fear of more violence, should anyone disturb the apparent calm made possible by pretending to forget.

The atmosphere that engulfed the country in those frightening days is still vivid in my memory. Even in Jakarta, the capital, where I lived at the time, the dramatic change was painfully obvious, although there were no massacres to speak of in the city. Overnight we became social outcasts as Jakarta was transformed into a city under armed occupation. It seemed that almost everyone I knew was being arrested. Friends had to flee their homes and many came to us for refuge; it was hardly a safe house as Suharto lived round the corner. At work, no one wanted to speak to me, and mobs of youths roamed the streets attacking the homes of communist suspects.

I well remember a PKI friend who came to see me in November 1965. As the arrests gathered pace in Jakarta, he returned home to his native village in Central Java hoping to escape arrest and seek refuge. Little did he know that the killings were in full swing there. He was too shocked to tell me what he saw except to shake his head and mumble: 'It's terrible, quite terrible. I had no idea.' He had come seeking refuge but there was nothing I could do to help. Within weeks, he was arrested by the army and spent the next fourteen years in jail. If such things are still so vivid for me, how much more they must be for those who lived through the massacres, after seeing loved ones and neighbours cut to pieces; it's hardly surprising that they prefer to concentrate on other things.

Let me add that my personal experiences were nothing as compared to the experiences of hundreds of thousands who remain voiceless. It is not fear alone that prevents them from speaking, but the pain of the memories they have to live with.

The vast majority of tapols rounded up in the late 1960s have now been released, but some still remain in prison, serving sentences passed down in grossly unfair trials. Most are serving life, but there are five men who were sentenced to death and have been on death row for more than twenty years. During the 1980s, many were executed regardless of appeals from overseas and human rights activists at home for the death sentences to be commuted. It mattered little to Suharto, the only man who could have saved their lives, that he was sending these men to their deaths after they had already served up to twenty years in prison.

But these are not the only victims of political repression in Suharto's Indonesia. The largest group of tapols today are from liberation struggles. They include scores of East Timorese, held for opposing Indonesia's illegal annexation of their country; much farther to the east, there are scores of West Papuans being held who also want to rid their country of Indonesian military occupation, while in the far north-west, on the tip of Sumatra, scores of Acehnese are also languishing in prisons for having raised the banner of independence.

Along with these are dozens of Muslim political prisoners who were rounded up and tried after army clampdowns on 'aberrant' Muslim sects. The Tanjung Priok massacre in September 1984 and the Lampung massacre three years later created new generations of political prisoners. They are what the regime describes as the 'extreme right' prisoners, by contrast with the communists who are the 'extreme left'. For this regime, people in the middle are also extremists if they happen to be liberals or advocates of human rights.

Pro-democracy activism has produced its own generation of political prisoners. Most of these have been found guilty of defaming the president or convicted under the so-called 'hate-spreading' articles of the Criminal Code. Students who defend the rights of farmers against unlawful land expropriation, and workers who defend the right to strike and the right to set up their own trade unions, have spent years behind bars. The latest addition to the many hundreds of tapols is a group of journalists who published alternative journals without government licence, after the Government withdrew the licences of the country's three most prestigious weeklies in June 1994.

When I arrived back in London in November 1971, little did I realize then that my decision to start campaigning against human rights violations in Indonesia would draw me into such a complex mix of problems. When I, along with friends and members of my family, first set up TAPOL in 1973 as a campaigning group in Britain, the focus was on pressing for the release of the PKI tapols, but there was an inevitable logic to the process. Persecuting communists was only the start. The repressive apparatus and laws used to crush the main enemy were soon turned against every other perceived political threat to the regime.

These memoirs of the years I spent in prison focus on that early wave of repression, but they are intended to show the reader how the Suharto regime treats all those whom it regards as a danger to 'national stability'. My own experiences sensitized me to the sufferings inflicted on so many others who, in support of their own causes, have bravely challenged the policies of the Suharto dictatorship.

On a more personal note, I see myself as someone who became a human rights activist because of my own bitter experiences at the hands of a harshly repressive regime. During the Sukarno era there were human rights abuses a-plenty, though not on anything like the scale of the regime that followed. I regret to say that in those days, I looked the other way. The enormity of what happened after 1965 confronted me with something that I could not ignore. My release and enforced return to London gave me the opportunity to take up the cudgels for the victims I had left behind. Since then, human rights activism has become the focus of my life. Although I became a victim because of my associations with the Indonesian Communist Party, I have never confined my work to supporting victims on the left. I firmly believe that to be truly democratic any society must recognize and protect basic individual and collective rights for all, regardless of gender, belief, political conviction or social standing.

During my years in detention, I developed a deep and lasting hatred for the Indonesian army and all its works. Being in army detention for three years brought me face to face with soldiers of all types; it is an experience that I shall never forget. To this day, I still cringe when I see photos in the Indonesian press of army officers and men. Having seen for myself the depths of their brutality, their capacity to abuse the law and regulations with impunity and use the state machinery to their own advantage, it has never been difficult for me to comprehend the lengths to which these uniformed monsters will go to destroy, maim or torture human beings at will for the achievement of their political aims. It has never been difficult for me to believe the horrific reports I sometimes read about what soldiers have perpetrated in East Timor, in Aceh or in West Papua, or their crimes against so many Indonesians.

Most of the chapters in this book describe my own experience of detention along with the rather unusual story of my release. There are some autobiographical snippets here and there and I have devoted a lot of space to the stories of many of the people whom I met during the three years which I spent in four very different places of detention in Jakarta. I have tried at the same time to provide the reader with an explanation of the political circumstances that led to this tragedy. I felt that the memoirs would not be complete without an account of the Untung coup attempt and the Suharto coup of October 1965. This comes in Chapter 6. My account is necessarily brief but I hope that it will give the reader a short introduction to an event of historic importance which is so sorely neglected in the literature about Indonesia currently available in the bookshops.

I am especially grateful to friends who gave me invaluable suggestions while I was preparing the manuscript: Maggie Helvig, Shirley Shackleton, Liem Soei Liong and Tom Soper.

I dedicate this book to the hundreds of tapols I met, men as well as women, who befriended me and who hoped that, if I ever had a chance to get out of the country, I would be their voice in a world where Indonesia is little known and the victims of Suharto's New Order are largely ignored.

LONDON, May 1995

CHAPTER 1

Arrest

It was late afternoon when they came to arrest me. I was giving an English lesson to two young women. This was how I had earned a living for three years after I lost my job at the Foreign Ministry in the crack-down on the left when General Suharto took control of the armed forces in October 1965.

A man in civilian clothes walked into the front room and was already seated when I entered. He sat with his legs sprawled out.

'Are you Ibu Carmel?' he asked.

'Yes, what do you want?'

It was odd for him to address me in this familiar way though we had never met before.

'You'll have to come along and answer a few questions', he said, as I sat down. 'It won't take long.'

Now that we were both seated, I saw another man get down from the jeep that was parked in the drive. He had been watching through the window, waiting to make his presence felt once he could be sure I was at home. Unlike his colleague, he was in uniform, a corporal, heavily armed. He walked through the front door into the room where we were sitting and sat down without saying a word. He stared at me as he held his weapon upright on his knee.

'Where do you want to take me?' I asked. 'Have you a warrant, coming in like this?'

The first man was getting impatient. 'Stop wasting time. Please hurry up.'

For three years, I had realized that something like this could happen. Many of my friends were in detention and Bud, my husband, had been arrested, then released, twice, and had spent altogether two years inside.

'Should I bring anything with me? A toothbrush? A change of clothes?'

The Lieutenant shrugged his shoulders: 'If you like, but it probably won't take long.' Uncertain whether he was trying to reassure me, I decided to take nothing, as if to show that I thought he was telling the truth.

As we were talking, Bud entered the room and stood, shoulders slightly bent, watching the scene. Tari, my daughter, and Anto, my son, were there too, watching from behind a low wall that separated the front room from our dining and living rooms behind. Tari, at seventeen, knew very well what was going on. In the early days of this nightmare she had been taken into custody for nearly 24 hours and had watched her friends being tortured by soldiers. Anto was five years younger but he knew what had happened to his Dad though he may not have thought that his Mum could be arrested as well.

Bud looked strained. It would have been more sensible for him not to have shown himself as the soldiers had only asked for me and must have had no idea that he was at home.

Since his second release, I had seen him get tense whenever he came into contact with anyone from the army. Now he was very tense, but very worried about me. He spoke to me in a whisper.

'Perhaps I should come with you, to see where they take you.' Not a very good idea, I thought, but I felt relieved as I hated the thought of going off alone with the two soldiers.

The Lieutenant stood up, in a hurry to leave.

'All right. You might as well come too. I suppose you're her husband, aren't you?'

Since they had no warrant for my arrest, there was nothing to stop them arresting him as well. But Tari could see what was happening and tried to intervene.

'Show them your release document, Daddy. They can't take you away again, can they?' She turned to go and fetch the document but Bud stopped her.

'Don't bother. It won't help.'

Bud had been released on the orders of General Panggabean, the deputy commander of the army. But he knew that he could be detained again at any time. Poor Tari so much wanted to help, but Bud realized there was nothing he could do to prevent his rearrest.

All the while, my two pupils were waiting in the room where we had been sitting. Goodness knows what they were thinking. I had never said a word to any of my pupils about our status as political outcasts in Suharto's New Order. I saw them out as gracefully as I could, saying as they left: 'Give me a ring before coming for your next lesson.'

As Bud and I left the house and clambered onto the army jeep, Tari and Anto stood on the verandah, watching us go. We would often sit there in the evenings chatting, as we watched the traffic go by. Now they stood there watching us leave under armed guard. It broke my heart to leave them like this. As we were being driven off, I saw Bud's mother, a small, frail woman, come out as well, her face strained, unable to say a word. His sister Par was there too, as well as Ira, our servant, who had been with us for many years. She looked really agitated.

Many friends asked me later whether either of the children cried as we left. I was so shocked by what was happening to me that I hadn't noticed. I can't remember now what I was thinking as we walked out of the house but, as the jeep drove off, I wondered what they would say to each other as they went inside and closed the door. Anto would probably be too shaken to cry and Tari would control her emotions so as not to upset him. Mbah, their grandmother, would probably start moaning with anxiety, rubbing her breast as she often did when emotions overcame her. Auntie Par, Bud's sister, would find some words of comfort for Tari and Anto. No one would want to eat much for supper and they would probably lie awake all night, straining their ears for signs of our return. It had happened twice before, when Bud was driven off, the first time in October 1965, the second time in March 1966, only ten days after his first release.

We were being taken to a military command post where we were ordered to alight. I recognized the building. It was the office of the Hsin-hua news agency which I had visited in better days, to teach some of the journalists English. Early in 1966, it was taken over by the army after diplomatic relations with China were severed.

The building looked deserted; there was no sign of any soldiers. We were taken to the rear of the house and ordered to wait in a small office. After a few minutes, an officer came down from upstairs, looking as if he had just woken up. He wrote our names in a book, Bud's as well as mine. It made no difference to him that his men had turned up with two captives instead of one.

I sometimes wondered what would have happened if Bud hadn't come out as I was being arrested. The unit ordered to arrest me could not have known that he had been released but they would have soon found out. Or would they?

After some brief formalities had been completed, we were taken to the front of the building. No one said a word about what would happen next. As I was soon to find out, they never did.

There was another vehicle waiting for us, this time a Land Rover. Now where were we going to be taken? As a detainee's wife for two years, I was familiar with most of the detention centres in Jakarta. But as the Land Rover drove off, I realized that we were not going in the direction of any of the places I knew. After going down several back turnings, we were soon speeding along a road in the direction of a suburb, Kebayoran, south of the capital.

This time, we had a larger escort. The two men who had come to the house were nowhere to be seen. Bud and I sat, side by side, in the back, surrounded by four heavily armed soldiers, with two more in the driver's cabin.

We said nothing to each other but Bud must have been thinking what I was thinking. Why had we not acted faster on our plans to leave the country? After his release in December 1967, we had decided that it was useless to remain in Indonesia. Neither of us would ever be able to get a job. Until October 1965, he had been an Assistant Minister at the Ministry of Sea Communications; I was a researcher in international economic relations at the Foreign Ministry and also did some university teaching. But the crackdown and purge after October 1965 meant that nothing was now open to us. The only thing open to me was to teach English, for which I had no formal training. But I had to confine myself to finding private pupils and make sure they knew nothing about my political difficulties.

As we sped along, I tried to relieve the tension by striking up a conversation with the guards, so I asked the man opposite where they were taking us. The answer was terse.

'I don't know. Stop asking questions.' His rudeness cut me to the quick. Indonesians were usually very courteous, even deferential to me, a foreign woman.

I fell silent and glanced out the back of the vehicle at the streets as they receded into the gathering darkness. We had now turned onto the main thoroughfare to Kebayoran. We drove past brightly lit, modern buildings and the new sports stadium built during the heyday of the former President, Sukarno. The road was lined with dilapidated huts and untidy hoardings. There were three traffic lanes but the Land Rover zigzagged from lane to lane, overtaking cars left and right. The driver was in a hurry; this was an army vehicle careering along, so other drivers kept out of the way. I gazed at the people along the road: pedestrians, motorists, cyclists, becak-drivers pushing hard at the pedals of their three-wheeled cycles with one or two passengers in front, at street-vendors jogging along, their wares bearing down heavily on the poles they carried on their shoulders. All very familiar, but now, suddenly, I was here and they were there. I wondered how many of them knew what was going on in their midst. Maybe they or their relatives had had similar experiences, or worse. In many parts of the country, especially in Java, few families had come through the last three years unscathed. But no one would say anything. The country was in the grip of collective amnesia.

As I gazed and wondered, a gruff voice interrupted my thoughts.

'Cover up your eyes!'

At first I didn't understand. Blindfolding was the last thing I had expected. As Bud dug into his pocket for a large handkerchief, one of the soldiers rebuked me for not responding faster. The thought that they were taking us to a secret destination suddenly struck me with fear, which I had not felt until that moment.

Someone, I don't know who, found a hankie and tied it round my head. I started screaming: 'Where are you taking us? Why are you doing this?' One of the soldiers, embarrassed by the noise I was making, tried to calm me down.

'Don't get upset, Ibu. Everything will be all right.'

But nothing anyone said could reassure me. The shock was too great and I became hysterical. This had never happened to me before and I couldn't stop screaming. Then it was Bud's turn to try and calm me down.

'Never mind if they want to kill us. At least we're together.'

Were our prospects really as bad as that? Then one of the men in the front cabin yelled 'Stop making that row. Everyone's staring at us.' But I was beyond caring what anyone said.

As we sped along, it felt as if we had left Jakarta far behind. Maybe Bud was right. They were going to take us to a remote spot and finish us off.

Then the Land Rover turned right, rattled down a gravel drive and came to an abrupt halt. Someone pulled my blindfold off and I found myself being taken through a huge, darkened shed with a very high ceiling. Bud was no longer anywhere to be seen and had been taken to another part of the compound. Some days later I realized that I had once visited this place. It was a film studio owned by a progressive film company. Taken over by the army like so much else, it had now become a secret interrogation centre.

It was quite dark by now. I was taken through the shed to a courtyard which looked even darker, because of the bright rays of light that I could see through windows along one side of the yard.

I was ushered into a small room full of soldiers, some in uniform, some not. One of them was just dressing. There were a few campbeds that looked as though they had just been slept in. These were the frontline intelligence troops, out and about at all hours of the day or night to round up more suspects. Nearly three years had passed since Suharto launched his crackdown against the Indonesian Communist Party, yet operations against communist suspects and anyone 'thought to have been directly or indirectly involved in the 1965 coup attempt' were still going on.

Some of the soldiers were surprised to see me, a white woman, caught up in this business.

My name was registered again, but this time in a large book with columns going across two pages. Name? Address? Nationality? Age? Gender? Organization? Member of the PKI?

I had calmed down by now. As I answered the questions, I looked round at the faces that surrounded me. Suddenly, I saw a familiar face; it was a young fellow, not in uniform, with a long face and thick, wavy hair. He was standing near the table where I was seated, looking at me intensely as if he was challenging me to remember who he was. Not having a very good memory for faces and names, I couldn't remember where I had seen him before. I wondered momentarily whether I should smile at him but decided not to. It had not taken me long to conform to one of the unwritten rules for detainees: never show signs of recognizing anyone unless you are sure it's safe.

In this case, I needn't have been so cautious. I later found out that before October 1965, he was on the staff of the secretariat of the central committee of the PKI. After 'the event', he went into hiding for about two years. When he was eventually arrested, he was badly tortured and 'persuaded' to become an informer. He was now working for army intelligence, helping to identify his former comrades. I had no idea how much he knew of my links with the PKI secretariat, as an English translator of documents and sometimes giving my assessment of economic problems.

The only time I had met him in the old days was as a member of IPPI, the left-wing school-pupils' organization of which Tari was a member. On that occasion, he had promised to 'keep an eye on' my daughter. Now he was keeping an eye on me.

By this time, army intelligence had recruited quite a number of informers from the PKI. Some may have been agents before 1965 but most had been unable to withstand all the brutality. For anyone facing interrogation, it was very demoralizing to recognize a former comrade among your tormentors.

After taking down my particulars, they told me I could go; I was taken to a room next door, facing the courtyard. This was the room for women detainees. A soldier unlocked the door and told me to enter. Hanging down from the middle of the ceiling was a very bright electric lamp, so bright that it made me blink. The walls were painted white and looked very clean. The floor was tiled and there was not a single piece of furniture in the room: no beds, no chairs, no cupboards, just a few straw mats. Along one side were two windows looking out onto a corridor along which I had just walked and then onto the pitch-dark courtyard.

Two women were sitting on mats in opposite corners of the room. One was busy writing and the other was suckling a new-born baby. The mother was rather fat and had her legs stretched out in front of her, rocking the baby to and fro. As I entered, she looked up at me; her face was expressionless, pale and haggard.

The other woman paused for a moment as I came in. There was a faint smile on her face which I did not return; I realized that I had met her before too but I couldn't remember where. No one said anything.

The soldier who had brought me in pointed to an empty mat in another corner and ordered me to go and sit down. There was another, unoccupied mat with a handbag on it, belonging to someone out of the room. As I sat down, the guard went out and locked the door behind him.

My three years of detention had begun.

CHAPTER 2

The Women's Room

It was a few moments before anyone spoke. The two women in the room seemed to be waiting until the guard was out of earshot. After he had gone past the window of our room back to the office next door, the woman with the baby spoke to me across the room in a whisper.

'Did they blindfold you on the way?'

'Yes, it came as a terrible shock.' I knew she could see I had been crying. 'Why did they do that?'

'They do it to everyone. This is a new detention centre and no one is supposed to know where it is.'

As she spoke, she looked at the baby in her arms. It was sleeping now, so she pulled her breast gently from its mouth and laid it down on a folded sarong on the mat beside her. The baby was so tiny, it couldn't have been more than two weeks old.

'You didn't give birth here, did you?' I asked, horrified at the thought.

'No. I was arrested yesterday morning with my husband. We were among the first to be brought here. They didn't want to let me bring her but I couldn't leave her with the other children. They wouldn't have been able to look after her.'

'Oh my goodness, did you leave your children at home all alone?'

She turned her face away and I realized that I had upset her for she brushed at a tear with the back of her hand.

The other woman, who was writing when I entered, had said nothing but she was staring at me. That faint smile was still there on her face; she looked more relaxed and fresher than her companion.

With the baby's mother too upset to speak, she began. 'Don't you remember me?'

'No, I'm sorry, I don't. We may have met but I can't remember.'

I really couldn't remember, but even if I had, I would have answered in the same way. Since the events of 1965, I had hardly met any communist or left-wing friends. If, here in this place, I acknowledged that she was a friend, it might confirm what I was trying hard to reject, that I belonged here.

'I once came to a lecture you gave on economics', she said, 'and I saw you once at SOBSI head office. I worked there in the women's section. Don't you remember?' SOBSI was the left-wing trade union federation which was banned immediately after the 1965 events, together with the PKI and a large number of mass organizations.

'Oh', I said. Was she trying to trick me? It was embarrassing to hear her talk about my visits to SOBSI, so I turned away, not wanting to continue the conversation.

Noticing my embarrassment, she spoke to me again, this time in a softer voice. The smile was still on her face.

'They know everything about you, Zus Carmel. It will be better for you to tell them everything frankly.' She was addressing me as Zus, the Dutch word for sister.

I didn't know what to say. I was as much confused by her advice as shocked by what she had told me. Was she saying that people here knew about my associations with the PKI? It was something very few people knew anything about. Had there been a betrayal? Why was she advising me to speak frankly?

In my bewilderment, I turned for guidance to the baby's mother, to see if she would confirm the other woman's words. I saw her purse her lips slightly and there was an imperceptible shake of her head, but she said nothing. She looked down at her baby and brushed a mosquito away from its face. I understood her message and said nothing more.

The silence continued for several minutes. I noticed that the other woman was busy writing again. Now I could see that she wasn't writing a report or answering questions; she was drawing a diagram with squares connected by lines, the sketch of an organizational structure. Every few moments, she would pause for a while before writing something in one of the squares. When I realized what she was doing, I turned my eyes away, not wanting her to see that I was looking at the paper on her lap.

I turned away to look at the window and saw a soldier standing, staring at me. He seemed surprised to see the new prisoner. There was nothing unfriendly about his stare, only curiosity. But it made me feel very uncomfortable, very vulnerable sitting on the floor, exposed to this man's stare. He had a weapon hanging from his shoulder, not a rifle but something larger. I ought not to have been surprised; this was an army detention camp and officers could be expected to carry arms, but the sight of it made me shudder, the thought that I was being guarded by armed men, that if I got up and ran through the door he could lift up his weapon and take a shot at me.

After standing there staring at me for a few more moments, he walked away into the darkness. I felt relieved that he had gone.

I looked round the room at the empty mat with the handbag. 'Where is she?'

The baby's mother replied: 'Upstairs being interrogated. They arrested her only this morning and she's been up there most of the time since then. Poor woman. They're probably giving her a rough time.'

I fell silent again. I didn't want to hear any more. Everything I had seen or heard in the past few minutes only emphasized the bleakness of my circumstances. I was a prisoner, worlds away from home, from my family, from the lessons, from the life I had been living for the past three years.

A mother who had been dragged away from her children, a trade union activist who had turned collaborator, a woman upstairs being tortured, armed men outside. How could I ever adjust to all this?

I suddenly felt exhausted and wanted to lie down. I had no pillow so I stretched out on the mat and lay down on my back. I felt extremely uncomfortable lying on the hard floor. I was embarrassed, lying there in a room without curtains. The guard might look in again. I felt more vulnerable to be seen by those men lying down than sitting up, so I sat up again, curled my legs sideways and sat facing the wall with my back to the other women.

When I was arrested on 3 September 1968, I had been living in Indonesia for more than sixteen years. My first thoughts after my arrest were a mixture of fear, regret, disappointment, self-recrimination, frustration, anger. I had known since the start that I could be arrested.

Yet, even so, when it happened to me I was quite unprepared for it. I felt ashamed of myself for having broken down on the way and began to think that I had made a terrible mistake ever to have got involved in politics. Back in England, politics did not involve personal risks, but in Indonesia things were different. In the years I had been living here, since 1952, things had changed and were less risky for people on the left – until October 1965. I had been lulled into thinking that as an English woman, an intellectual, a government employee, a university lecturer, I would never get into trouble. Why had I been so lacking in foresight? Had I been wrong to come to Indonesia? Even as the questions formed, I rejected them. Why should I blame myself? Like millions of others, I had been swept along by events over which I had no control.

Being British I had had no knowledge of Indonesia in my youth, but my association with the country went back many years, to the time soon after the Second World War when I attended several international student conferences in London and Prague. In 1946, I struck up a friendship with the first Indonesian I had ever met. His name was Suripno. He was very good-looking, with jet black hair and a winning smile. There was a large birthmark in the middle of his forehead, so exactly placed that I thought at first that it was a mark of rank or distinction. We went on a trip together to Yugoslavia and took part in an international youth brigade to help build the Youth Railway. On one of the many student get-togethers, I saw him perform a classical Javanese dance, with poise and grace. I had no idea at the time that he was a Communist Party leader. Several years later, he was shot dead in Madiun, East Java, with ten other leading communists after a violent clash between the PKI and the army.

In 1947, I got a job in Prague at the secretariat of the International Union of Students (IUS). There I began to mix with the Asian crowd, Indians, Burmese, Vietnamese, Chinese and Indonesians. I had many other friends too, Czech, Yugoslav, Romanian, but I felt more at home with the Asians.

In November 1947, I was sent to India by the IUS to help prepare the South-East Asian Conference of Youth and Students in Calcutta. The three months I spent in India were exciting and sometimes tense. I was in Calcutta when Gandhi was assassinated. The atmosphere created by this tragedy was unforgettable. Walking in the street soon after the news broke, a friend advised me to look solemn like everyone else. Indians would be offended if they thought that an English woman was not sharing their terrible grief.

The conference was a very militant event attended by students from many countries, including Kuomintang China. Later, commentators from the West falsely accused us of making plans for armed rebellion in Burma, Malaya, Thailand and Indonesia.

It was during this trip to India that I first came face to face with brutal repression. On a visit to Bombay, I saw Indian troops firing on a public students' meeting that I was attending. I fled, along with hundreds of people, as the troops used tear gas to disperse the crowd. I got a dose of it myself as I took refuge in a doorway. In Calcutta, I saw armed hooligans attack a hostel where some of the conference delegates were staying; two student helpers were murdered in front of my eyes. It fell to me as the only representative of the IUS present to officiate at the funeral. I had never attended a funeral in my life.

After the conference, I travelled to several South-East Asian countries with other delegates. In Burma, I visited an area under the control of a pro-communist peasant movement. I spoke about the international student movement at Chinese schools in Bangkok and met revolutionary

Chinese student leaders in Hong Kong. In May 1948, I visited Kuomintang China for the 4 May celebrations (marking the first mass student demonstrations in 1920), at the invitation of the Chinese revolutionary students' organization, and spent several days being chaperoned from city to city by clandestine activists who always kept at a distance to avoid detection. I spoke at a number of student meetings on university campuses, surrounded outside the walls by security forces. My speeches expressed solidarity with the students at a time when Kuomintang repression was at its height.

I was exhilarated by the trip, feeling that I had done a great job for the IUS. But back in Prague I was met with glares of disapproval. For reasons I could not understand, my visit to China had angered the Soviet and Czech people in control of the IUS. Years later, I realized that already in 1948, long before the emergence of the Moscow–Beijing split, the Soviets were deeply suspicious of the Chinese revolution.

However, the Asians in Prague were delighted with my trip and my affinity with them grew even stronger.

There was at the time a large group of Indonesian students in Prague, whose company I enjoyed. They were relaxed and sociable, full of fun and always having social events with lots of singing and dancing. They were delighted when I sang Jewish folk songs. They told me about the birth of the Indonesian Republic in 1945 and the wars with British and Dutch troops who were trying to restore Dutch colonial rule. Several of the Indonesians in Prague had come there from Holland after giving up Dutch Government scholarships, in protest at the second Dutch aggression against Indonesia in 1948.

That was the year when I met and fell in love with Bud. He had come to Prague after attending an international youth conference in Warsaw. Back home, the Mohammad Hatta Government under Sukarno as President launched a punitive attack against the left wing and the PKI in September 1948, resulting in the murder of many communists, including my friend Suripno. Bud had been granted a scholarship to study at Charles University in Prague and took a course in political science. My first recollection is of seeing him at the IUS office, looking miserable and cold in a thin, tropical suit. He was too proud to tell anyone that he had nothing suitable to wear to protect him from the rigours of the Prague winter.

We got married in Prague in 1950. The Indonesian crowd wanted to dress me up like a Javanese bride, so I let them get on with it, though I was only too glad they decided not to shave back some of the hair on the sides of my forehead. My features were so un-Javanese, I must have looked a sight. That was the only time in my life that I wore Javanese traditional dress.

Soon after my daughter Tari was born in June 1951, Bud got the opportunity to go back home with an Indonesian youth delegation that had come to Europe to attend the World Youth Festival in Berlin, travelling via Beijing. I was not able to attach myself to the delegation, so I made my way to Indonesia by returning home to London, then travelling aboard a Dutch liner to Indonesia. The three months I spent in London were strained. My parents had not been able to accept my decision to marry a non-Jew, and the fact that Bud was a Muslim made it worse. Once I had made up my mind, my father refused to have anything further to do with me. My mother tried to talk me out of it with all kinds of warnings. If I had only stopped gallivanting around the world, this wouldn't have happened. Didn't I know that Muslims could have four wives? Would I like living with people who ate with their fingers?

But during this trip back to London with Tari, now six months old, it was my mother who was first won round when she visited me one day at the home of my eldest sister, Lebah. Later, when my father inadvertently met me with Tari, his objections melted at the sight of his grandchild.

Conciliation between my parents and Bud came very much later, when he made his first trip to England in the early 1950s. He was the first Asian they had ever met. Once they got to know him, they were easily able to take their son-in-law to their hearts and were not ashamed to admit that they liked him.

The day I arrived in Indonesia with Tari, Bud met us at the quayside with a group of friends. I knew none of the people there and was not able later to recollect their names or faces. The excitement of arriving in my new homeland had made it impossible for me to register anything. After the long drive into Jakarta, we arrived at our first home, a tiny room in a hostel for officials of the Ministry of Communications, just large enough for a double bed and a cot. The only sitting space we had was a small verandah outside the room. My most vivid recollection of that first day was sitting at a small round table piled high with fruits of all descriptions, most of which I had never seen in my life.

Suddenly my thoughts were jolted back to the present as the door was unlocked and thrown open, hitting me in the back. A young woman entered and sat down on the empty mat, in great distress. Her escort, a man in plain clothes, came into the room and stood looking down at her with his hands on his hips.

'You've got till tomorrow to think it over.' From where I was sitting,

I could not see his face but his voice was ringing with contempt. 'It's ridiculous to say you can't remember.'

The woman sat holding her head with her hand. She didn't look up at him but nodded as she said 'I'm trying to remember. Please leave me alone.'

'You're lying', he barked back, and without saying anything more he turned and walked out of the room, locking the door behind him.

She sat on her mat quite still. Her blouse was hanging out of her skirt and the lower buttons were undone. She had very long, plaited hair that trailed on the floor behind her. The lower part of her plait was untied and dishevelled and strands of hair had fallen onto her forehead. She wiped some wisps of hair from her face with one hand, and with the other she started rubbing her breast. She was not crying; she seemed too shocked to cry.

As soon as we saw the man go past the window on his way to the office next door, the baby's mother was by her side. She had shuffled as quietly as she could along the floor, hoping that no one outside would see her move. I later learnt that they were close friends and had been students together in Moscow.

'Are you all right? Do you want a drink? Are you in pain? Did they beat you?'

Our new room-mate said nothing, shaking her head as she continued to massage her breast. After a few moments, she took a sip from a cup of tea that had been offered to her, but still remained silent.

The other woman had returned to her mat and took her baby into her arms for it was whimpering again.

The newcomer straightened herself, did up her buttons and pushed her blouse into her skirt.

'They stripped me naked', she said. 'I told them I could remember nothing. The brutes.' She lay down on her mat, using her handbag as a pillow, and said nothing more.

The room went quiet again.

My thoughts turned back to the time when I decided to get married. My Asian friends in Prague were worried that I might not be able to settle down in a strange country. Had I ever thought of the problems I might have getting to know my Indonesian in-laws? Would I ever get used to having servants in the house? Did I realize that I would be mixing with people who behaved differently and had different customs? And how would I cope with the heat?

Such problems never entered my head. I had fallen in love and was going to get married; the natural thing was to go and settle down in my husband's country. Why all the fuss? I am not the type to worry about the future. When things happen and problems arise, I usually manage to cope.

It is difficult to recall my first impressions of Indonesia. In those days, Jakarta was a sprawling, untidy city with striking contrasts between rich and poor. There were densely populated kampungs, where the poorest people lived, existing within easy reach of affluent residential districts. Close as they were, they were worlds apart. The kampungs lacked sanitation, drainage and electricity. But the squalor was hidden by luxuriant foliage. The worst thing for me were the filthy canals running alongside the narrow paths between the houses; these were used for garbage disposal and as a public loo, and were a breeding-ground for mosquitoes. I was also shocked at the sight of so many beggars on the streets, some of whom sat with malformed children by their side.

There was little in the city that interested me; culturally, it offered little to a Westerner – few cinemas, some ramshackle theatres, no concert halls. It was a long time before I began to enjoy Javanese cultural performances.

I never regretted my decision to go to Indonesia. I was soon offered a job as a translator at the Antara national news agency. I was persuaded to take the job within days of my arrival even though I knew hardly a word of Indonesian. They sat me down at a table in front of a typewriter with a dictionary and told me to get on with it. For the first few weeks, one of my colleagues would check my work, but then no one bothered any more. Indonesian is a fairly simple language to pick up and I was soon able to translate short items of news. There were a few memorable occasions when I made terrible mistakes. I remember the Hungarian trade attaché protesting because of a terrible mix-up with his clients because I had got the tense wrong in a report about the arrival of some goods.

After two years, I began to get bored with translating so I got a job at the Foreign Ministry doing economic research. In my spare time, I did translations for the Communist Party and occasionally wrote articles on economic affairs. I was never officially inducted as a member of the PKI but I met party leaders quite often and gave them my assessments of economic policy. These were the days, before 1965, when the PKI had what looked like a solid alliance with Sukarno. Political developments seemed to be moving in the direction of radical change and I often felt elated that I was on the winning side.

After taking a master's degree in economics at the University of Indonesia in Jakarta, I started lecturing at state and private universities while continuing to work at the Foreign Ministry. All this kept me extremely busy. I could never have done it without the help of my sister-in-law, Par, who lived with us for long stretches of time. And we could afford to have servants to help with all the housework.

I was something of a novelty. Plenty of Indonesians were married to Dutch women, but English wives were few and far between. To most Indonesians, Europe meant Holland and white people were always expected to speak Dutch. I was always being addressed in Dutch and soon got used to the surprise on people's faces when I said 'I'm sorry I don't understand. Please speak to me in Indonesian or English.'

I think that being English made it easier for me to assimilate. I never mixed with the Dutch community and there was no expatriate English community to speak of in Jakarta; even if there had been one, I would not have felt comfortable in their company. So, all my friends and acquaintances were Indonesian and my working life and leisure time was all spent in Indonesian company.

It was a life-style that led me irresistibly to political activity and, ultimately, to prison. But, even in those first moments of shock, I never regretted anything.

The door suddenly swung open again. A soldier stood holding the door knob as the young man with the familiar face whom I had spotted earlier rushed past him into the room.

He came up close to me on the mat and yelled into my face 'Kasman, you're wanted upstairs!'

Now I knew for certain that I had been betrayed. This was the name by which I was known only to some PKI leaders and staff members of the Party's secretariat. No one else knew that name in the old days.

I stood up and followed the two men out of the room.

CHAPTER 3

Interrogation

They didn't take me upstairs but led me to the room next door which, I soon discovered, was often used for interrogations. Many times, during the next fortnight, we were to hear the distressing sound of detainees being questioned and beaten there.

I was told to sit down in front of an interrogator. I don't remember feeling scared even though I had just seen my room-mate return from a session in such a state. I think I was too keyed up, too preoccupied with coping with the immediate present to bother about what might happen in a few moments' time.

The interrogator was a young soldier with a fresh, open face, not at all unfriendly. He seemed to be treating his job with some indifference. I didn't meet many interrogators like him. He wasn't in uniform, though I couldn't tell who were soldiers and who were civilians.

Several men in open leather jackets were standing behind me, lounging against the walls or the door. In front of me, to the right, standing with his hands on the table and looking very tense, was the young man with the familiar face. He wanted to make sure I was aware of his presence. This was Datong. He and his wife had been close friends of Tari's. I was later to discover that he had worked at the PKI secretariat in 1965 and went underground after October. It was clear that he had been well enough placed in the movement to become a useful source of information for the army.

The interrogator took up a pen, wrote my name down on a blank sheet of paper and began.

'When did you join the HSI?' This was the left-wing university graduates' association which I joined soon after it was founded. It was banned after Suharto seized control, along with many other organizations accused of being communist.

'In 1963', I replied.

'What was your position?'

'I was on the central executive and I chaired its economics section.'

'Why did you join the HSI? You knew it was a communist organization, didn't you?'

'No, I didn't, and, anyway, it's not true. There were communists and non-communists among its members.' I could hear the men behind me sniggering and making grunts of disbelief.

'But why join the HSI? You could have joined another organization, couldn't you?'

'I did. I was a member of ISEI [the Indonesian Association of Economists], and the Association of Women Graduates as well. But the HSI was different because it included people from many disciplines. Anyway, that was my choice.'

He started asking me for the names of HSI leaders. They were always wanting people's names. They certainly knew the composition of the organization's leading bodies, for these had been well publicized at the time. Yet even though I knew they knew, I couldn't bring myself to mention the names of people who might still be at large. I just mentioned people who I knew had been arrested or who had been killed during the massacres after 1965.

It's just as well that I have a bad memory for names; after mentioning ten people or so, I could truthfully say 'I can't remember any more'.

The interrogator left it at that, saying I could think it over during the night and give him more names tomorrow. But then came the bombshell.

'When did you become a member of the PKI central committee?'

'What? That's absolute rubbish. Whoever told you I was a member . . .'

Suddenly, there was a loud crash on the table. It was so unexpected that I jumped in my chair and put my hands to my throat with a gasp. It was Datong.

As he banged his hands down hard on the table in front of me, he yelled at me 'That's a lie. I know all about you.'

I looked him in the eye, trying to keep calm, although inside me things were far from calm; my heart was thumping like mad. 'If you scream and shout, and bang on the table like that, how do you expect me to answer any questions?' I spoke slowly but realized that my throat and mouth were parched; he had really shaken me.

I looked at the interrogator again and fell silent for a few moments. I needed to restore my cool. I began to hate Datong with such intensity that it was a relief to look at the soldier seated in front of me.

'It's absurd to think I was a central committee member. You've got too high an opinion of me. I wasn't even a member of any lower party organ.'

'You worked for the PKI international department, didn't you?' Few people knew about the things I had done for the Party's international department. Did Datong know? Perhaps a friend in the Party had betrayed me. It seemed pointless to deny it.

'I did translations for the department and people were in contact with me, but I was never a member.'

'What about your husband? He was part of the department, wasn't he?'

'Why don't you ask him. He's somewhere around, isn't he?'

The interrogator wrote something down as I spoke. He must have realized they had made a mistake and I was never again questioned about being a central committee member.

Was that the reason they had picked me up? If so, they ought to have released me. But things didn't work like that. It was now up to them to construct another case against me; if one charge didn't stick, they would think up another one.

'Were you sworn in as a party member?'

'No, never', I replied, quite truthfully.

In Britain, I had been a member of the Communist Party but my membership lapsed when I moved to Prague. In Indonesia, I never applied for party membership. I was in contact with some party leaders, especially in the last years before 1965, but never actually joined. The PKI was a legal organization throughout the 1950s and right up to October 1965, but with the ever-present danger of a sudden reversal of its political fortunes and mass arrests, it was considered unwise to expose all of its members and sympathizers. The PKI had gone through periods of violent repression in September 1948 and in 1951. Its legality was fragile and there was a strong undercurrent of anti-communism in the country throughout the Sukarno era. There must have been quite a number of semi-clandestine members like me.

When I joined the HSI, I was part of a group that functioned as a party cell to discuss the general direction of the organization. Communist parties throughout the world used to have cells like this to try to keep control of organizations, a method certainly employed by other political parties as well.

Army intelligence placed great emphasis on forcing people to speak about their swearing-in ceremony. They wanted to know who had sworn someone in, at whose house this happened, who was present, who else was sworn in at the same time. Information like this dragged ever more people into the net. In my case, I had nothing to say, but I later met several people who had been arrested simply because someone had confessed to having been sworn in at their home.

While they were still pressing me about oath-taking, a soldier came to say that everything was ready upstairs. I was ordered to go upstairs and all the men in the room, including Datong, went up behind me.

Followed by this retinue of thugs, I went through a dark shed, up a short flight of stairs and into a huge room with a high ceiling. It could have been a meeting hall, but I later realized that this was the film studio I had once visited with my sister Miriam, who worked in the film industry, when she came to see me many years ago. Although it was shrouded in darkness, I could see tables and chairs scattered around. There was a single light at the far end of the room. As I walked towards the light, I realized that there were many men half hidden in the shadows, some in uniform, some in leather jackets. At first, I wondered what they were doing there, but it soon dawned on me that they were part of the process, helping to create the right atmosphere for my interrogation. They stood around, waiting for cues, responding to what I said with jeers and catcalls. Although it didn't happen in my case, they were also there to beat and torture the victim.

When I reached the table, I came face to face with a man whom I knew to be one of the most ruthless and cunning of army interrogators. It was Atjep, the man I had met two years earlier when Tari was arrested. She was fifteen at the time. Some hours after she was taken into custody, I was summoned to the place where she was being held.

Tari was arrested because the army were looking for some of her friends in IPPI. They first drove her to a 'safe house' where IPPI activists had been hiding, but fortunately no one was there at the time. Then she and a girl-friend were taken to one of the most notorious interrogation centres in Jakarta at the time, which I then knew as 'Posko', or 'command post'. There, the two girls sat alone for several hours. Then a heavily built man, breathless and sweaty from a torture session, took them to a room where a close friend, Hari, was being badly roughed up. They tried to get Tari to talk about him but she had nothing to say. As they continued to beat him in her presence, her blouse was splattered with blood, even though Hari was standing several metres away. Later, on her way back to the room where she was first taken, she saw another young friend who was in great pain; part of an ear had been bitten off by one of the torturers.

Now here was I seated before the man who had caused her so much distress and whose name struck terror among political detainees. He was a small, seedy-looking man, slightly bald with reddish hair. He must have been Eurasian by birth. He had sharp features, piercing eyes and a repulsive arrogance about his mouth. He had the face of a man who had grown used to not believing anything anyone said. I never saw him in uniform and never discovered his army rank, though it was probably quite senior. He once worked as a chauffeur at the US embassy in Jakarta; my hunch is that this was a cover for intelligence work he was probably doing for the CIA. Whenever I saw him, he was always surrounded by an armed escort.

As I sat down, he leaned back on his chair. He was holding a pipe in his hand. Before saying a word he raised the pipe to his lips and began to play a mournful Sundanese melody. There is something eerily atmospheric about the music of the Sundanese people of West Java, which I always associate with the mystery of dark nights in the countryside. The pipe he was now playing was reminiscent of that atmosphere.

'Remember me? Remember the pipe? We're old friends, aren't we, Ibu Carmel?' He spoke slowly, in fluent English.

'Of course, I remember you. How could anyone forget?'

'Don't you remember hearing me play my pipe outside your house? I've been there quite often recently, keeping an eye on you.'

I had first heard him play his pipe when he summoned me during Tari's arrest. The pipe was part of his distinctive style as interrogator, creating an atmosphere of apparent, almost hypnotic calm that could suddenly be shattered by brutality.

Now, as he spoke, I remembered hearing the pipe late at night as I sat in the front room or on the verandah. Our house stood on a corner, opposite a grass roundabout where becak-riders and street-vendors would congregate in the evening for a chat, a smoke or a snooze. I had sometimes wondered whether it could have been Atjep but had never stopped to think why he would want to watch my house. All my political friends had long since stopped visiting me and, although I had an inkling that PKI people had started organizing underground, I had no idea who was involved or what was going on.

'Well now, Kasman', he said, placing emphasis on the name by which very few people knew me, 'tell me about your links with the PKI.'

'There really isn't much to tell and anyway you seem to know it all already, so why ask?'

'It would have been better for you if you had told me all about it the last time we met. We would have been more lenient with you.'

'That's a lie. Why should I have said anything when I knew very well you would have arrested me? Don't take me for such a fool.'

When he summoned me at the time of Tari's arrest, he had plied me with questions about my links with the PKI.

The moment I finished talking, he lurched across the table towards me and spat out words like bullets from a machine gun. The atmosphere created by the pipe had suddenly been transformed.

'Why were you forever criticizing the Government's economic

policies before the coup? It was the communists that put you up to it, wasn't it?'

'I criticized the Government because I thought its policies were wrong. I didn't need the communists to tell me that.'

His line of investigation was beginning to become clear. I was being accused of helping to create an atmosphere of discontent and unrest, 'ripening the situation for revolution'. The army was always looking for proof that the communists had been planning to launch a coup for many months during the so-called prologue to the October 1965 events. My part in this, according to Atjep, was on the economic front. For a year or so before October 1965, I regularly contributed articles to the Antara news agency, criticizing the Sukarno government's economic policies. These were written for the general reader and had become quite popular. They were reproduced in a number of national and regional newspapers, giving me quite a reputation as a commentator on the economy.

The coup attempt launched by Lieutenant-Colonel Untung and others on 1 October 1965 had, in their own words, sought to protect Sukarno against army officers who wanted to oust him, but Suharto initially portrayed their movement as anti-Sukarno, as an attempt to remove the legitimate government. Gradually, however, it was Suharto who began to discredit and outmanoeuvre Sukarno. In March 1966, Suharto forced Sukarno to surrender all his powers, and by 1968 he had installed himself as President. Sukarno had been removed from power and was placed under house arrest. From then on, no efforts were spared to vilify the former President.

Yet here I was, being accused of subversion because I had criticized the policies of the man whom the army had removed from power. As they saw it, my articles were part of the 'prologue' to the coup attempt and therefore subversive.

'Now don't try to deny it', Atjep yelled. 'It was Aidit who got you to write those articles, wasn't it? He told you what to say. I know all about your correspondence with him.'

This was becoming ridiculous. I had started writing my articles after years of frustration because proposals I submitted as an economics researcher at the Foreign Ministry had gone unheeded. I wasn't going to let Atjep give Aidit, the PKI chairman, the credit for that.

'I doubt whether Aidit fully understood the points I was making. He certainly never told me what to write', I said.

'You were expressing a Marxist point of view, weren't you?'

'Rubbish. You'd better read the articles before saying things like that.' I could tell he hadn't read them as my analysis was very much in the tradition of Western economic thinking.

'All right. Tell me what your criticisms were. What proposals did you make?'

I felt that things were moving my way.

'Do you want me to give you an analysis of relative price structures, of the pros and cons of devaluation during an inflation, of the meaning of disguised devaluation, or the history of Indonesia's currency policy? I can if you like, but you may find it a bit boring.'

'All right, all right. We'll find time for that later.' (We never did.) 'But now I want you to answer one simple question: what is your opinion of the Marxist analysis of the Indonesian economy?'

'I'm not aware that there has ever been one. Stalin may have written a lot about India or China, for all I know, but I'm not aware of anyone writing a Marxist analysis of the Indonesian economy. You'll have to give me time to look into that.'

He repeated the question with great deliberation. Goodness knows what the thugs slouching in the shadows were making of all this. After some further attempts along these lines, Atjep suddenly changed tack.

'All right now', he said. 'What about Effy? When did you last meet her?'

Effy was a young woman I had met casually before October 1965. She had been living in a hostel attached to the PKI's central academy for Marxist studies, though I don't know whether she was a student or a lecturer. When it was burnt down by mobs during the wave of attacks on party buildings in early October 1965, she came to see me with another friend and asked me to take them in. Effy stayed for several months. I knew that she was part of an underground network but was not involved in anything myself, and she left my house to avoid incriminating me. She and her comrades may also have considered my place as being too close to the enemy, with Suharto's private residence just round the corner.

'Oh, Effy. Yes, when was it? Quite a while ago. She came to see me to wish me a happy birthday. I remember it well because she got the date wrong and came too early, though she had the month right, June.'

'June!' The effect was electrifying. Atjep leapt up from his chair and Datong jumped to his feet. The men around me joined in the chorus of surprise.

'Where was she living? How was she dressed? Did she have anyone with her?'

I realized that I had made a terrible mistake. Her visit had been rather brief. She had indeed come, thinking it was my birthday but also to tell me something about the clandestine work she was doing. I told her I didn't want to know. I had long since realized that the communists had committed many blunders since 1965 and had not been able to adjust to

23

working underground. With Bud in and out of prison, there was little I could do to help; and anyway, it would be dangerous for people in the clandestine movement to make contact with our family.

But from Atjep's reaction, I realized that I had told them something they hadn't known, that Effy was in Jakarta as recently as last June. I could have kicked myself for this.

'She didn't say where she was living. If you are after her, and I'm sure she knows that, she'd hardly be likely to tell me that, would she?'

Atjep was now getting very aggressive, shouting at me across the table, waving his arms and brandishing threats. Some of the men stood up and crowded in on me. Things were becoming very tense.

I knew nothing more about Effy and I was glad of it. I shudder to think what would have happened if they had started beating me or stripping me naked. I doubt whether I would have been able to withstand torture. Even shouts and thumping on the table had turned my throat dry and sent my pulse racing. I was not mentally prepared for this kind of pressure.

After a few moments, the tension eased and Atjep said he would give me till tomorrow. He seemed pleased with the clue I had let slip and now wanted to let the matter rest, though he brought it up again later on. This blunder caused me a great deal of distress and lay heavy on my conscience. I knew that it was best to say as little as you could when being interrogated, but it took me a long time to learn how.

The session was coming to an end. Atjep asked a few questions about Tari and Anto, saying 'how sorry' he felt to have dragged us both away from the children. I took this as a veiled threat that he might take Tari into custody again if I failed to co-operate. Before I left the room, I asked him how long he intended to keep me in detention.

'Not long', he said, 'but it doesn't depend on me. He's the one who will decide.' He pointed to a man slouching on a couch just behind me.

I had noticed this man watching me intently throughout the interrogation. I now turned round and looked at him properly and what I saw still stands out in my mind as the most ghastly face I have ever seen in the flesh. He was dark with a long-shaped face, unkempt hair and bulging eyes that were full of menace. There was a constant sneer on his face. He had rings on the fingers of both hands, all of them carrying large stones. These were part of his armoury, for inflicting lacerating blows on torture victims. When my eyes met his, his mouth shaped into a vicious grin, enjoying the joke Atjep was playing on me, and he nodded as if to say 'Yes, I'm the man'.

He was the commander of the camp and his behaviour was as menacing as his appearance. But more of him later on.

As I got up to go, Atjep started to apologize for the lack of amenities. 'Sorry, we can't give you a room more like your own at home.'

'Please don't start apologizing', I said. 'If you were really sorry, you would let me go home. And when am I going to be allowed to meet my husband?'

'Sorry, that's against the rules', he said.

As I returned to the room, I realized that they had very little on me. There was no way they could implicate me in what they claimed was the PKI's coup attempt. There was nothing they could pin on me about working underground after 1965 as I had done no political work at all for nearly three years and my pre-1965 connections with the Communist Party had been peripheral.

I felt disappointed about the way I had been betrayed and unhappy with myself for the slip-up about Effy. I returned to the room feeling hopeful that they would have no reason to hold me for any length of time. I still had a lot to learn.

CHAPTER 4

Life in a Detention Camp

When I returned to the room, my room-mates were lying down but not asleep. As soon as the guards left us alone, they offered me something to eat and drink. It was already late and I hadn't eaten since lunch, but I couldn't eat anything now. The tea they gave me was cold and tasteless but it greatly refreshed me.

I wanted to go to the toilet and needed permission for this. There were two lavatories on the other side of the courtyard. It was dark and I could not bear the thought of going out alone with a soldier, so I asked one of the women to accompany me. With her help, I groped my way into a pitch-dark cubicle. It was not difficult to know where I had to squat because of the awful stench. There was just a hole in the ground. I wouldn't have minded that but it was brimming over with shit. The place was kept like that the whole time I was at this centre. I was constipated throughout the time I spent there because I couldn't bear the thought of going to that dreadful place.

Once back in the room and locked up again, I began to consider how I could settle down for the night on the floor, with no pillow or cover.

'Can you manage?' asked one of the women. She could see my predicament but had nothing to offer.

'Yes, I think so', I replied hopefully.

As I was trying to settle down, a camp orderly must have seen my discomfort through the window. A young boy came in and gave me a man's dressing gown and a small hand towel.

'Here, use these to cover yourself, Ibu. You'll be able to sleep better.' I was very grateful for this kindness though I couldn't help wondering what had become of the man whose belongings were so generously being given to me. I said nothing to the other women about what had happened upstairs but sat thinking about the awfulness of my situation.

There was a single, very bright bulb hanging from the ceiling which was kept on all night. After a while, I lay down, feeling exhausted and drained of energy. I slept fitfully and heard men coming and going outside, shouting to each other across the yard. This was the flurry of activity that followed an order to rush out and make some new arrests. Then I heard the door of our room open and close; the woman with the long hair had been called away again for interrogation. The noise of the guards when they came in for her was such as to make sure that we all knew what was going on. Not long after, another woman was brought in. She had come from Surabaya, East Java, more than 700 kilometres away.

As the night wore on, I heard a commotion in the room next door; a detainee had been brought in for interrogation. The muffled voices and yells merged with my own dreams of boys thumping on tables and men wagging their fingers at me menacingly.

Towards morning I fell into a deep sleep and when I woke up it was broad daylight. The bright tropical sun had chased away the gloom outside our windows and for a moment I almost forgot where I was.

I was brought back to the present by a guard standing at the door.

'Up you get and be quick about it. It's your turn to go to the toilet and the well.'

My neck ached from sleeping without a pillow and my hips were stiff from lying all night on the cold, tiled floor, but I got up fast and hurried after the other women, clutching my small towel.

The courtyard which I was seeing for the first time was surrounded by lush, green foliage. Along two sides there were banana trees and palm trees in haphazard profusion, separating the compound from the neighbouring gardens. There was a well in the far-right corner, partly concealed by hawthorn bushes and a cherry tree. At the opposite end was the high wall of the shed where I had been interrogated the night before, and along the foot of the wall there were piles of sand, bags of cement, a roll of wire netting and other material, in readiness for an extra wing and specially designed cells. The former film studio needed extra buildings to transform it into a proper detention centre.

I could see chickens flapping around in the garden next door and beyond a fence at the bottom of the yard topped with barbed wire was a small, ramshackle factory with used tyres scattered around, just the kind of surroundings you could see over many back fences.

'Be as quick as you can', said one of the women as I lingered at the well to swill my mouth. 'The guards get nasty if we take too much time.'

As soon as we had finished our 'toilet', we were hustled back to the room, behind lock and key. Moments later, I realized the reason for the haste. A group of male prisoners appeared at the door of the shed, escorted by an armed guard, and crossed the courtyard to take their turn at the well. Among them I saw a man I knew, a musician from Ambon, a dark, rugged-looking fellow like most Ambonese, who always had a smile on his face. I used to see him outside Salemba Prison when I went there taking food for Bud during his first periods of detention.

'That fellow over there is a choir conductor, isn't he?' I asked of my room-mates. 'I used to buy sweets from him outside Salemba Prison. I thought he'd been released long ago.'

'It makes no difference', said one of the women. 'They are re-arresting many people these days. One fellow here says this is his fourth arrest.'

When the group went back to the shed, another group appeared. I noticed Nuriah, the baby's mother, give a start as she spotted her husband. I saw another familiar face, a man I had known in Prague in 1950. In those days, he was the leader of a communist youth organization, PESINDO, but he had left it long ago following political disagreements. Since then, he had gone into business and had become quite successful; now he was stocky and looked as though he had been living a good life. From what I had heard, he stopped associating with communists about ten years ago. I wondered why they were arresting a man like that.

Bud was in the third group of men to appear. He looked haggard and ill at ease. He must have had a bad night, getting used to the idea that he was in for the third time. I could see that he was trying hard to pretend that he was not looking for me. Then, while he was down at the well, someone must have told him where the women's room was for, on his way back, he glanced in our direction and I saw his fingers move imperceptibly to show that he had seen me at the window. It was painful seeing him like this and I turned my head away.

I started to think about what he had done the day before, virtually offering himself for arrest, in order to be a comfort to me. It made me feel sick in the stomach.

More groups followed for their turn at the well. Most of the detainees, I was told, had been picked up in Jakarta in the last couple of days. The others had been brought to the capital from East Java where they had been arrested in the past few months. One of the detainees to appear was short and fat, his legs hardly strong enough to bear the weight of his body. He panted heavily as he walked across the yard. Half way across he stopped. After asking the guard for permission, he squatted for a few moments to catch his breath. He was Chinese and one of the women told me he was originally from Solo in Central Java. He now had an antiques shop in one of the main Jakarta shopping centres and had been arrested because someone had confessed to being sworn in as a party member in his house more than a decade ago. I saw him get up slowly and walk to the well with great difficulty. Why on earth drag such a man into all this?

During the morning, things at the centre were quiet. Nuriah told me that, as night approached, things would 'warm up' and more interrogations would take place. The 'intel' officers preferred to work at night. Darkness provided cover for their activities and detainees were more likely to be confused, having questions fired at them in the glare of a bright light, surrounded by gloom and darkness.

As we chatted, I learnt that the centre had been set up by the army's central intelligence unit, Satgas-Pusat, which was in charge of the huge new influx of detainees rounded up when a communist base had been discovered in Blitar, East Java. There had been many reports in the press about Blitar in the past few months, with photos of underground tunnels and cleverly concealed entrances. Many communist leaders and activists and deserters from the army had taken refuge there after fleeing from the massacres and the mass arrests in 1965. The army was jubilant because the discovery of the Blitar base led to hundreds of arrests. The newspapers had given prominence to photographs of the battered corpse of a man I knew very well, Oloan Hutapea, a member of the Party's politbureau. Another victim was Surachman, leader of the PNI, the Indonesian national party. Both men had been shot dead by soldiers. The sight of Hutapea's body had transfixed me. I would have preferred not to look but I could not help studying the photo because I wanted to convince myself that it was really him. What must his wife and children have thought when they saw it? I knew him in the old days as a very confident man, always optimistic about the future but now it had come to this.

The first person to be summoned for questioning from our room that morning was Ting Suwarni, the woman who had been drawing the charts the night before. I later discovered that she had been working on a chart showing the organizational structure of SOBSI, and wondered how many more people would be rounded up because of her revelations.

As soon as she left the room, Nuriah whispered to me 'She's a big shot, if you please, a member of Parliament. In the old days, of course. I wouldn't like to live with her conscience.'

As Nuriah chatted on, I realized that she had quickly adjusted to the detention regime. I was to spend a great deal of time with her in the next year or so and valued her keen powers of observation. She could quickly size up the guards and was always the first to know who was who. She seemed to have a sixth sense, knowing everything that was going on and when the more sympathetic guards were on duty. In conditions like this, she was an invaluable companion.

'Before "the event" [that was how everyone referred to the events of October 1965], I was studying in Moscow with my husband. We both graduated in 1965 and returned home in August. Neither of us had the slightest idea of what was going on but now we've been arrested for involvement in the coup.'

They had been sent to Moscow on state scholarships, she to study Russian literature and her husband to study economics. They had been promised employment on their return home but 'the event' had changed all that. Neither of them had got a job, so she made a living teaching in an elementary school and dressmaking. Her husband was the younger brother of D. N. Aidit, the chairman of the Communist Party whom the army depicted as being the 'mastermind' of the Untung conspiracy. No one in Indonesia would dare to employ anyone with a name like that. It was this family connection that had landed them both in jail. For him, this was the second arrest.

When Ting returned, she had a large blank sheet of paper which she put down on the mat beside her. She was in her late forties, rather plain looking; she had no family and had devoted her life to working for the movement. I had the impression that she was connected with the Blitar base, but she never said anything about it. After being arrested somewhere in East Java, she was savagely tortured, stripped naked, beaten and forced to stand with the legs of a chair on her feet while a soldier jumped up and down on the chair. This form of torture is commonly used by the army. After having to endure such ordeals, she succumbed and was now feeding information to her persecutors.

As she settled down, she turned to me. 'The Party made terrible mistakes, Zus Carmel, and we're all paying for it now.'

No one could disagree with that, I thought. But the Party could not be held responsible for the millions of people who had suffered after 1965. She was herself a victim and was trying to rationalize her collaboration. I couldn't help but feel distrustful of her, but decided to keep my thoughts to myself. So she went on.

'It's all very well to kidnap six generals, but why kill them? Political assassinations have never achieved anything. Don't you agree?'

I did agree, very much, but I could not understand her assumption that the Party had been responsible for the murder of the generals.

'Surely no one from the Party would have given orders for such a thing to happen. I can't believe it.'

She smiled faintly, shook her head and said nothing more. Then she picked up the sheet of paper and began writing again.

For several months in 1968, around the time of my arrest, many people were taken into custody. This new wave came as the result of an operation, 'Operasi Trisula', launched by the army to destroy the clandestine base that had been set up in South Blitar, East Java. After the mass killings, arrests and purges that followed the events of 1 October 1965, many communists, sympathizers and some left-wing army officers went underground and made their way to South Blitar where they set up a base involving several thousand people, hoping to launch a movement against the Suharto regime. They had built an underground network of tunnels, inspired by the tunnel warfare organized by the Vietnamese people's army. I never knew whether they planned to organize guerrilla warfare or to use the base to organize politically against the regime. But before they could get anything going, army intelligence got wind of their plans and dispatched thousands of troops to surround the base. Several leaders were killed during the assault and hundreds were rounded up.

The wave of arrests in South Blitar caused waves of arrests in other parts of the country as army torturers succeeded in extracting information about former contacts in the PKI. One of those arrested in South Blitar was a good friend of mine, Iskandar Subekti, a member of the PKI's international department with whom I had worked closely. I was told that he mentioned my name which led to my being taken into custody. Whether or not this was true, I had no reason to feel any bitterness towards Iskandar. He later went on trial, along with several of his Blitar comrades, and was sentenced to death in 1972. These men had to endure long terms in prison, always knowing that they could be executed at any time. In the late 1980s, more than twenty years after being arrested, two of his comrades were executed. It was not yet time for Iskandar to face the execution squad but he never knew when his turn would come. In the early 1990s, he fell gravely ill, but this did not earn him compassionate release; he died on death row in 1993.

The interrogation centre where I now found myself was called Satgas-Pusat, the special central intelligence task force, which was set up to handle the new wave of Trisula arrests. Whatever Effy and her group's connections with Blitar, it was clear from the arrests which swept through Jakarta that the repercussions of the Blitar crackdown were felt in many parts of the country where clandestine groups had been working successfully for some time.

My own arrest on 3 September 1968 was not my first encounter with the army. I was first summoned for interrogation in late October 1965 when

I was picked up from home and driven off in an army truck, along with several men and one other woman. We were taken to a nearby army command. The moment we arrived, the men were taken to the back and registered as detainees. The other woman and I were told to wait in the office of the intelligence officer. Fortunately for me, he was not happy about the arrests and felt that the least he could do was to find a way to let the two of us go.

I had just been given a letter by my doctor for a hospital bed because he had discovered a tumour on my left breast. The officer interrogated me for a while, but when I produced the letter he went to see his commanding officer and convinced him to let me go. He also found some argument to let the other woman go and phoned her husband to come and pick her up.

He ushered us out of his office to the waiting car. 'Get out of here fast', he said. 'Once your names are registered and they take you to the back, you'll never get out of here.'

This same officer turned up again when I was moved from Satgas-Pusat. Now he was a detainee, apparently accused of being a Sukarnoist or a PKI sympathizer. I recognized him the moment I saw him; he was in very bad shape, shortly after a ferocious torture session. Soldiers who were rounded up as political prisoners were always treated particularly harshly.

Not long after my first summons, I was called in again, this time to answer questions about the whereabouts of my former boss, Dr Subandrio, who was still Deputy Prime Minister at the time. This session didn't last long and left me baffled. It was not till several months later that Dr Subandrio was arrested, tried and sentenced to death in 1966. Many years later, his sentence was commuted to life. He was released from prison, an ailing and fragile shadow of his former self, in August 1995.

After my brief conversation with Ting Suwarni, I dozed off. I was woken by a man standing by my side, a prisoner who was holding a plate of food. Clad only in underpants and a thin vest, he offered me the food with a smile. A soldier had opened the door to let him in and held the door, waiting for him to leave. As he bent down to give me the food, he whispered very softly 'Greetings from Bud.'

Before I could gather my senses to thank him, he had disappeared and the door had been locked behind him. I felt comforted at the thought that, even here, with guards and intel officers everywhere, contact could be made.

CHAPTER 5

A Brief Visit Home

In the afternoon things began to get busy again as officers turned up for duty. I was summoned by an interrogator and given a long list of questions to answer in writing. I returned to the room with several sheets of paper and a pen, and skimmed through the questions. When did you first hear about the coup? What were your reactions? What are your views about the Communist Party and its programme? What advice did you give the former Deputy Prime Minister, Dr Subandrio, when you were working at his economics secretariat before the coup? Who visited you at home before the coup? After the coup? Give the names and addresses of your ten closest friends.

How should one deal with questions like these? What right have these people to know my thoughts, so as to use them to build a case against me? Why should I tell them anything at all about myself? But if I showed defiance by refusing to answer, what would this do to my chances of early release? I agonized over these dilemmas, not realizing that whatever I said or didn't say would make no difference to my prospects. Once they had arrested me, they were not going to let me go and there was nothing I could do, one way or the other, to change that.

As I sat staring at the questions, I became conscious of an officer leaning on the ledge of one of the open windows. He was glaring at me with a sinister grin on his face.

'Don't make anything up now. Try telling the truth for a change.'

Trying not to be provocative, I said 'Please don't disturb me. I need to concentrate.'

In a flash, he pulled out his pistol and aimed it at me. His bulging black eyes were livid with anger as he yelled at me. 'Concentrate? You bitch! How dare you answer me back? You're a prisoner here. You'd better realize, and quick, that I can kill you right now if I want to.'

I dropped the pen and stared at him. My mouth went completely dry. This was the man Atjep had pointed out to me the day before as the one who could determine my fate. After a few moments, he relaxed and walked away from the window without saying another word, pushing his pistol back in its holster.

When he was well out of earshot, one of my room-mates who had watched the scene in silence whispered 'You must be careful with him. That's Bonar, the camp commander. He's a vicious brute and he has a wicked temper.'

From then on, I was conscious that whenever he was present in the camp, everyone became tense and uneasy. As soon as he turned up, warnings would be whispered: 'Look out. He's come.' He usually turned up for duty late in the afternoon and stayed till early morning. When we woke up in the morning, he was never around and we could spend a few hours at ease, though we remained alert in case he turned up unexpectedly. Bonar was one of those officers who, by his very demeanour, was groomed to strike fear in their victims. He swaggered arrogantly and seemed always to be ready to draw his pistol at the slightest provocation.

Later that day, I was summoned to the large shed where I had been interrogated the day before. Atjep was sitting at the table but this time he was alone; this was not going to be an interrogation session.

'I'm going to have your house searched. I shall allow you to go with the men to fetch some things for yourself and your husband and to arrange some family affairs with your children.'

'That's very generous of you', I said, 'but I'd prefer to go home to stay. How long are you going to keep me here?'

'For the time being at least, but let's hope it won't be for long. We try, whenever possible, not to keep both husband and wife in detention. It's bad for the children.'

Although I had no reason to believe anything he said, I found his words reassuring. It meant nothing, however, and I later discovered that he was one of those who repeatedly opposed my release.

I returned to the room and soon afterwards Bonar came to fetch me. Although the thought of going anywhere with this brute scared me, I was elated that I would be seeing Tari and Anto again. As we walked to the Land Rover, I could see that he was in a different mood now. He was able to switch on and off, normal and relaxed at one moment and flaring into a vicious temper the next.

When we reached the vehicle, he got into the driver's seat and told me to sit in front, next to him. Seven or eight heavily armed soldiers climbed into the back and, before we drove off, one of them blindfolded me. We started down the drive and turned left onto the road, but we had hardly gone more than a few hundred metres when the engine spluttered to a stop. I could hear Bonar pushing his foot against the starter, turning the ignition key on and off and pulling at the brakes, but the engine would not start. His temper exploded when he realized that the petrol tank was empty and I heard him swearing at 'you idiots' in the back who hadn't refilled the tank. He got down from the driver's seat and ordered one of the men to fetch some petrol from a pump nearby. Then he rushed over to my side of the vehicle and hissed, his voice almost hoarse with fury, 'Take that thing off your face, quick. Look at all those kids gawking at you.'

Happy to oblige, I pulled the blindfold off. As I blinked I saw a crowd of schoolchildren and passers-by standing a short distance away, staring at me in amazement. It doesn't take much in a Jakarta street to attract a crowd of spectators and I could now see that this was quite a busy thoroughfare. I must have looked quite a sight, sitting there blindfolded in a stationary army vehicle. The spectators were even more surprised to see that I was a foreign woman. As soon as they realized how angry Bonar was, they hurriedly dispersed.

'Stupid fools!' Again Bonar was spluttering with anger, whether at the people in the street or his soldiers I could not tell. Anyone witnessing this farce would know that there was an army security camp nearby, but we couldn't move till someone arrived with a tin of petrol. I felt a bit better sitting looking ahead through the window and gazing at the passers-by, though I took care not to look behind. It was like a momentary respite from a nightmare. I had no idea where I was though I realized now that this must be on the outskirts of Jakarta. It was in fact Kebayoran Lama, one of the oldest suburbs, south of the capital.

When the petrol arrived, we drove off and I was not blindfolded again. Bonar became quite chatty and asked me about my name. I told him my father had named me after a mountain mentioned in the Bible. He seemed impressed, then sniggered and muttered something about 'communists having biblical names'.

The drive back home took quite a while and I enjoyed every minute of it, seeing ordinary people and breathing free air. It was not yet dusk as we drove through the suburb of Kebayoran which was quite familiar to me, with its wide streets and modern, well-built houses, each surrounded by large, neatly trimmed gardens. In those days, this was the most popular residential area for more wealthy people, well-to-do business-men and their families, up-and-coming generals and top-ranking civil servants.

As we approached our destination, Bonar barked orders to the men about the search, ending with the words 'And mind you don't make a mess. I'll shoot anyone who dares to nick anything.' I knew that he was trying to impress me.

We sped past the sports stadium and came to the older part of downtown Jakarta. We swung round the traffic roundabout in front of the capital's tallest building, Hotel Indonesia, and drove alongside one of the canals towards Jalan Teuku Umar which is where we lived. This was an élite, residential area where many ministers, generals, ambassadors and other powerful people lived.

It was a wonder we had still been able to hold on to the house we had been living in since 1959. Before we got it, the house belonged to a Dutch insurance company but became government property when all Dutch businesses were taken over in 1959. We had rented it ever since.

Several of our nearest neighbours were senior army officers, including General Pangabean, deputy commander of the army, and General Abdul Haris Nasution, the former armed forces chief. I was aware that several people in the army wanted to requisition the house but the Jakarta municipality had so far blocked their attempts, objecting to the military taking over houses that were regulated under its tenancy rules. Some friends thought that Bud's and my arrest was part of a plan to seize the house in our absence. I knew of quite a few people who had been arrested simply to enable officers to grab their houses. This might have been a factor in our case, though I doubt that it played a major role. As it happens, the house was eventually taken over, but that happened much later on.

As we were approaching the house, Bonar spoke. 'Now listen. You're not to talk to anyone in the house about anything except household affairs. You'd better look out, we'll be watching.'

As the Land Rover drew up in front of the house, I saw Tari looking out through the front window. A moment later, Anto appeared beside her. They must have been waiting for something to happen, for news of our whereabouts or for one of us to return. For a moment, they were overjoyed to see me, but as armed soldiers pushed past them through the front door, the looks on their faces changed.

The men quickly spread through the house. They drew all the curtains and slammed shut the side and back doors. Everyone in the house was ordered to gather in the central part of the house. It came as a relief to me to see that Mbah was not there. She had gone to stay with her youngest daughter. The very presence of soldiers always shocked and dismayed this gentle and kindly woman; she was small in build and her lined, oval-shaped face usually bore a faint smile. My sister-in-law Par was there with her three stepchildren, Retno, Agus and Yoyo. Par's husband Mudjajin was also under arrest. He worked on the railways and was arrested when the SBKA, the railwaymen's trade union, was banned. He was in detention in Semarang, Central Java, but they had lost their home and the family had been living with us for some time.

Before I could say anything, Bonar made his purpose clear in a commanding tone of voice. 'We've come to search the house. Don't ask your mother anything. Anyone who's not a member of the family must leave immediately.'

Tari, Anto, Par and I went to the front room and sat down, happy to be back together and not caring much about what the soldiers were doing. The house had been searched before and we knew from experience that there was no point asking to see a search warrant. We could only stand by and watch as they flung open cupboards and drawers and threw everything onto the floor in their search for 'evidence'.

Suddenly, we heard Bonar shouting. 'Who the hell are you? What do you think you're doing here?'

He had found Bobby, Tari's boyfriend, who had been very helpful in times of crisis; the day before, he had come to the house as soon as he heard of our arrest.

'I'm a close friend of Tari's. Please let me stay. I only want to . . .'

'Get out quick, or I'll shoot. You heard what I said, didn't you? Only relatives can stay in the house.'

It had taken a great deal of courage for Bobby to stand up to this brute, but there was no arguing with Bonar and his gun. Tari told me later that Bobby waited at the side of the house until the soldiers and I had left. Another friend of Tari's came to the house later and they both stayed overnight to keep Tari and Anto company.

Tari had met Bobby at the local church and they remained close friends till she and Anto left Indonesia nine months later. There weren't many people ready to take the risk of being friends with the families of tapols. Apart from Par and Mbah and another older sister, Partimah, Bud's brothers and sisters kept away from the house and did nothing to help Tari and Anto in those difficult years. Bobby was one of those rare individuals who stood by them.

As the soldiers continued their search, I was able to convey to Tari that I had no idea where we were being held because we had been blindfolded. This must have upset Tari but, as always, she looked cool and collected. Par sat there saying nothing; after a few moments she got up to fetch me a glass of water. After I had given her some advice about several things and explained where I had put away some money, Tari got up.

'I'd better keep an eye on them to make sure they don't take anything.'

Then Bonar came and told me to fetch some clothes for Bud and myself. When I went into the bedroom, I saw Tari leaning against the doorpost with her arms folded, watching the soldiers' every move. When one of the men asked her where we kept our notebooks and address books, she replied 'I've got no idea. Look for them yourself.'

The search had been going on for about half an hour when Bonar came and told me they were going to dig up some of the floor tiles in the bedroom to make sure there were no weapons hidden underneath.

'You're wasting your time', I said, 'and think of all the mess you'll make.'

'That's our responsibility. We'll pay for anything that needs repairing.' (They never did.)

Someone found an iron bar in the shed at the back and the soldiers started hacking away at some tiles in the front bedroom. After a great deal of exertion, they managed to remove six tiles and the concrete underlay, which revealed nothing more than sand and water-pipes. They left a pile of rubble and quite a deep hole just in front of the bedroom sink. They seemed to be convinced that we had no weapons stashed away and Bonar looked pleased with himself and his men for this great discovery. The only folder they grabbed contained the documents about our tenancy – a hint of what they were really looking for, perhaps – and an anti-communist book in a bookcase that had the word 'communist' on the title page.

As Bonar was making preparations to leave, he suddenly remembered that he had not found the folder containing my economics articles that Atjep was so interested in. He asked me where they were kept.

It was an ill-judged snap decision on my part but it seemed important to me that Atjep should see them, if only to prove how nonsensical were his accusations. I was hoping that the collection would be returned to me but they never were. I lost these and everything else I had written during my productive years before October 1965.

Bonar looked triumphant as he grabbed hold of the folder, sat down and started skimming through the first few pages. Whatever it was that he read, he seemed engrossed for a few moments, nodding his head, as if it confirmed what he thought. Suddenly, he stopped, slammed the folder shut and pushed it under his arm.

'Now, we can go.'

The discovery of the folder seemed to have put him into a good humour and I took the opportunity to ask him to allow me to take a few books back with me.

'Okay, take two or three and we'll see about it when we get back.'

I went to a bookcase which was in great disorder and grabbed three books which I thought harmless enough to pass their censorship. I chose the Bible, a book about Shakespeare and the *Iliad*. Hoping that my luck would hold, I asked whether I could take a pillow back, but this time he refused.

'It's against the rules', he said, 'and anyhow, communists don't need pillows.'

As we drove off, I looked back and saw Tari, Anto, Par and her children and Ira, the servant, watching me disappear. Although the house was not empty of people, it seemed to me that it was over-shadowed by a feeling of desolation, almost like a household in mourning.

Back in the house after I left, Tari passed the night wondering what would happen next. She went to school the next morning, to the Catholic girls' school, Santa Teresa, to which I had shifted her after she was subjected to a great deal of abuse at the state school. The events of October 1965 had shattered all her friendships at school because her father was under arrest and her mother was a 'suspect'.

When Tari told her headteacher that both her parents had been arrested, the woman became very agitated, especially when Tari explained she had no idea where we had been taken. She rang the parents of some other pupils to ask their help; they came rushing to the school and took Tari to several district military command headquarters asking for information. Eventually, they visited the Jakarta military command and met an officer who confirmed that we had been arrested. He knew where we were and promised Tari that any food supplies she brought him would be passed on to us. We did actually receive one food parcel from home but it had been in transit so long that some of the food was inedible.

Night had fallen by the time we approached the interrogation centre. Despite all that had happened on our outward journey, Bonar ordered the soldiers to blindfold me again. He didn't want his superiors to know about the security slip-up and behaved as if the location still had to be concealed from me.

As I alighted, Bonar took the three books away from me. He would have to check first, before letting me have them.

My room-mates were delighted to see me back and showered me with questions about my adventure. My stories brought some cheer into our lives, especially the one about the empty petrol tank. Anything that made Bonar look a fool was more than welcome. The next morning, an orderly came and handed me a book.

'But I brought three books. Where are the other two?' I asked.

'You're only allowed to have this one', he replied, and left me holding the Bible in my hand.

CHAPTER 6

1 October 1965 and
the Suharto Coup

I was held at Satgas-Pusat for two weeks before being transferred to another detention camp. My stay there was a period of perpetual fear and anxiety, of hearing about the arrival of new detainees at all times of the day and night, of hearing them being tortured and seeing them immediately after their sessions with the torturers, covered in blood or with other signs of physical abuse.

Like all detention centres used for newly arrested people, Satgas-Pusat was designed to keep the inmates in a constant state of terror in order to crush their morale. The terror was not confined to the interrogation sessions: officers and rank-and-file soldiers on guard duty were constantly on the lookout for pretexts to punish detainees for the most trivial 'offences' against the regulations. The purpose was to remind us again and again that we were prisoners and should never forget this. The powers under which we had been detained were extra-judicial and the army were answerable to no one but themselves. We had no rights at all. There was no such thing as legal representation, either now or at later stages of detention.

It was here that I first became aware of the extent to which some communist activists and leaders had become collaborators. In most cases, these were people who were unable to withstand the unremitting torture to which they were subjected. The PKI had functioned until 1965 as a legal Party; each member knew many others and could be forced, under duress, to provide a great deal of information by the thugs employed to take part in interrogations. By 1965, many in PKI circles were confident that the Party was edging towards power by peaceful means. The idea that the Party might be plunged into a period of clandestinity was far removed from people's thoughts. Under such circumstances, activists were unprepared for the physical and psychological pressures to which they were subjected by army interrogators and torturers. Most collaborators came from the ranks of the more senior activists in the PKI or left-wing organizations.

On top of this, army informers had for several years wormed their way into the PKI and won the trust of many activists. By 1965, there had been a lot of counter-intelligence between the Party and the army. Once the army gained the upper hand, intelligence units used their own informers to great effect as decoys and to infiltrate the underground networks that were created after 1965. Informers were also set to work to comb through the reports of interrogations in search of points that might help the interrogators pursue new lines of questioning. Without their help, the army would never have been so successful in smashing the left-wing movement and frustrating all efforts to create a sustainable underground movement to organize against the military dictatorship.

Another thing I experienced here at Satgas-Pusat and throughout the whole of my incarceration was a sense of bewilderment and disappointment among many who had spent most of their working lives in political activism closely related to the PKI. Few people – perhaps nobody – really understood what had happened in October 1965, in particular the role of the PKI top leadership in those events. Sometimes we would spend hours discussing it and trying to understand what happened. It was not till many years later that I was able to piece together the facts.

So, what *did* happen on 1 October 1965? To the military regime, the victors, it was a coup attempt engineered by the PKI, their justification for the unprecedented onslaught against the entire left-wing movement which left hundreds of thousands dead, and hundreds of thousands more rounded up in detention camps and prisons. Within days of 1 October, the army coined a name with which to incriminate the PKI – the 'G30S/PKI' (G30S being the abbreviation of 'Gerakan 30 September' or 30 September Movement). Suharto's New Order has never relinquished this name which lies at the heart of its claim to legitimacy, and never will.

During the months before October 1965, the air was rife with rumours of a possible move against President Sukarno by top-ranking anti-communist generals who were fearful of the mounting strength of the PKI. Sukarno had for some time been engaged in a precarious balancing act, trying to keep the PKI and the army in tow. His policies, particularly on international affairs, were close to those of the PKI, pro-Beijing, anti-US and seeking to place Indonesia – and himself – at the head of a new international constellation, the Newly Emerging Forces against the Old Established Forces. For the US, Britain and other Western powers, Indonesia appeared to be on a headlong slide to the left. While the PKI, with a membership of three million, enjoyed the political support of organizations whose joint membership probably exceeded fifteen million, the army had all the fire power in its hands as well as control over a sizeable sector of the state-run economy. A proposal by the PKI, endorsed by Sukarno, for the creation of a Fifth Force, an armed people's militia, plunged some army generals into a state of apoplexy, especially as rumours abounded that China might be willing to supply small weapons to arm the force.

Early in August, Sukarno suffered a relapse from a kidney complaint that had been troubling him for years. This raised the political stakes as fears of another, perhaps fatal, relapse made the question of the presidential succession extremely acute.

The army itself was far from united, not to speak of the disputes between different branches of the armed forces, particularly between the army and the air force. Within the army, there was a band of middle-ranking officers associated with the Diponegoro Division based in Central Java who were deeply hostile to the army high command. The discontent centred on the view that the generals in Jakarta, many of them also from Central Java, had betrayed the true spirit of Indonesia's fighting force and had been sucked into a life of affluence and corruption. There were rumours too of a CIA-backed 'Council of Generals' intent on toppling Sukarno. At many levels, and in many of the divisional commands, the army was split between Sukarnoists and those who wanted him out because they saw him as a tool of the PKI.

The 'coup attempt' on 1 October took place as the army was preparing to celebrate Armed Forces Day on 5 October and battalions had come to Jakarta from Central and East Java to take part in the annual parade. Leading the action in Jakarta were Lieutenant-Colonel Untung, commander of the first battalion of the Tjakrabirawa Regiment, the presidential guard; Colonel Latief, commander of the first infantry battalion of the Jakarta territorial command; and Brigadier-General Supardjo, commander of the fourth combat command in West Kalimantan. The intention was for the operation in Jakarta to be followed by actions of like-minded officers against senior officers in Central Java.

The plan in Jakarta was to kidnap seven generals so as to pre-empt the CIA-backed coup which Untung and his group were convinced had been hatched against Sukarno. Some of the plotters later insisted that there was no intention to murder them but rather to take them to the presidential palace and force them to give an account to Sukarno of their disloyal intrigues. In the event, three were killed by the kidnap squads when they were captured in their homes at around 3 a.m. on 1 October. Three others were killed after being taken to the Halim Perdanakusumah air force base outside Jakarta. The seventh general, Abdul Haris Nasut-ion, escaped by scaling a fence into his neighbour's garden. His four-year-old daughter Irma was fatally wounded when shots were fired inside the house by the kidnappers, and a sentry on duty in front of his house was kidnapped and later killed.

The Jakarta plotters had set up their headquarters at a training ground located at the Halim air force base known as Lubang Buaya, or Crocodile Hole. The bodies of the seven victims were all disposed of by being thrown down a 30-foot deep well in Lubang Buaya. This training ground was being used at the time to train members of the PKI's youth organization, Pemuda Rakyat, as part of a nationwide scheme to give para-military training to young people across the political spectrum. Members of Gerwani were also at the ground to take care of auxiliary duties in the kitchen. Members of youth organizations affiliated to the other political parties were also being given military training elsewhere in the country.

By dawn on 1 October, troops from two battalions which were in the capital for the army day celebrations, the 454th from Central Java and the 530th from East Java, had occupied several key positions in Jakarta including the state radio, RRI, and had surrounded the presidential palace. The Untung Group, the G30S, broadcast several pronounce-ments during the morning and into the early afternoon. In his first pronouncement, Untung, who had assumed the leadership of the group although he was lower in rank than the other two leading plotters in Jakarta, stressed that the movement was 'solely a movement within the army directed against the Council of Generals', aimed at preventing a CIA-backed counter-revolutionary movement by the 'Council of Generals which has stained the name of the army and harboured evil designs against the Republic of Indonesia and President Sukarno'. Later that day, the Untung Group announced the creation of a 45-member revolutionary council of whom half were from the armed forces and the rest mostly middle-of-the-road politicians. Only two were communists.

Although the stated purpose of the G30S movement was to protect Sukarno, the President was not named a member of the revolutionary council, making it appear as though his government was being replaced. This threw the real intentions of the Untung Group vis-à-vis Sukarno into confusion. This was later to be used to very powerful effect by those who crushed the movement.

By mid-morning, Major-General Suharto, who had not been targeted by the plotters, had mustered forces which easily succeeded in re-capturing the radio, winning over the commanders of the two renegade battalions and dispatching a unit of special troops to occupy the Halim airbase. They captured many of the troops and non-military personnel there while others who managed to escape fled in all directions. This was in fact the start of the Suharto Coup.

Earlier, while the kidnap squads were at work, the Untung Group had taken three key personalities to the base, keeping them well away from the training ground where the action was based and where the bodies were disposed of. They were President Sukarno, D. N. Aidit, chairman of the PKI, and Air-Marshal Omar Dhani, commander of the air force. They had allegedly been taken to the base for their own safety. As events unfolded and Suharto's troops moved in on Halim, they all had to flee. Sukarno refused to comply with a request from the plotters that he take a plane to Central Java where officers colluding with the Untung Group were planning their own operations; instead he went to his palace in nearby Bogor, West Java. Aidit took the only safe option open to him and went by air force plane to Yogyakarta in Central Java where he rapidly became isolated and lived for weeks as a fugitive.

Within days, the political climate in Indonesia had changed beyond recognition. The bodies of the murder victims were exhumed and buried in a frenzy of national mourning, focusing almost exclusively on the alleged role of the PKI in the tragedy. The PKI was proclaimed the mastermind of the G30S 'coup attempt'. Suharto and Nasution, the surviving general, made great play of the fact that Aidit had been at the airbase and that members of the youth and women's organizations, both close to the PKI, had been there too. There was also what the army condemned as a highly incriminating editorial in the Party's daily *Harian Rakyat*. From then on, the alleged role of the PKI became an indisputable fact, the official version which even today cannot be publicly challenged in Indonesia.

PKI offices and the homes of its functionaries came under attack by anti-communist mobs. Although in the months and years ahead, thousands of members of the armed forces, including many from the army, were arrested and held as Sukarnoists or undercover PKI contacts, Suharto quickly turned attention away from the fact that the Untung movement had been composed of army officers and had mirrored a deep conflict within the force. PKI-as-mastermind meant that interpretations of the G30S as an internal army affair have never been allowed to surface.

The only newspapers allowed to publish filled every edition with gruesome accounts of how the bodies of the murdered generals had been mutilated by 'fiendish communist women' at Lubang Buaya, who had also engaged in frenzied sex orgies with the troops. These stories about depraved women were instrumental in stirring up anti-communist passions in the cities and in the countryside, as the army began its slaughter of communists and communist suspects later that month, leading to the killing of up to a million people by March the next year. President Sukarno repeatedly insisted publicly that autopsies of the murdered generals had not confirmed that the bodies were mutilated, the eyes gouged or the penises slashed off as the army claimed, but his statements were deafened by the hysteria of anti-communist lies churned out by the press. Many years later, a leading academic on Indonesian affairs, Ben Anderson, discovered the autopsies by chance and published them in April 1987. The documents fully confirmed Sukarno's statements but they have never been published in Indonesia.

The autopsies had been carried out on the orders of Suharto who knew better than anyone that, according to forensic evidence, the sex organs of the victims were intact and the corpses had not been mutilated. When I entered Bukit Duri in 1970, some of the young women who had been in Lubang Buaya on that fateful night were still being held for their alleged involvement in these fabricated events.

So, what was the role of Suharto, then a major-general and in command of the strategically crucial army command, Kostrad? The first and most obvious question is: why was he not targeted for kidnapping by the Untung Group? And why was Kostrad, the unit best equipped and trained for the rapid deployment of special troops capable of crushing an Untung-type rebellion, not occupied by the troops that were briefly under Untung's command? The unit's headquarters were located along the north side of Medan Merdeka, a square situated in the centre of Jakarta, just opposite the radio on the south side and a short distance from Sukarno's palace on the east side of the square. It beggars belief that the rebels simply forgot to include Kostrad in their plans.

At seven in the morning of 1 October, Suharto left home and drove along streets that were guarded by G30S troops, reaching his office without hindrance. He was able, within minutes, to put into operation a plan to thwart the Untung movement. By early afternoon, he had assumed *de facto* command of the armed forces, replacing the murdered General Yani in defiance of an order issued by President Sukarno as Supreme Commander, while still at Halim, to appoint General Pranoto Reksosamudro to the post.

One member of the Untung Group in particular, Colonel Latief, was familiar with the combat capacity of Suharto's troops, having a day earlier been in charge of a dress rehearsal for the 5 October parade. He knew also that Kostrad was in possession of the army's most up-to-date communications system that had recently been supplied and installed by US contractors.

Latief provides another clue to Suharto's role in the 'coup attempt' that paved the way for the real coup. At around midnight on 1 October, just hours before the kidnap squads set out from Halim, Latief met Suharto at the bedside of the General's son who was undergoing treatment at the military hospital, to inform him that the kidnaps were about to begin. In several interviews some years later, Suharto himself drew attention to this meeting, though on each occasion he gave conflicting accounts. He must have realized that information about his late-night contact with the Untung Group had surfaced and he needed to come up with an explanation of his own. In one interview, he alleged that Latief had intended to bump him off at the hospital but got cold feet at the last minute, in another that Latief had come to the hospital to keep track of his whereabouts and movements. At his trial in 1976, Latief gave his own account of the meeting, saying that he had informed Suharto of the forthcoming action. Why did Suharto do nothing to warn his superiors of their impending fate?

Equally important are Suharto's known personal ties with Untung and Latief. The first ten years of Suharto's career in the army were all spent with the Central Java divisional command, and in the mid-1950s he became its commander. Untung and Latief had both served under him in Central Java. Latief played a crucial role in an action under Suharto's command, to march on the city of Yogyakarta in 1946, at a time when it was still under Dutch occupation. Latief and his wife had become close personal friends of the Suhartos. They had visited them socially on two occasions in the weeks just prior to 1 October 1965. Untung had served under Suharto as a paratrooper when the latter was in command of a special operation in 1963 to land Indonesian troops in West Papua before US-backed moves forced the Dutch to cede the territory to Jakarta. While Untung was serving as commander of the 454th battalion, when Suharto was in command of the Central Java division, Mrs Suharto found him a wife and she and her husband travelled from Jakarta to attend Untung's wedding.

During his period as a senior general in Jakarta under the command of the murdered army chief, General Yani, Suharto had held himself aloof from the generals at the army high command. He had his own quarrels with General Nasution, who dismissed him in 1956 as commander of the Central Java division for involvement in a smuggling operation. He saw General Yani as a rival who had been appointed commander of the army over his head. He shunned the flamboyant and cosmopolitan life-style enjoyed by Yani and others at headquarters that was despised by their puritanical subordinate officers in Central Java. Since his days as commander in Central Java, Suharto had recruited a clique of officers who handled his many financial projects and managed his own intelligence operations. All this set him apart from the generals seen by the Untung crowd as scheming to topple Sukarno. More important, it gave him the wherewithal to engage in his own politicking and intrigues.

And what of Aidit and his, or the PKI's, alleged role? How did he, or it, become entangled in the G30S plot? Or did they?

Aidit's physical presence at Halim was portrayed by the army as proof that he had engineered the events, though no one was able to prove that he played an active part in anything that occurred during the night. Another proof of alleged PKI complicity was that the Party's daily *Harian Rakyat* came out on 2 October with an editorial that expressed guarded support for the Untung Group's actions. The strangest thing about this, however, is that late on the afternoon of 1 October, the Jakarta military command shut down all newspapers in the capital save two that were mouthpieces of the armed forces, *Angkatan Bersenjata* and *Berita Yudha*. The 2 October issue of *Harian Rakyat* was the only non-army newspaper to slip through the net, suggesting that the army wanted it to appear and may even have drafted or tampered with the incriminating editorial.

The most crucial question of all is: why should the Party have seen any advantage in staging a coup together with army officers? The Party looked very strong politically and was getting stronger by the day; its alliance with Sukarno was solid enough to bring it enormous gains by continuing along the path of peaceful transition that it had been pursuing for years. The Party had won sizeable victories during national and local elections in the 1950s with around 20 per cent of the votes. This placed it on a par with three other political parties. At the time of the Untung coup attempt, there is no evidence that the Party did anything to mobilize its huge mass following to back up the activities of the officers. On the contrary, on the day of the event, Party activists, insofar as they were told to do anything, were instructed to 'go about your work normally'.

Things were complicated for the PKI because Aidit had a secret intelligence unit called the Special Bureau (Biro Khusus) which was under his personal control, outside the Party's constitutional structures. Syam Kamaruzzaman, the man who headed the bureau, fed information to Aidit, leading him to believe that a successful move by 'progressive army officers' would bring about a favourable turn in the Party's fortunes. Insofar as anything is known about Aidit's intentions and actions leading up to 1 October, they suggest that he was confronted by an event within the armed forces that was pressing ahead, under the control of army officers who were pursuing their own political agenda to resolve internal army conflicts. His actions were limited to deciding the Party's response. Where he may come in for criticism is the inadequacy, or even futility, of that response, and the soundness of his judgement in accepting Syam's word. Aidit's day-to-day dealings with Syam were so secretive that no one else on the politbureau was kept informed. As politbureau member Sudisman stated in his trial, the Party had complete confidence in Aidit to handle the matter.

The special bureau was a body whose existence was known only to a tiny handful of Party functionaries. Its task was to handle the Party's political and intelligence work within the armed forces and gather information about friendly or 'progressive' officers. Given that Syam was in control of the flow of information between Aidit and 'friendly elements' in the armed forces, he held the key to everything that happened. Although he had been associated for many years with Aidit, and Aidit appears to have had complete trust in him (a point that was made to me repeatedly by Aidit's wife, Dr Sutanti, when we were together in Bukit Duri prison), he turned out to have been on the payroll of the Jakarta military command's intelligence unit.

Syam was at Halim during the fateful events there and acted as the go-between between Untung and his co-plotters and Aidit. By all accounts, there was never any direct contact between Aidit and the plotters; everything was handled by Syam. And later, during the dozens of special military tribunal trials that took place under Suharto's supervision, Syam was a willing and loquacious witness, holding forth on the deeds and intentions of Aidit.

Unlike Untung and Supardjo who were both executed very soon after being sentenced to death, within months of 1 October, Syam was kept alive for twenty years. He is said to have boasted to co-prisoners, who were puzzled about his prolonged survival, that each time he thought his execution was imminent, he would tell the authorities of another PKI contact in the armed forces which would lead to further investigations involving him as witness. Finally his luck ran out and he was executed in 1986.

After October 1965, nothing was heard of Latief for several years. He eventually emerged in the early 1970s, a prisoner in Salemba Prison, Jakarta. He had been badly wounded during his arrest early in October; he was gravely ill for many months but finally recovered. He was not brought to trial until 1976. Unlike his co-plotters, he was not sentenced to death but given a life sentence. Someone somewhere in the regime seems to want to keep him alive.

As for Aidit, Suharto was determined that he should be put to death with all dispatch. The story of Aidit's murder has been told by the officer who perpetrated the crime at Suharto's behest. In fact, the officer, Colonel Yasir Hadibroto, is so proud of his feat that he has related the events leading up to Aidit's death no fewer than three times, in 1980, 1983 and 1985, all published without a shred of remorse in the Indonesian press.

When Aidit fled from Lubang Buaya to Central Java, he encountered great difficulties establishing contact with PKI activists in the province. By the third week of October, army troops were rampaging in Central Java; the massacres had begun and most communist leaders were either murdered, arrested or on the run. Some PKI activists who met him said that he was planning to turn to Sukarno for help, calling on him to work out a political solution to the tragedy. Aidit was a minister without portfolio in Sukarno's government and on one occasion attempted to travel back to Jakarta to attend a cabinet meeting at the palace early in October, but it was impossible to arrange transport for him. Another PKI leader, Njoto, who also held ministerial rank, attended the meeting, was arrested as he left the palace and was later shot dead. With the single exception of Sudisman, who was tried, sentenced to death and speedily executed, all the members of the Party's politbureau were executed summarily.

Colonel Yasir, commander of the fourth infantry brigade of Kostrad at the time, was given instructions by Suharto a few weeks after 1 October to go with a unit of men to Central Java and 'deal with' Aidit. Yasir told *Kompas,* one of Indonesia's leading dailies, in 1980 that he tracked his prey down with the help of a young man who had served as Aidit's personal bodyguard but who was in fact in the pay of the army. The man had been detained but was released from prison to re-establish contact with the unsuspecting Aidit. It was this man who escorted Aidit to his last hiding place, in a village not far from Solo where he was arrested by Yasir's men on the morning of 22 November. He was held for several hours, during which time an officer took photographs of their 'prize captive'. Yasir told *Kompas* that he later received prints of these photos but no negatives.

I have no idea where the negatives ended up. But six prints were sent to me by an anonymous sympathizer in 1979 and were reproduced in the newsletter of my organization, *TAPOL Bulletin,* in November 1980.

A few hours after his arrest, Aidit was bundled into an army vehicle and driven to the spot where Yasir's men had set up base, but not before a major from divisional command headquarters in Semarang had got wind of Aidit's arrest and had driven down south to meet Yasir and suggest that Aidit should be placed under detention at headquarters, so that his arrest could be reported to Sukarno. Knowing that this was not what Suharto wanted, Yasir feigned agreement, suggesting that they drive in convoy, with the major driving the front vehicle, but Yasir turned off the road and took Aidit to his base where he ordered his men to strap him up, stand him in front of a well and shoot him dead. His body was thrown down the well, covered up with leaves and burnt. Banana trees were planted to cover up any evidence of the crime.

The Major had lost track of the convoy but, on hearing the gunfire, turned back, found the base and asked Yasir where the prisoner was.

'He's been dealt with', said Yasir.

'That's terrible. Someone will have to answer for this', said the Major.

'Why? He's been dealt with. This is a time of war, isn't it?' was Yasir's reply.

All that was now left was for Yasir to report the successful completion of his assignement to Suharto, so he went to Yogyakarta two days later to meet his boss.

He described the whole operation to Suharto, then said 'Is this what you meant when you said we should "deal with" him?'

Suharto smiled and said nothing.

Later, on retirement, Yasir was appointed Governor of the province of Lampung, one of the many assassins who have held positions of high office in Suharto's New Order.

Aidit's brutal murder was only one of hundreds of thousands of murders that were taking place at the time. As Suharto knew only too well, it was extremely important as it meant destroying crucial evidence that only Aidit could have produced about how the PKI had been tricked into becoming entangled with the Untung plot. With Aidit dead, it was now left to Syam to testify in numerous trials 'on Aidit's behalf'.

Aidit's wife told me she knew nothing about the way her husband had died. She had not even been officially notified that he was dead.

After crushing the Untung plotters, Suharto began his carefully contrived plan to destroy the PKI and to remove Sukarno, gradually grabbing the reins of state power from his hands. The destruction of the PKI proceeded rapidly and was completed within six months. The ousting of Sukarno took two-and-a-half years to complete.

The PKI was physically annihilated by the massacres that swept through all parts of the country, striking with particular severity in Central and East Java, North Sumatra and Bali. In all regions, the killings were initiated by the army, which was able to instigate civilian mobs allied with local political groups to join in the blood-letting. A steady flow of cable traffic between the US embassy in Jakarta and Washington, released under the Freedom of Information Act, shows conclusively that the US was well aware of the killings, approved of them and even sent emergency supplies of small firearms to arm the killers.

Tens of thousands of the victims were people who had been taken into army custody. Many PKI members and suspects arrested in Jakarta were trucked off to nearby army-run plantations and killed. This was the fate of a close colleague of mine, Porkas, whose wife could not trace him after he was arrested. She had heard he had been taken to an unknown destination in West Java. I met her when I was visiting the central headquarters of the military police in Jakarta seeking information about Bud's release prospects. This was her fifth or sixth attempt to trace him but she never discovered exactly what happened to him.

Many thousands of prisoners taken into custody all over Java were trucked to Nusakembangan, the prison island off the south coast of Central Java. A young boy who lived on the island, and whose father had been Deputy Director of the prison, later revealed that some 30,000 prisoners were transported to the island in the two years after 1 October. He said that prisoners were dying at a rate of twenty a day from malnutrition and disease. Every night dozens were taken away to Pasir Putih on the western tip of the island, shot dead and buried in mass graves by special police brought to the island from Cilacap, the nearby harbour on the mainland.

Most of those slaughtered were poor peasants and villagers who were taken from their homes and put to death by troops armed with small arms or slain with knives, machetes, often decapitated and impaled, or their bodies thrown into rivers. President Sukarno stood by helpless as the massacres engulfed large areas of the country, repeatedly pleading for a return to sanity. He refused to comply with calls for the PKI to be outlawed and even tried to restore the unity he craved between nationalist, religious-based and communist parties, the concept known as Nasakom. In December, when the massacres were in full swing, he commissioned a nine-man team to investigate the scale of the slaughter. It came up with a figure of 78,000 dead, although one member of the team, later interviewed by US journalist John Hughes, believed that the true figure was ten times as much.

Was he really saying, Hughes asked, that he believed the figure to be 780,000?

'Yes, that's right. You mustn't forget that when we talked to officials and village headmen, they were trying to downgrade the figures of people they'd killed. On Bali they gave us a death figure of 10,000. I believe it

*was nearer 100,000. There was covering up elsewhere, too. So I calculate
that about ten times as many people were killed as we actually reported.'*

JOHN HUGHES, *The End of Sukarno* (Angus and Robertson, 1967), p. 185

Oei Tju Tat, a minister in Sukarno's cabinet, was a member of the
fact-finding commission. In his autobiography, published in 1995, he
explains how he managed to separate himself from the group and meet
local political leaders to check whether the figures they were being given
were accurate. He, too, confirms that the figures he was given privately
far exceeded those recorded in the official report.

In any case, the killings continued for several months after the
investigation was completed, so it is no exaggeration to put the estimated
death toll at one million. The Western powers did nothing to condemn
the armed forces and Suharto, still less seek an accounting of this terrible
crime against humanity. Far from it. At the end of October, a week after
the killings had commenced, US Secretary of State Dean Rusk cabled
the US ambassador in Jakarta saying that the 'campaign against the PKI'
must continue and that the military 'are [the] only force capable of
creating order in Indonesia'. A month later, Washington provided the
army with small arms dubbed 'medicines' to expedite the killings.

The West welcomed Suharto's rise to power, the annihilation of the
PKI and the downfall of Sukarno because it opened up Indonesia and all
its resources to unhindered Western investment. The US press welcomed the reversal of the political situation in Indonesia as 'a gleam of
light in Asia' and 'the best news for years in Asia'. The *Wall Street Journal*
congratulated Suharto for using 'strength and finesse'.

As for Sukarno, Suharto needed to move with circumspection, knowing full well that the army itself harboured many Sukarnoists while other
branches were actually commanded by officers who still looked to the
President for leadership. Sticking to the Javanese method of *alon-alon, asal
kelakon* (slow but sure), Suharto managed, step by step, to wrench power
from Sukarno, taking his time while purging the armed forces of
unreliable elements.

Already on 2 October 1965, having refused to allow General Pranoto
to take command of the armed forces as proposed by Sukarno, Suharto
sought and obtained an order from the President to 'restore security and
order'. A week later, on 10 October, he consolidated these powers by
setting up his own special command, the Command for the Restoration
of Security and Order, Kopkamtib, an extra-constitutional security and
intelligence agency that took over the task of political persecution and
control. Kopkamtib drafted its own regulations and guidelines, issued its
own decrees, arrested and detained people and determined the criteria

for their continued detention or eventual trial. The existence of this agency, which was replaced in 1988 by a similarly powerful agency called Bakorstanas, turned Indonesia into a military security state, under *de facto* martial law.

Wielding these special powers, Kopkamtib effectively outlawed the PKI and several dozen left-wing mass organizations six months before Suharto had seized the necessary powers from Sukarno to ban them formally.

From October 1965 till March 1966, the army kept the country in a state of perpetual political and economic turmoil, using the army-backed student and school-pupil action fronts, Kami and Kappi, to demonstrate on the streets, whipping up passions against the PKI and heaping blame for all the country's ills on Sukarno. The President was even accused of having backed the Untung plot, although in the early stages Untung and his co-conspirators had been accused of having staged their coup *against* Sukarno.

On 11 March 1966, while a cabinet meeting was in progress, the presidential palace was surrounded by troops of Kostrad under Kemal Idris. Warned that his life was in danger, Sukarno fled by helicopter to Bogor where he was pursued by three army generals who presented him with a written order ready for his signature, assigning special powers to General Suharto. Although the order did nothing more than instruct Suharto 'to take all necessary steps to guarantee security and calm and the stability of the running of the Government' (Sukarno would have been unlikely to sign away full powers), Suharto used it to ban the PKI and numerous organizations, to arrest fifteen cabinet ministers and begin to reshape the cabinet and government policy. Two months later, Supersemar, as the 11 March Order became known, was confirmed as a state decree by the country's supreme assembly, the MPRS, which was convened in special session by Suharto, after more than half its members had been purged or killed. This document has since been used by Suharto as the formal transfer of power from Sukarno.

During the succeeding months, the trials of three of Sukarno's closest political associates in his cabinet were staged. These were in effect proxy trials intended to discredit the President. Throughout the whole process, Suharto avoided anything that might lead to open confrontation with Sukarno; during this period, conflict within the armed forces was so intense that the danger of civil war was never far from the surface. For Suharto, it was essential to avoid such a catastrophe, not because he feared yet more loss of life but because he feared that an open conflagration might strengthen the hand of 'radical' army officers who had for months been baying for Sukarno's blood.

With Sukarno's position now disintegrating fast, Suharto convened a second MPRS session in March 1967 at which Sukarno was stripped of his designation as 'President-for-life' and Suharto was appointed 'Acting President'. This was followed a year later, in March 1968, by a third special session at which Sukarno was stripped of all his powers and Suharto became President. The Suharto Coup, for which the Untung plot had wittingly or unwittingly paved the way, had now completed its course.

Sukarno was held under house arrest from then on. Even close relatives were rarely given access. He died in June 1970, without ever having the opportunity to give his own verdict on Suharto's rise to power.

CHAPTER 7

Morale at a Low Ebb

There was a great deal of mutual suspicion among the prisoners, especially during these first days, which made it difficult, with few exceptions, to establish any companionship with others who were suffering the same fate. Much of the time, I felt lonely and defenceless against a system of evil that had me in its grip. Each of us with our own fears had few emotions left to sympathize with others.

The only woman in our room I drew close to was Nuriah. She had a very practical approach to life and was always ready with advice. She was a tower of strength in moments of crisis. When people came back to the room in pain or physically damaged in any way, she was the one best able to comfort them or treat their injuries. She had what I can only describe as a sixth sense and always seemed to know before anyone else what was going on. I valued this greatly because I am not very perceptive and often failed to pick up signals or notice remarks made by officers during the course of the day. A few days after we first met, arrangements were made for her baby to be taken home and be cared for by a relative; and this was the only time I can recollect when she broke down. She was occasionally asked to help with chores outside our room, particularly in the kitchen, and this gave her access to all kinds of stories and rumours about the camp. She told me that there were regular showings of pornographic films for officers so as to encourage them to be unrestrained in their use of sexual abuse and gross indecency when interrogating women.

Shortly before I was transferred from Satgas-Pusat, a row of cages was constructed inside the shed, to the left of our room. These cages were not yet in use by the time I left, but I later heard that they were used to isolate and humiliate detainees. Alone and in the eye of the guards at every moment of the day, some of these men and women went insane, some attempted suicide even though their tormentors deprived them of the means of inflicting physical harm on themselves. The only way of telling whether a person had succumbed was to see whether they remained in the cages and whether they were restricted to a punitive diet of unpalatable rice.

55

The night after my brief visit home, I slept even more fitfully. To add to our discomfort, one of the guards on duty had a transistor radio on full blast all night and walked past our windows a number of times, with his radio under his arm.

When I awoke the next morning, I was horrified to see a man stripped to the waist, dangling by his wrists from a tree near the well. His wrists were pulled just high enough to keep him touching the ground with his toes. His body was covered with swollen, red weals and his head hung down on his chest. Occasionally, a guard would walk across the courtyard or along the corridor past our room, ignoring him. To see other people moving around normally, unconcerned about the sufferings of this man, made the scene even more horrific. It was more than I could do to go to the well or cross the yard to the toilet while he was still hanging there and I avoided looking out of the window. Later, when we were escorted on our morning visit to the toilet, it was a relief to see that he had been taken away. I never discovered his name but we later heard that he was a low-ranking army officer who, until his arrest, had worked at the army's recruitment office and was accused of having helped young communists to join the army. Many thousands of soldiers and officers were arrested after 1965 and accused of being PKI agents or Sukarnoists.

As the day wore on, I tried to get the tortured man out of my mind as I sat answering the inquisitor's questionnaire. But, that afternoon, there was another incident that shook me profoundly. I had just finished writing and was lying on my mat, trying to rest when we heard angry shouts in the courtyard. I looked out and saw a detainee standing outside one of the toilets, being harangued by Bonar.

'How dare you answer me back? You're a prisoner here, don't forget.' He screeched the words over and over again, *kamu tahanan*, using *kamu* for 'you'. Officers were always addressing us as *kamu*. This is an acceptable form of address among friends but is very offensive when used between adults who have no grounds for familiarity with each other. Bonar lost no opportunity to remind us that we were prisoners, unworthy of respect and utterly at his mercy.

The man refused to be silenced by Bonar, insisting that he wanted to go to the toilet. Then Bonar started pummelling him with his fists but the man refused to budge. By now Bonar was livid. He barked an order to the guard on duty to summon others to help him deal with this infraction. Five or six soldiers turned up, all carrying rifles. They seized the man by the arms, dragged him along the ground to the centre of the courtyard and started laying into him with their fists, rifle butts and boots, as Bonar stood a short distance away, shouting at them to 'give him a good thrashing'. I sank to the floor unable to watch the scene, but there was no way I could avoid hearing the sound of beating, the words of abuse and the groans of the victim. After several minutes of this, the noise and the voices receded towards the shed as they dragged the defenceless man back to his room.

Then things went quiet again . . .

———————————

A few days after my arrest, two more women joined us in our room. The first to arrive had been a member of the MPRS, the upper House of parliament. Like all left-wing members of both Houses, she was expelled from parliament immediately after the Suharto takeover; her husband, a member of the lower House, had also been arrested. During Bud's first and second arrests, I had often met her outside Salemba Prison in Jakarta when I used to take food to him three times a week.

Although these were called *hari bezoek* or 'visiting days', they were not visiting days at all. We were permitted to bring food parcels but were not allowed to meet the detainees. Visits were permitted only once a year on special days like Christmas or Lebaran, the end of the Muslim fasting month. Sometimes even annual visits were cancelled for selected prisoners.

The hardship and sufferings of the wives and children of detainees are a story in themselves. The vast majority of these women had no means of support or regular income and were cold-shouldered even by close relatives, who were afraid of being tainted by contact with prisoners and their families. Some women managed to survive by setting up food stalls and selling home-made cakes. Others turned to dressmaking, but few were able to earn enough to keep hunger from the door. Some, in desperation, handed their children over to relatives or neighbours. In many cases, the children were hounded from their schools – as Tari had been – and were unable to get places in other schools.

Prison 'visiting days' were occasions for chatting to other wives or relatives, exchanging gossip, and gleaning what we could about the prospects for release.

'Is your husband still in Salemba?' I asked our new room-mate after she had had time to settle in.

'Yes, and what about Mas Bud? He was released, wasn't he?'

'Yes, but they picked him up again, together with me. He's here now, somewhere upstairs.' Little had changed, I thought, except that we were meeting now as fellow detainees rather than detainees' wives.

A day or so after she arrived, something very unusual happened. After we had returned from our early morning toilet, we were suddenly ordered to lie down flat on the floor and keep still for a few minutes. We had to do this again several times during the next few days. At first, we could not understand what was going on, then realized that each time we had to lie down, someone was taken across the courtyard who, for some reason, was not allowed to see us in the room.

After three days of this, another woman joined us. Her left eye was black with bruises and, as soon as the guard had gone, she sank to the floor, obviously relieved.

'They told me there weren't any other women here. They said all the women here had been killed and their bodies had been buried under a heap of sand in the shed.'

For three days, she told us, she had been held in strict isolation in a tiny room upstairs. She slept at night on a table with a guard sleeping on the floor underneath. Enormous pressure was used to force her into submission. She was stripped naked by torturers who deliberately started punching her breasts, knowing that she had recently given birth and had been unable to suckle her baby for days so that her breasts were full of milk and particularly painful and sensitive. She got a black eye when one of the thugs punched her hard in the face with his fist, striking her eye with a huge ring on one of his fingers. This had broken a blood vessel in her left eyeball. She was in a state of shock when she joined us, though she gradually calmed down, greatly relieved to be with other women.

But her problems were not at an end. They arrested a cousin of hers whose address they had forced out of her. She was summoned for a confrontation with him in the room next to ours. They stripped her naked in front of him while he, also stripped naked, was beaten by another woman detainee, the former member of the upper House of parliament, who was ordered to beat him by one of the torturers. As this frightful atrocity proceeded, I sat cowed in my corner trying to drive the sounds out of my head. But there was no closing my ears to the orders being yelled, the sound of the rattan stick being lashed against bare flesh, and the screams of pain. When things like this happened within earshot, a deathly silence fell in our room.

As for my own 'case', nothing more happened after I handed in my answers to the questions I had been asked. There were no further interrogations, except for a rather unexpected brief encounter with Atjep. He appeared one day in the courtyard and I was summoned to go and talk to him.

'Did you have anything to do with the Gilchrist Letter? It wasn't you who wrote it, was it?' he asked.

'What on earth makes you think that? I did no such thing', I replied.

This was a confidential cable dispatched in March 1965 by the British ambassador in Jakarta, Sir Andrew Gilchrist, to the Foreign Office about 'our local army friends', hinting that the British were informed about an army plot to eliminate Sukarno. The document fell into the hands of the BPI, the state intelligence agency headed by Dr Subandrio, concurrently Foreign Minister. It was drawn to Sukarno's attention in May that year and was widely commented on. The Gilchrist Letter helped to stir up speculations in Jakarta, reinforcing the rumours of a council of generals that was plotting to depose Sukarno. Britain had reasons of its own to despise Sukarno, who had initiated a campaign of *konfrontasi* with Malaysia in 1964, after the British colonies in northern Borneo were united with Peninsular Malaysia against strong opposition from Jakarta. The crucial sentence read: 'It would be as well to emphasise once more to our local friends in the army that the strictest caution, discipline and co-ordination are essential to the success of the enterprise.'

Army intelligence insisted that the document was a forgery produced by the BPI, part of a series of pre-October 1965 events that, according to them, had been designed to create an atmosphere of tension. Many years later, Sir Andrew Gilchrist wrote to an Indian academic, confirming that the letter was not a forgery and confirming that it was 'one found by the Indonesians in the wreckage of the British Embassy'. But here was Atjep, trying to pin this one on me because I had worked closely with Dr Subandrio for many months before October 1965. This was the first and last I heard of the Gilchrist Letter during my detention.

One evening, when things at the camp had not yet heated up, we were sitting bracing ourselves for whatever horror would occur next when Bonar suddenly appeared at one of the windows. He stood leaning on the ledge and looked at each of us in turn, leering. What kind of mood was he in now? Had he come to bully, to intimidate or threaten, or to ridicule and gloat?

'Well, well. How are you all feeling this evening? Quite well and happy, I hope?'

Happy! His taunts were sometimes more cutting than his tempers.

'We'll only be happy when you release us and let us go home to our children', one of the women said.

The leer did not leave his face but he nodded slowly – a habit of his when he wanted to impress us.

'There's no going home for any of you lot, you dirty communists. This isn't like any other place. Once here, you'll never get out alive.'

Had I thought about it calmly, I would have realized that he was playing on our vulnerability. But any sense of calm and rationality had by now been destroyed. None of us said anything.

After a pause to let his words sink in, he said 'Hey, you', pointing at me, 'how old is Tari?'

'Seventeen.'

'That's a nice age for a girl to be left alone at home, isn't it? What's going to become of her?'

'I don't know', I replied, 'but I'm sure she'll be able to look after herself.'

'Ugh, rubbish! She'll be out on the streets soon enough, selling herself to make a living. And what about your daughters', he said, turning to the other women. 'Two years old? Four years old? In fifteen years, they'll be grown up, all of them, and out on the streets. Prostitutes. And you lot won't be there to look after them, will you?'

I felt so vulnerable that his words hit me like a knife. Would we really be here for ever? And what would happen to the children?

'Ever heard of Eichmann?' he asked, looking at me.

'Yes, he was the man who planned the annihilation of the Jews in the German concentration camps', I replied. 'Of course, I've heard of him.'

'Eichmann, that's me, commander of this camp. I've read all about him. A great fellow. He's my model.'

I stared at him, hardly believing my ears. After a few moments, he swaggered off chuckling something to himself about Eichmann and concentration camps.

By now it was already more than a week since I had last seen Tari and Anto and the separation was getting me down. It was unbearable to be cut off from any news of home, and I could well imagine how hard it was for them, knowing nothing about the two of us. I spent much of the time worrying about how they were coping.

His words were senseless but I find it difficult to describe the mood of desolation that overcame me. And I was not alone. Nobody in the room spoke after he left and the atmosphere was laden with gloom. I spent the night dozing off occasionally, unable to dispel the fear that I would never leave this place alive, never see the children again. I woke next morning in a fit of sobbing. I managed to calm myself but broke down every time anyone said anything to me. I could not lift myself out of this depression for the whole day.

Late that afternoon, I saw Bud crossing the courtyard. He glanced in my direction as he always did and noticed that I was utterly miserable. On his way back across the yard, I saw him speak to one of the guards. Then, quite unexpectedly, the guard came over and entered the room.

'He wants to tell you something. I'll let you out but please be quick.'

I went out and stood just near enough to hear Bud's words.

'Please don't cry. Don't worry about the children. They'll learn a lot through all these experiences. They'll grow up much more quickly and grow wiser in the process.'

I could say nothing in reply. I only nodded and tried to smile through my tears. The guard escorted me back to the room, whispering as we went: 'Cheer up, Ibu. Things aren't all that bad. Why don't you try singing, to keep your mind off things?'

It had been foolish of me to let Bonar get the better of me like this. I took their advice to heart. Never again during all the years of my detention did I suffer the fears and heartaches of that dreadful night and day.

CHAPTER 8

Transfer to Another Camp

During the two weeks I was held at the Satgas–Pusat interrogation centre, we were kept in the dark about what might happen to us. It was a new centre and none of the detainees there had yet been transferred to other centres. When you live without knowing your short-term or long-term prospects, a great deal of time is spent watching for signs of something to happen. As I discovered later, one of the things to watch out for was signs of transfers or release, but here we had nothing to go by and our imaginations were always running away with us.

The food we were given was not bad, much better than anything I got during the rest of my detention. The cooking was done by women detainees who were held in another part of the camp. I was conscious of the fact that some PKI activists who were collaborating with the interrogators were living with their wives in married quarters, and these were the women who worked in the kitchen. Nuriah was sometimes called out to help and it was here that she picked up gossip that she shared with us.

I vividly remember the night before my transfer. We had heard that Bonar and the other intelligence officers would be away from the camp on operations. So, in celebration of their absence, we had a fit of exuberance. Moments like this are rare, like outbursts of gaiety coming as a relief to the intolerable tension. Caution is thrown to the wind, all inhibitions are shed and you become convulsed with laughter at the silliest of jokes, or behave like children for no apparent reason. On that evening, my room-mates and I had such a fling. I was the one who started it when I began singing 'The Blue Danube'. One of the women took up the refrain and we both jumped up and started waltzing round the room. It was as though we had forgotten where we were as we pranced round and round, egged on by the others who joined in, clapping and singing. It didn't last long. We were soon warned 'someone is coming', so we sank, panting, to the floor. But we all felt much better for it.

Many Indonesians have a strong belief in premonitions. So, when three of us in the room were summoned the next morning and told to put our things together, someone said 'That's what comes of all that singing and dancing last night'. Whether this was supposed to be a premonition of things getting better or worse I don't know, but, for me, transfer from Satgas-Pusat was a tremendous relief. Anything was better than this, I thought.

When tapols are moved, they are given no advanced warning. I later got used to the routine as I was transferred on numerous occasions. A soldier would turn up and bark 'Get your things together, quick. We're waiting.' He would stand there watching, to make sure there were no farewells or parting messages. They wouldn't even say that you were going to be moved, or where you were going, or why. It would just be 'Get in the van! Be quick!'

This was a deliberate strategy to keep detainees in a state of anxiety and uncertainty, breeding fear and demoralization. I doubt whether it had much to do with security; it was much more part of the psychological warfare against defenceless prisoners.

After we got into the waiting Land Rover, I saw a group of men waiting to get in and Bud was among them. They actually allowed us to sit next to each other although Bonar, who was supervising the move, warned us not to talk to each other. As we were about to be blindfolded, Bonar put out his hand and shook hands with Bud: 'No ill feelings, I hope. I was only doing my duty.'

'Okay, okay', Bud replied, rather pointedly.

As we drove off, I again experienced the horror of being driven to an unknown destination, but when we were allowed to remove the blindfolds I realized that we were travelling back into the centre of Jakarta, to a detention camp where Bud had been held during his first period of detention in 1965. He had been taken from home a few days after returning to Indonesia from Japan where he had gone on a government mission. He had gone to Japan just after the October events at a time when the anti-communist hysteria was at its height. Responding to a summons from the army, he went to a military command office and was taken from there to the place where we were now being brought. They told him to sit in a room and wait. He waited till late afternoon when an officer came in.

'You're under arrest. We're not going to let you go home.'

This happened at a time when people were being rounded up in their thousands in Jakarta, and the homes of communists or sympathizers were being mobbed and ransacked. In the countryside, the killings had begun.

Seven of us were transferred from Satgas-Pusat, three women and four men. When we arrived, we were ordered to stand in line outside a door leading to the office. After a while, an officer came out and eyed his new charges with a look of unconcealed contempt. He was a heavily built man with a thick moustache and bleary, red eyes under a pair of bushy eyebrows, reminding me of an English sergeant major. As we stood in the blazing heat, he spoke to us about our new 'home'.

'Relations between us will be okay as long as you remember how to behave. You are prisoners here and I warn you not to forget it.' In his short speech of welcome, he made it clear that he would be treating us as guilty men and women. According to his simple logic, the fact that we had been arrested was proof of our 'involvement' in the G30S/PKI.

'You must have done something wrong or our men wouldn't have arrested you. Is that clear?' he said, glaring menacingly at us.

'Yes', we replied dutifully.

We were summoned into the office one by one and our meagre belongings were thoroughly searched. Then we were told to go and join the other tapols. As I entered the compound, a crowded, derelict place, I was conscious of numerous pairs of eyes watching me. I was struck by the silent, unfriendly stares that met me as I crossed a narrow corridor and entered the women's room. Actually, people were not really being unfriendly; this was the natural pose of tapols towards any newcomer, guarding against tell-tale signs of recognition should you happen to see an old acquaintance.

The place was packed full of people. Some were sitting on the floor playing cards or doing nothing; some were standing and chatting or leaning against roof pillars. Others were squatting before an enormous wood fire, cooking, or bending over a tap in the centre of the compound, washing plates. Along the back, I saw five or six people standing in a queue. They were waiting to use the only toilet in the compound.

Most of the male prisoners were dressed in underpants and thin vests, some little better than rags. We were cooped up with hardly an inch to move. What a contrast to Satgas-Pusat! There we lived in strict isolation with nobody being allowed to meet anyone except for people sharing the same room. But here all the tapols were mingled together. To get anywhere, to the bathroom, the toilet, to the fire or the tap and to the office, you had to pick your way over people's bodies or between their legs, stooping down to avoid brushing your head against clean or half-clean clothes hanging from wall-pegs or on lines, for want of a better place to keep them. As you edged your way along, it was 'Sorry, did I tread on you? A thousand apologies . . .'

This detention centre was a converted residence, probably inhabited formerly by Dutch families. The house itself was now an army office.

Along the sides of the yard at the back were rooms that had been the servants' quarters, four rooms along one side and two along the other, which were now occupied by tapols. The largest room was near the gate, probably the former garage; this was occupied by a team of soldiers who guarded the place. All the rooms were packed with tapols, ten or more, men or women, in rooms no larger than about seven by ten feet. Along the two corridors covered by a roof but opening out onto the yard were dozens of men who lay down or sat up, shoulder to shoulder. When it rained, the corridors were flooded with water. In some places, the floors were tiled, in others they were concrete, but all were full of crevices that housed numerous insects. The sun never shone into the rooms as the only windows opened out onto the covered corridors. The longer corridor, which must have been about 50 feet long, accommodated 25 men – a space of two feet each.

In the centre of all this confusion was a raised, covered platform with an open oven where a fire was kept burning for most of the day. Some prisoners who received extra supplies from home would cook rice or other dishes to supplement the meagre rations provided by the army. Along the top end was a forecourt where tapols received visitors, sitting on mats on the ground.

When we moved here, there were about a hundred prisoners in a space that should not have accommodated more than twenty. Some of the men told me that sometimes earlier that year the overcrowding was so acute they had to sleep in shifts, some sitting up hugging their knees while others slept for a few hours. At times, the overcrowding became so bad, with more than 130 people, that some of the men preferred sleeping in the yard to being cooped up in the unbearably stuffy, mosquito-ridden rooms and corridors. During the rainy season, with the likelihood of heavy showers at night, special permission had to be sought for tapols to sleep in the offices, but they were only allowed to shift there after it had started to rain. Whenever a downpour started, there would be a mad rush as men sleeping in the yard or along the corridors jumped up, grabbed their mats and other belongings and hurried to take shelter in the office.

This was Likdam, the headquarters of the Jakarta military command's special investigation unit. It was located in Lapangan Banteng, not far from one of Jakarta's main markets, Pasar Baru. Many of the shops there were owned by Chinese or Indian businessmen who presented the officers at this unit with a fruitful source of income. In former days, they spent much of their time picking up traders on a variety of trumped-up charges and then asking for money as the price of release.

But now it served primarily as a transit centre for tapols. When people were arrested in Jakarta, they would first be taken to an interrogation centre where information would be dragged out of them. Then they would be moved to Likdam to be sorted out; a few would be released but the majority would be transferred to prison for indefinite detention.

One of the officers once tried to explain to me the difference between various detention camps; the interrogations here, he said, were not 'operational' as in Satgas–Pusat but 'juridical'. He wanted to assure me that interrogators did not rough up their victims so much here because the main aim was to classify us into categories 'A', 'B' or 'C'. But what 'juridical' in fact meant was that the army performed the role of investigator, prosecutor and judge for each and every one of us. There was no part in all this for the legal profession. This was army detention from start to finish.

All the hundreds of thousands of arrests and detentions that had been going on since 1965 were based on the special powers exercised by Kopkamtib. A presidential instruction decreed by General Suharto 'on behalf of' Sukarno (still nominally head of state but already deprived of virtually all his powers) in May 1966 defined three levels of 'involvement' in the G30S/PKI affair:

- *Those clearly directly involved, who (1) planned, helped to plan or knew about the plan but did not report to the competent authorities; or (2) being conscious of its objectives, were involved in the implementation of this counter-revolutionary movement.*
- *Those clearly indirectly involved, who after knowing about this counter-revolutionary movement (1) displayed an attitude, whether in deeds or words, of approval for this movement, or (2) consciously displayed an attitude, in deeds or words, opposed to actions to suppress the movement.*
- *There are indications of, or it can reasonably be thought that there was direct or indirect involvement in the movement, including members of the outlawed PKI or of the executive boards of like-minded mass organizations or ordinary members of like-minded mass organizations who did not categorically oppose the movement.*

'A' category tapols were those against whom there was enough evidence to bring them to trial; 'B' category prisoners were those considered to have been PKI or mass organization leaders or activists, but against whom no charges could be brought because of the lack of sufficient evidence but who had to be detained indefinitely because of their direct or indirect involvement; 'C' category prisoners were regarded as followers of the PKI or banned mass organizations but who did not need to be held indefinitely and could therefore be released. Transfer to a prison meant that you were either 'A' or 'B' category. If you were released you must have been classified as 'C'.

Tapols were never informed of their classification. They could only draw their own conclusions from what actually happened.

Suharto did not introduce martial law nor did he declare a state of emergency. Instead, he used Kopkamtib to give army commanders at every level special powers. In the wake of his coup, the main aim was to crush the PKI and left-wing organizations. But the army's security agency had wide powers to act against all suspect organizations and movements and to interfere in a variety of political, social and economic activities. Kopkamtib remained in existence until 1988 when it was replaced by a security agency called Bakorstanas with broadly the same powers. Commanding officers of military commands in the provinces, districts, sub-districts and villages were, and still are, vested with these special powers, answerable to no one but their superior commanding officers.

Among their most repressive powers are the powers to arrest and interrogate, torture and detain anyone suspected of being opposed to the Government.

Little did I realize, when I entered the women's room at Likdam on the day of my transfer in late September 1968 that this ramshackle, overcrowded compound was to be my home, my entire world, for the next fifteen months. Few people stayed there for more than a few months. As far as I could gather, the fact that I was English created complications for my captors and explains why they were undecided about what to do with me. I was probably classified very early on as 'B' but my transfer to prison did not happen for nearly two years.

Here at Likdam, I quickly became accustomed to the regular cycle of events. Once a month, there would be a transfer of prisoners to Salemba Prison for the men or Bukit Duri Prison for the women, bringing the number of inmates down to 60 or 70. Living conditions would get a little easier. We would not have to queue quite so long to go to the toilet or the bathroom. However, almost immediately, more prisoners would start arriving from other centres.

When I arrived, there were seven of us sharing a single room; within days, five more women arrived. With twelve in the room, it was almost impossible to sleep. We placed ourselves six on opposite sides of the room. We had to lie perfectly straight with our arms folded across our chests or held stiffly to our sides. The slightest move brought us into physical contact with the women on either side or at our feet. As I was taller than the other women, my feet protruded farther between the feet of the women on the other side and I had to be even more careful about not moving. I had four neighbours to worry about, not two.

No mats were provided; everything we had came from home. Indeed, throughout the time I spent in detention, not a single item of clothing, bedding, towels, not even a cup or plate, was ever supplied by the prison authorities. A large number of tapols had no relatives near enough to visit and had to rely on others to share a mat with them or were given things left behind by departing tapols. Some were reduced to sleeping on sacks or bits of rag.

None of the soldiers on guard at the camps showed the slightest interest in our conditions. This had been going on now for three years and I suppose they had got used to the squalor and deprivation. Anyway, we were all 'communists' and not deserving of anything better. Fellow-tapols who had had experience of centres in other parts of the country regarded conditions at Likdam as being comparatively very good. We had no idea in those days whether anyone anywhere outside Indonesia had any inkling of what we were going through.

However awful things were here, I was enormously relieved at being rid of Satgas-Pusat and Bonar. My room-mates inducted me into the general run of things and I was thrilled to learn that we were permitted to have contact with our families. Since the day I returned home with the search unit, I had heard nothing from Tari and Anto and had received only one parcel of food which I knew had been sent indirectly. This could only mean that they had not been informed of our whereabouts. The first thing to do was to send a message home. Things were definitely beginning to look a little brighter.

Bud was in a room on the opposite side of the yard. Now we could always exchange a few words without having to ask for permission. Some hours after our arrival I saw him standing near the door of the women's room, with a grin on his face.

'Have you been to the toilet yet?' he asked as I approached him.

It was a strange question, but he must have known about the troubles I had had with the toilet at Satgas-Pusat.

'No', I replied. 'Why do you ask?'

'It's great. You'll love it. Just a hole in the ground like before but it's deep and clean. A few tins of water and away it all goes', he said, making a clucking noise with his tongue.

It was the best news I had heard for days. After two weeks of being constipated, I was feeling that I could stand almost anything as long as I had access to a toilet that worked!

CHAPTER 9

Likdam, My Home
for Fifteen Months

On the evening of my arrival at Likdam, a man came to see me. He was holding a tattered exercise book and asked for my name and address. At first I thought he was a clerk from the office, but it soon dawned on me that he was a tapol like the rest of us. He was our 'RT' which is what the local chief in a residential area is called in the world outside. The camp RT was appointed by the camp commander as his liaison with the tapols. No one ever volunteered for the job; it was a thankless task. Whenever anything went wrong and people needed disciplining, he (women were never chosen) would be the first to take the rap, which could mean not only a severe reprimand but also a beating. He would even be held responsible if someone arrived late for the twice daily roll-calls.

Sitting cross-legged beside me, the RT explained that the inmates were divided into food groups and suggested that I join the women's group.

'Some prisoners get food regularly from home. Others get things less often but the majority never get anything at all. Food rations from the army are so awful that we try to make sure there are one or two well-supplied tapols in each group so that the food can be shared. Is that all right with you?'

It sounded fine. I knew that as soon as we had made contact, the family would try to keep the two of us well supplied with food.

'But what about telling my children where we are? Can I phone home this evening?'

The RT didn't like this at all.

'You can't do that. They'll never allow you to use the phone.'

He came closer and whispered in my ear. 'The soldier on duty now is very unfriendly. Tomorrow evening another guy will be here. One of the fellows here knows how to handle him so he'll ask him to phone home for you after the officers have left for the day. But please make sure to give him a tip. That's the only way to get things done round here.'

It was easy enough for people like us, living in Jakarta, who had phones at home. Those without phones had to ask a soldier to deliver a message to their family, which called for a bigger tip. For tapols whose families lived in other towns, there was no solution. We were not allowed to send letters, and, unless those outside were able to track down relatives who had been detained and make contact, the tapol would go for months, perhaps years, without contact.

Three days later, Tari and Anto came to see us for the first time, bringing us a plentiful supply of food. From then on, they came three times a week, every visiting day. I was worried about them coming so often but they insisted; we soon realized how welcome their visits were and how much we needed the food.

I knew very little at the time about how they managed to keep the household going. The money I had left at home, my takings from lessons and translations, soon ran out, so they had to find ways of earning money themselves. Par started making cakes and Anto set up a stall in front of the house. Tari had learnt to make yoghurt which I used to sell before my arrest, so she prepared this and went out selling it to local families and to some of the nearby embassies. We had rented a small pavilion at the back of the house to a US company, which brought in some cash every month. Apart from that, life was bleak for the children. But never once did they speak about their difficulties, always insisting 'Things are fine, so don't worry'.

. The food supplied by the army was dreadful. Twice a day, at midday and in the evening, we were given cooked food from a nearby army kitchen, half a small bowlful of rice and a small piece of *tahu* (bean-curd) or *tempeh* (a soya cake-like food). The rice was always dry and full of grit, and the pieces of *tahu* or *tempeh* were hardly larger than a postage stamp. Fried and well seasoned, both these foods are delicious and very nutritious, but they were served to us boiled without any flavouring except for some very hot chilli peppers. Sometimes the food was mouldy and inedible. Sometimes they would serve us a small helping of boiled cucumber which I always found revolting, or, as a special treat, a leathery piece of salted fish which I could never chew, let alone swallow.

The only thing we got in the way of beverages was boiled water. They never provided us with sugar; there was nothing for breakfast and never any fruit. They never gave us soap or clothing, mats to sleep on or medicines.

We were allowed to receive uncooked food from home and cook it in the camp. There were a few stoves but all the paraffin was supplied by relatives. The army did not supply us with fuel to boil the water we drank, even though Jakarta water is not drinkable unboiled. The light bulbs in the rooms and corridors all came from home and when a bulb needed replacing in the office, a soldier would come down and take one of ours. We also had to supply the officers and the guards with their mid-morning tea or coffee and sugar, and they sometimes came to us for food and medicine.

We were often required to do odd jobs for the soldiers, repairing their cars, giving massages, cleaning up the office. One day an officer came down and asked whether anyone around could do some typing.

'Why don't you go out and find a typist in the street? All you need do is arrest someone and your problem is solved', a tapol was heard to say.

The camp commander who had given us such an unfriendly welcome was called Adil, the word in Indonesian for 'justice'. How on earth he came to have such a name I can't imagine! Sometimes, he would come down to the compound to nose around, strutting along the corridors and peering into the rooms. If anyone happened to be eating when he appeared, he would look on, satisfied, as if he was personally responsible for the food we ate.

There were roll-calls every morning and evening, but occasionally he would summon us all for a special roll-call to rebuke us for some misdemeanour or brag about how well we were being treated.

'I've been in charge of this camp since 1965', he would often say. 'More than 7,000 prisoners have gone through my hands since then and not a single one has died. That's because we look after you so well, so don't forget it.'

Who knows whether he was telling the truth but he would not be able to make this claim for much longer.

The short, tubby old man whom I had seen puffing his way across the courtyard at Satgas-Pusat had just been transferred to Likdam and it was plain to see that he was extremely ill. He walked with great difficulty and even Adil took pity, allowing him to squat when we had to attend the longer roll-calls.

Pak Tasrim always had a smile on his face and never complained even though he was in terrible pain all the time. He loved chess and would often lie on the floor in his room, his head propped up against the bare, damp wall, watching his room-mates play, nodding approval at a good move or explaining the mistakes people made.

As his condition deteriorated, he was given permission to go to hospital for a check-up and treatment. We all expected not to see him again for some time. But he returned the same day and struggled back to his room. They had given him a bottle of pills and told him he was not ill enough to be treated in hospital. That same night, his condition worsened but the guards refused to call a doctor.

'He was examined a few hours ago so we're not going to call a doctor', said one of the soldiers.

The next morning, I met him outside the bathroom, leaning heavily on two other prisoners. They were taking him there to relieve himself. Minutes later, as we sat eating breakfast, a deathly hush spread through the camp. We heard men in the corridors talking in anguished whispers and soon understood what had happened. Pak Tasrim had passed away soon after returning from the bathroom.

Within minutes we filed into his room to pay our last respects. There he lay on the floor, with a few detainees sitting cross-legged by his side. Many hours were to pass before a relative came to take his body home. Not long after he died, someone managed to get hold of leaves and petals – goodness knows how – and the women made floral chains to adorn his body. All the Javanese and Muslim rites were carefully observed during the hours his body remained in our midst. His body was washed, his eyes closed and covered, his hands crossed on his chest. He was wrapped in a batik cloth and turned with his feet pointing towards Mecca. Prayers were said and incense was burnt. The room where he lay was cleared of all the belongings of his room-mates, giving him the space and peace in death that he had been denied during his dreadful illness.

Here we were, total strangers, but the death of this unfortunate man was more shattering for many of us than the loss of a close friend.

The women I lived with in my first weeks at Likdam were a mixed bunch. Some of my friends in Satgas-Pusat were transferred, including Nuriah, whom I was very happy to see. One room-mate had once been a leading functionary of Gerwani, the women's organization which was banned immediately after the events of 1 October. But she left the organization long before that time because it had criticized her for seeking a divorce and getting married for a second time. She didn't mingle much with the rest of us and was always expecting her husband, a local government official, to come and take her home. It was weeks before he did.

A younger woman in the room was her niece, a dreamy-eyed girl who spent much of the day telling us about her boyfriends. She would often lie on the floor and tell us that one of the tapols here had fallen in love with her. These fantasies seemed to suggest that she was really afraid that prolonged detention would damage her chances of getting married. Most young Javanese women found it difficult to contemplate a future without a husband. She had been arrested in her aunt's home because the army alleged that she was in contact with Gerwani members in Central Java. Because of this, the aunt treated her very unkindly and bore a deep grudge against her, believing that she had been arrested because of the girl's presence in her house – which was probably true.

Another room-mate was a trade unionist, a quiet, thin woman with a pallid complexion and a high-pitched voice. She rarely said anything to anyone. I got the impression that she had devoted most of her time and energies to her organizational activities. Nothing seemed to ruffle her and she never complained of anything. Her husband was also in detention but they had lost contact with each other and she never had any visits from relatives. I was to meet up with her later in Bukit Duri Prison. While there, she discovered by chance that her husband had died in detention although she was never officially notified.

Then there was a devout Catholic who spent several hours a day fingering her rosary. She was a born story-teller, but the story of her own arrest beggars belief. It all happened because of her former husband, who had been an activist in the left-wing veterans' association. They had got divorced long ago and her present husband was not connected with any of the banned mass organizations. Even so, troops came to pick her up and arrested her present husband as well.

Another of my room-mates was a domestic servant. She had never been to school and was illiterate. She understood nothing about coups or the G30S/PKI and the word 'communist' meant nothing to her. We could only guess that she must have been arrested for alleged connections with Gerwani, though she herself seemed to know nothing about the organization. She was always pleading with the guards to let her go home. One day a soldier started teasing her, telling her that she wouldn't be allowed home until she could produce a Gerwani membership card. The poor woman really believed him. Every afternoon she would dress herself up in her best clothes which other tapols had given her, gather together her few belongings, walk up to the front gate and ask for permission to go home. She was eventually released but not until she had spent about a year in detention.

Suwarni, another of my room-mates, was what I could call a 'prisoner of circumstance'. She was nineteen years old when we first met and had come to Jakarta from her home village in Central Java, in search of work. She moved in with her boyfriend, who shared a house with his brother, a member of one of the outlawed organizations. When soldiers came to arrest the brother, both she and her boyfriend and everyone else who happened to be in the house at the time were taken into custody. Not long after this happened, two of her brothers, who were also trying to find work in Jakarta, started looking for her and eventually traced her to an army interrogation centre. They went there hoping to meet her and were told to wait. After waiting for most of the day, they were placed under arrest. Now the three of them were here in Likdam, bewildered and helpless, with no relative in Jakarta to turn to. Since they weren't allowed to write home, it was many months before their parents, sensing that something was amiss, came to Jakarta and were finally able to locate them. Everybody in the camp knew their story and there was great relief when the three of them were released, after spending nearly nine months as 'political prisoners'.

I gradually fell in with the routine of camp life. We started the day with a communal bath, all the women going to the bathroom together. The bathroom was fairly spacious and consisted of a large tub of cold water. Standing on the floor, we showered our bodies and let the water run off through a drain in the corner. The bathroom was always in great demand because this was the place where we often had to urinate as well, because the only toilet for shitting was in constant use. I never found anything hygienically better than this in any detention centre.

Then I would spend a few minutes doing exercises in the yard. Soon after I arrived, a prisoner thought it would be a good idea for us to do communal morning exercises, before the officers arrived for duty, to keep us in good shape. But one day an officer turned up when we were exercising together and reported this to Adil. He regarded this as a dangerous form of 'organized activity' which had to stop immediately.

After doing my exercises, I took a brisk walk around the yard. I calculated that if I walked round the edge plus one diagonal crossing 50 times, I covered a distance of about two kilometres. A number of us would do physical jerks separately, but when Adil appeared – we always knew when he was coming by the sound of his Mazda car – everyone would disappear. I hated kowtowing to this man. If I happened to be in the middle of one of my rounds I would finish it as he entered, then saunter slowly back to the room.

When the officers were working in the office, we were not allowed into the yard and had to confine ourselves to the rooms and corridors. After breakfast – which for me most of the time meant bread which I bought from a street-vendor, and tomatoes from home – I would spend several hours doing needlework or knitting until lunch time. Often tapols would come and sit by me to practise their English. I made many friendships listening to people's life stories or sometimes hearing their descriptions of how they had got caught up in all this. Sometimes they would read aloud to me but we had no books or magazines except for the Bible and the Koran. Occasionally, a group would sit round reading a whole book aloud from the Old Testament. The Book of Esther was a great favourite, though it wasn't always easy to explain the meanings of the biblical English. Once a detainee managed to have a copy of *Reader's Digest* smuggled in, so we tore it up into its separate articles which made it easier to hide and meant that more people could read it.

Interrogations went on for most of the day – but never at night – and the rooms where they took place were close enough for us to hear what was going on. When someone was being beaten, the camp fell silent as we listened to the screams, groans and thuds. Often a detainee would return with cuts, swellings or bruises and others would be ready with rice poultices or other kinds of treatment to alleviate the pain. Compared to Satgas-Pusat, the treatment here was relatively mild, little more than verbal abuse, punches, kicks or a beating with a soldier's belt. Coming from that terrible place and other torture centres, we actually considered ourselves lucky to be here.

After office hours, when the officers had gone home, leaving us under the guard of a team of sentries, things became more relaxed and the yard became 'ours' again. I would spend the early evening strolling there with a detainee. We worked out a weekly schedule for those who wanted to practise their English. We could not plan to hold English classes – this would never have been allowed – so we did it on a one-to-one basis. I heard more Indonesian folklore and descriptions of different parts of the country during the time I spent in detention than in all the previous sixteen years I had lived in Indonesia.

The only communal activity allowed was evening Muslim prayers. Afterwards, we would sit and chat, play cards, or stroll, tell jokes or commiserate with each other. To the casual observer, we might sometimes have appeared to be quite a relaxed community. Most of the tapols were Javanese, who have a great capacity for hiding their emotions. Few would talk about their cases or their personal problems, what they feared about husbands, wives or children. I found it helpful not to think much about the future but to live in and for the present. The future seemed so bleak and empty.

We never knew from one day to the next what would happen to us and when things did happen we had to respond smartly. Releases occurred with the same degree of unpredictability as transfers to prison. There were always rumours circulating about lists of detainees who would be released, or transferred. Most of my fellow prisoners assumed that I would be released because I was English, even though I now had Indonesian nationality. I had my doubts but got used to jokes being made about the British Government sending a gunboat to rescue me from Suharto's clutches.

There were regular monthly transfers of tapols to prison, usually at the end of the first week. When the fateful day arrived, an officer would come down into the compound and read out a long list of names as we listened in silence. The ones whose names were called out would rush forward and stand in rows. Once they were all known to be present, they were ordered to go and fetch their things. Those of us who hadn't been called would help them pack and search in our own small stock of belongings, grab anything useful and push it into the hands of those about to depart: a few ounces of sugar, a bar of soap, a bottle of vitamin pills, perhaps an item of clothing. We knew that the first few weeks in prison were the worst. The newcomers usually had to spend time in a block with criminal prisoners where they were always treated badly, or in isolation, and not allowed family visits. There would be no food-sharing for quite some time.

The departing tapols would be hustled onto a truck waiting outside the gate; within minutes they were gone. No time for goodbyes to new-found friends who we might never see again. After the whole thing was over, we would return to our places, shaken by the experience, wondering whose turn it would be next. Why was so-and-so transferred and not so-and-so? You were arrested long before her; could this mean that you are soon going to be released? Those of us left behind might have been expected to rejoice at our good fortune but I always felt sad and despondent after these transfers. We could never look forward to anything good. All we knew was that this was a process over which we had no control.

Then, as the day wore on and we settled back into our emptier rooms and corridors, tired of analysing what it all meant, another group of tapols would arrive. In the next few days, other groups would come until the place was filled to overcrowding again and it was time to start thinking about whose turn it would be next for transfer.

CHAPTER 10

The Kalong Torture Chamber

Most of the people transferred to Likdam came from an interrogation centre in Gunung Sahari, Jakarta, the headquarters of a special unit established by the Jakarta military command in 1966 to smash the underground movement. The exploits of this unit – though not the methods it used – were widely reported in the press. Its most spectacular achievements were the arrest of Sudisman, the only member of the PKI politbureau not to be caught and murdered in 1965, and Brigadier-General Supardjo, the most senior army officer in the Untung Group that planned and carried out the kidnappings of the generals. Both men were later tried by Suharto's extraordinary military tribunal, Mahmilub, sentenced to death and executed.

This was the place where Tari had spent a few dreadful hours. From my own brief visit there when I was summoned by Atjep, I remembered it as a derelict house with nothing outside to distinguish it from the other houses in the quiet side street. It still bore the name-board of the social services union for becak-drivers which had occupied the building until it was requisitioned by the army. But the oppressive feel of an intel unit hit you the moment you entered the front door, the detached, sullen attitude of the soldiers on guard and the swagger of the officers in charge of operations.

The operation conducted from Gunung Sahari was called *Operasi Kalong* or 'Operation of the Bats'. As the name suggested, it functioned mainly at night. I knew from Tari's experience that this was a torture centre, but it was not until I met the detainees who came to Likdam that I got a true sense of what went on there. Every time new tapols arrived, we would hear more accounts of horrific torture sessions. Sometimes, a prisoner at Likdam would be summoned back to Kalong for further interrogation. A burly lieutenant whom we knew only as Bob would turn up and 'borrow' the person for a few days. The word in Indonesian is *dibon*, which means 'being exchanged for a voucher', a word I heard many times in detention. Whenever Bob appeared, a shudder would go through the camp.

When a new detainee arrived at Kalong, he or she would be kept in the interrogation room for days, sleeping on one of the tables and not allowed to mix with the other people. The unit was geared for rapid action and reaction, and the turnover of prisoners would sometimes be very high. Newcomers had to be isolated, shocked and demoralized and were forced to watch others being interrogated and tortured, a form of torment in itself.

During its first years of operation, Kalong was run by Atjep and Major Suroso, an officer who won rapid promotion in recognition for his successes in rounding up communist activists. The two of them had recruited and trained a team of tough, dedicated and ruthless torturers and had also been able to recruit a number of communist activists to assist in the interrogation of their comrades. By late 1968, when I began to hear first-hand accounts about the centre, two senior communists were playing a crucial role on the Kalong operations; they were widely despised because of their active participation in the torture of detainees.

One was S. who, until October 1965, had been the personal body-guard of D. N. Aidit; the other was B. from South Sumatra, who had been made a member of the party's international department only a short while before his arrest.

The commonest form of torture was the electric shock, first applied on the thumbs, then on other parts of the body, including the genitals. Another favourite was beating the victim with the long, spiked tail of the mammoth pari (stingray) fish. Several of the men arriving at Likdam bore the scars of newly healed wounds on their arms and backs. The physical state of one young man particularly horrified me. He was very handsome and had a lithe body and thick black hair; his skin was darker than usual for an Indonesian. When I first set eyes on him, he reminded me of a proud young Indian sitting astride an elephant. But one day, when he was stripped to the waist, I saw fresh scars all over his body, hideous thin, white streaks across his dark skin where the tail had torn through his flesh. He was the younger brother of a PKI leader and had been beaten mercilessly to make him divulge information about his brother's whereabouts.

Some tapols who joined us from Kalong bore psychological rather than physical scars. One man who slept just outside our room always had an empty stare on his face. He could have been taken for a simpleton. He spent the whole time cooking and doing chores for his food group. He only ever spoke when spoken to and responded like an automaton to whatever people asked him to do. The torturers had used electric shock on his genitals to devastating effect. He was a victim of mistaken identity; they mistook him for a communist member of the upper House of parliament, the MPRS. Although the confusion was cleared up, he remained in detention because he happened to be a member of the banned peasants' union, the BTI.

I heard exactly the same stories from everyone who arrived from Kalong. Even after the initial interrogation sessions were over and the newcomer could now join the others being held in the compound, conditions were intolerable. The detainees were segregated into groups and were forbidden to talk to anyone in another group. There were plenty of informers spying on the detainees, most of them former comrades, who were constantly on the lookout for breaches of camp discipline. Torture went on all day and night. There was a term for the shrieks of the torture victims – *lagu wajib* or 'obligatory song'. In the evenings, the inmates were required to watch television, except for the news bulletins when the set was turned off. Perhaps this kind of regime was maintained to prevent the tapols from spending the evenings in discussions with each other. It is really frustrating watching people on television living normal lives when you yourself are held behind barbed wire in a detention camp. When I later had the chance to watch, I sometimes felt like screaming at the people inside the box and wanted to tell them things they would never read in the Indonesian press.

What was particularly disturbing about Kalong was the number of communist cadres who were now working for the army. But there were plenty more whose courage defies belief. One who stands out for me is Sri Ambar, a member of SOBSI and one of its leading women activists. She had succeeded in escaping arrest for about nine months after October 1965 but her husband was caught and their home was mobbed and destroyed by a gang of young men. I first heard about Sri when I moved to Likdam. She had come there from Kalong about a year earlier. Stories about Sri were legendary. Even the guards spoke about her with awe. One soldier told me she was so distraught when she came to Likdam that the mere sight of a uniformed soldier would cause her to scream 'Get away from me, you brute!'

Later, when we met in Bukit Duri Prison, she told me about everything that had happened to her.

After her home was destroyed, she and her two daughters moved in with her mother. One day she met a former comrade in the street. In the course of a chat, the man asked her where she was living. She took the precaution of not giving him her address, mentioning only the district where she was staying. As it turns out, that was more than enough. Little did she know that he was working for army intelligence. He went to the local government office and scanned the photos of local residents handed in when applying for identity cards. He found hers and was able to direct the army to her mother's home. Other activists had just been arrested during an operation against the underground and, under torture, one told the army that she was helping to distribute illegal pamphlets. While she was certainly a victim of betrayal, she agreed that her own lack of vigilance was partly to blame.

As soon as she arrived in Kalong, she was interrogated but denied everything. They brought in the man who had betrayed her and ordered him to repeat his allegations in her presence. Still she refused to confess. They were both stripped naked and flogged in an attempt to find out who was lying. By now it was late in the evening. They were both taken to a yard in the middle of the camp, tied to a tree by their wrists and left dangling with their toes just touching the ground till morning. As she hung there in great agony, an elderly civilian employee at the camp crept up to her while the guards were out of sight. He held a cup of hot, sweet tea to her lips for her to sip. Then he took a jar of balsam from his pocket.

'Excuse me for touching you', he said, as he rubbed her body with the ointment.

After this, the torture sessions continued daily, till one night, things came to a head. Atjep who took personal charge of her interrogation was enraged by her stubborn refusal to talk. On this occasion, she had been stripped naked as usual and was being beaten in the presence of some of her male colleagues, when Atjep suddenly shouted 'Let her have it'.

One of the torturers pulled out a knife and plunged it into her left thigh, causing a long, deep gash. One of the other prisoners in the room who saw this fell unconscious at the sight of so much blood, but she herself could hardly feel the pain.

'You sadists', she yelled, then bent down and, scarcely conscious of what she was doing, she pushed the two sides of the gash together, to try to stop the bleeding. But Atjep would not let things rest and nodded in her direction to the man who had knifed her. He made another plunge at her with his knife, this time in the right buttock. By now, she was so weak from loss of blood that she fainted.

When she came to, she was lying in a military hospital and was told that she had been brought in two days earlier. The first doctor to examine her said she had only herself to blame. But other medical staff were more sympathetic and told her that the doctors on duty had been shocked to see how badly injured she was. Apart from the deep knife wounds, there were many other injuries and bruises on her back and neck. Two days after the gashes on her legs had been stitched up, a doctor came to say he would have to remove the stitches. When she protested, he told her that the doctors on duty when she arrived had complained to army headquarters about her condition. An investigation had been ordered and the doctors had been instructed to remove the stitches so that they could measure the length and depth of the gashes.

'The removal of the stitches was more painful than anything I had suffered', she told me.

She heard later that Atjep was suspended from duty while the inquiry was under way and spent some time in detention.

Long before she had fully recovered, she was discharged from hospital and ordered to return to Kalong so that the interrogations could continue. When she next turned up for questioning, her two daughters were in the room and were being beaten. They had recently been taken into custody and had been asked to give information about people who used to visit their mother at home. When they refused, the decision was made to confront them with their mother. As she stood and watched, the girls shouted 'Mother, don't say anything. Never mind if we have to go through this.'

Sri kept quiet as the girls were beaten. The two of them were taken away and she heard nothing more about them for several months. Later she was told that one of her daughters was being held at another camp run by Kalong. The younger daughter, who was under ten years of age, was taken away by an army officer who said he would look after her. Sri was never able to discover what happened to this child or where she was taken. Up to the time I last saw Sri, the quest to find her daughter had led nowhere.

The loss of her child was the worst tragedy of all for Sri. She told me that whenever she was brought before interrogators or army officers, the first thing she always did was to ask them where her daughter was.

There was to be yet another confrontation, this time with her mother. The elderly woman had been detained and was accused of helping her daughter. The army had no respect for her parental bond with Sri. She was quite fearless and made no secret of her views when interrogated in Sri's presence:

'Did you help your daughter and give her shelter after the coup?'

'Yes, of course I did. Why shouldn't I?'

'Didn't you know the security forces were after her because she was scheming against the Government?'

'That's nothing to do with me. She's my only daughter and it's my duty to help her in every way I can when she's in trouble.'

'But didn't you realize you would get yourself into trouble by helping her?'

'I don't care about that. I'm her mother and that's all that matters to me.'

While all this was going on, the soldiers were slapping her face, punching and beating her. Undeterred she turned to Sri and shouted 'Don't take any notice of what they are doing. You must do what you have to do. All this doesn't matter.'

Sri's mother remained in detention for several months together with her granddaughter, the older of Sri's two daughters.

Some years later, when I was being held in the same prison as Sri, she heard that her mother had died of a brain tumour. Together with her, we mourned the passing of a courageous woman. She may have known little about politics but would not allow anyone to shake her faith in her daughter.

Sri was kept in the interrogation room at Kalong for so long that she witnessed a great deal of torture. She told me she saw a soldier bite off the ear lobe of Tari's friend.

'How could he possibly do such a thing?' I asked her.

'One of Atjep's most brutal thugs held the boy's head in his hands, dug his teeth into the fleshy part of the ear and bit it off. Then he spat it onto the floor. That's how he did it', she said.

Another scene had shaken her profoundly. As she was sitting in the interrogation room one day, a young boy was brought in. He had been caught carrying messages which the interrogators had reason to believe were intended for Sudisman, the PKI politbureau member who was still at large, in hiding somewhere in Jakarta. They beat him mercilessly, to force him to say where Sudisman was hiding, but he said nothing. Sri was struck by the dignity of the boy as they flogged him without respite.

'It was remarkable. He stood there, his head held high, defying these sadists.'

Then they tried to undermine his confidence by telling him they had obtained plenty of information from people in the party leadership so he might as well tell them all he knew. They mentioned a name, Sujono Pratiknjo, a PKI central committee member who had just been captured. He held a key position in the clandestine movement and had worked closely with Sudisman. The boy could not believe someone so high up would betray Sudisman and was convinced that they were bluffing. Sujono was brought in, but still the boy showed no sign of weakening.

'Now', said one of the interrogators to Sujono, 'tell us about the underground organization you've set up in Jakarta.'

Sujono walked to a blackboard, picked up a piece of chalk and began to draw a diagram of the underground network, indicating the cells that had been created and writing down the names of people in the cells. He also described the ways each of the cells kept contact with Sudisman.

As Sujono was busy scribbling, Sri looked at the boy. She saw him quiver. All his poise had gone; he was limp with horror. Torture he could stand but not the sight of such treachery. Sudisman was captured the very next day and the underground network crumbled to pieces.

Later I found out more about this incident and the tragic consequences for the underground movement. Immediately after Sujono's betrayal, one of the young couriers escaped from the detention centre with the help of his close comrades and rushed to Sudisman's hideout to warn him to flee. Sudisman refused to believe that Sujono had betrayed him and thought this was a ploy to force him to leave his hideout. But within hours Sudisman was arrested.

For Sri, the worst of her memories was witnessing the treatment of another courageous young activist caught carrying messages from Central Java to Jakarta. She had seen him in the prisoners' compound and he had whispered words of admiration for all her courage.

She was in the room when they started flogging him. They aimed at his back and neck, the most vulnerable parts of the body. I was told by prisoners who had gone through such beating that the only way to protect yourself is to bend the head back as far as possible against the top of the spine. The flogging grew in intensity and Sri tried not to watch. She stared at a piece of paper in front of her, trying to concentrate on anything but the atrocity going on in her presence. But when she heard him fall, she turned round to see what had happened. He was lying prostrate on the floor; thick white foam was oozing out of his mouth. When she rushed over to him, the torturers did nothing to hold her back. They seemed stunned by what they had done.

She bent down and just managed to hear him whisper a girl's name, probably the name of his sweetheart. A few moments later, the boy was dead.

Not long after all these experiences, Sri was summoned to appear as a witness at Sudisman's trial but she refused to testify. She held her hand cupped behind her ear to indicate to the judge that she could not hear properly and told the court that her hearing had been impaired by torture.

Many years later, in 1975, Sri was tried and sentenced to fifteen years. After being released in the early 1980s, she lived in Bogor, West Java, with her husband who had spent fourteen years in detention without trial. They managed to survive from the proceeds of a small stall which they set up with the help of Amnesty members in Austria, but after her husband died she stopped writing to the group. Now a widow, she lives somewhere on the outskirts of Jakarta and has begun to lose her mind, hardly surprising for someone who has lived through such a terrible ordeal. But the legend of Sri Ambar's unshakable courage is still spoken of with awe by all those who knew her in prison.

CHAPTER 11

My Fellow-Prisoners in Likdam

Once, in the camp where I was held after Likdam, the commander confided to me that he was puzzled.

'Why do prisoners always look so miserable? I treat them humanely. I talk to them as a friend but it makes no difference. They go on looking miserable.'

This was Lieutenant-Colonel Prijo Subagio who occasionally called me in for a friendly chat. Try as he might, he could not understand that there was a yawning gap between him and us, an inability on his part to understand that he and the system he represented were the problem.

People responded in a variety of ways to political imprisonment. Some stuck to their ideals and remained firm, which sustained them in the face of physical hardship and torture. Others resigned themselves to being in prison, seeing it as a 'consequence of the struggle which we must put up with as best we can'. But there were many, especially those who were more or less ignorant about politics, who regarded their misfortune as the 'hand of fate', karma, an ordeal inflicted by the gods for past misdeeds. They firmly believed that those responsible would one day get their deserts. I heard a story later, in the women's prison, that was all about karma. The wife of a soldier who had maltreated many women under interrogation was suffering such severe labour pains that he feared for her life.

'Go and ask forgiveness from the women you maltreated if you want your child to survive', his wife implored. So he rushed to prison and begged forgiveness from his victims. None of the women refused. The child was delivered safely.

Some tapols had a tremendous reserve of will power, not because of political conviction but simply from a determination to come to terms with a situation that was out of their control. Many were overwhelmed by a sense of powerlessness and constant grief. One woman I shared a cell with for several weeks woke up every morning bemoaning her fate.

There were many reasons why the tens of thousands of tapols felt their sufferings so deeply. The vast majority were held for years without being charged and with no prospects of ever being tried or released. We all knew that an 'A' category tapol was regarded as a 'heavy case' and more serious than 'B', but at least you would be tried and have a chance to defend yourself. If you got a fixed-term sentence, your chances of being released might be better than those classified as 'B'. Five years after the 1965 events, there were still about 100,000 tapols in Indonesia, but there had only been a few hundred trials.

From the moment of their arrest, tapols thought only of the present, and 'the present' hardly changed from one day to the next. There was nothing anyone could do about it, no access to lawyers, no basic rights, no one to look to for help. In prison, we knew nothing about any moves outside to support us. In 1968, two men set up the first human rights group in Indonesia, Lembaga Pembela Hak-Hak Asazi Manusia (Human Rights Defence League); for many years they waged a lonely campaign.

One of the men was J. C. Princen, who, in February 1969, told a Jakarta newspaper that 2,000 or 3,000 people had been killed by army units in the previous three months in the district of Purwodadi, Central Java, and many more were in detention and were being tortured with electric shocks. Princen's exposure created quite a stir, but was quickly hushed up after journalists went to investigate. This was the first time that anyone had spoken out about massacres, detention and torture, condemning them as grave human rights abuses.

The other man was the lawyer Yap Thiam Hien, who had spent some months in prison himself. In 1975, he made an impassioned plea on behalf of the tapols during the trial of a communist named Asep Suryaman:

> The tapols are treated like the dregs of society, deprived of the most elementary rights . . . . They have no power and no voice, no right to complain or protest against their interminable imprisonment, against torture, insult, hunger or disease.

> 'We are like leaves on a tree, just waiting to fall to earth and become one with it', said one tapol. 'Help us to get our freedom back, to rejoin our unprotected families. Help us at the very least to be brought to trial so that this soul-destroying uncertainty can end. Whatever they want, we are ready to sign, so long as we can be released.'

It was not that people outside the prisons didn't know what was happening. So many people had been killed and captured since 1965 that literally all sections of the population were well aware of the tragedy. Most communities had been affected and few families were unscathed by the terror. People had been struck by fear and felt just as powerless as we on the inside.

When I first went to Indonesia, I was struck more than anything by the friendliness of Bud's close-knit family and the circle of people I came into contact with at work and in our neighbourhood. In truth, I found it difficult at first to get used to the idea that family ties meant having relatives coming and staying for weeks or months on end. We always had one of Bud's sisters or his mother staying with us. I sometimes craved the privacy of being just with my husband and children, of having a sitting room where I could sit alone in the evening.

The anti-communist hysteria that swept the country within days of the 1965 events changed all that. Suddenly those of us who were on the wrong side of the political divide were pariahs, treated, as Bud used to say, as if we were suffering from a contagious disease. Relatives, including Bud's own brothers, were terrified of coming to the house. They never visited Bud in prison nor did they come to find out how I was coping with life as a detainee's wife. Even after we were both detained, they preferred to keep their distance. I lost most of my friends; even friends from the movement thought it best not to stay in touch for fear of being accused of *gerpol* (guerrilla politics), a new word created by the New Order which could apply to almost anything.

I had a friend, a Dutch woman, the wife of Taher Thayeb, a well-known communist and member of parliament. He spent many years in Salemba prison and then at the Buru Island forced labour camp, the place of exile for tens of thousands of Indonesia's 'highly dangerous communists'. His wife lived alone and was unable to fend for herself because she had terminal cancer, yet none of her many brothers- or sisters-in-law ever lifted a finger to help her.

Once, when I visited her, she said 'During the German occupation, many Dutch people, including me, gave refuge to Jewish people, knowing that we were taking terrible risks. Why is it that in Indonesia, where social cohesion is supposed to be so strong, no one cares about what happens to us?'

Our house was in one of the more affluent residential areas. The sense of community was not very strong and people took little notice of what was happening next door or across the road. While this led to a sense of isolation, a redeeming feature in times like these was that no one paid much attention to the comings and goings. In the crowded kampungs, social pressures were enormous. There was no escaping the watchful eye of the local RT, the neighbourhood chief; even residents would turn in their neighbours to the army if they were thought to be doing strange things or receiving unusual visitors. For tapol families, it was all a question of survival, lying low, never drawing attention to yourself, never causing offence, keeping out of other people's way. Such a life-style does not make for happy faces.

At Likdam, those of us who had made contact with our families were permitted to have visits three times a week. These were the days when Prijo Subagio might have seen some happy faces. Like everyone else in the camp, I always looked forward eagerly to visiting days, wondering each time who would come to see me and what news they would bring. These days were special not only for the fortunate few who got visits but for the whole camp.

Visitors entered by a gate that was visible in all parts of the camp. As visiting time drew near, all eyes were on the gate. As soon as anyone appeared, word would go round that so-and-so's wife, or husband, or child, had arrived.

'Hurry up! Brush your hair! Put on a clean shirt! Don't go out looking like that! Here's your mat. Don't keep them waiting.'

The visitors would first hand over the food and anything else they had brought to soldiers who would feel inside the baskets with their hands, open the tins of food, cut up the loaves of bread; they were looking for sharp implements, pencils, or the many other things we were not allowed to have. Every scrap of wrapping paper was removed from bars of soap or packets of cigarettes – the ban on anything that might come in handy for writing was particularly strict. I could never get used to getting my supplies, which had been prepared with such loving care at home, in a state of disorder after being mucked around by the guards. Then the visitors and their tapol would sit together on a mat for ten minutes or so until their time was up, watched discreetly by dozens of pairs of eyes peering from behind the pillars or the lines of clothes hanging in the corridors.

Once the visitor had gone, the lucky woman or man would return with plenty of stories to tell. We celebrated each other's joys and lamented over the sad news some visitors brought. For the rest of the day, this would keep tongues wagging, mulling over the latest crop of problems, giving advice, commiserating.

The majority of prisoners rarely received visitors, and some never at all. For them, visiting days were a painful reminder of what they were missing. Sometimes, a visiting family would try to help a detainee trace a relative. Occasionally, someone would turn up at the camp wanting to trace a relative who had been arrested, or who had been transferred from a camp without anyone knowing. These were Indonesia's 'disappeared' of whom there were tens of thousands.

Some visiting days brought scenes of great poignancy that I will never forget. There was one man in Likdam, a journalist, in his mid or late thirties who seemed much older than his age because of the dejected look on his face. Some time before his arrest, his wife had left him and their two children, a girl aged ten and a boy two or three years younger. Like most of us, he lost his job after October 1965 when the paper he worked for was banned. He was not arrested until early 1969, and when the soldiers came to pick him up he had no alternative but to leave the two youngsters at home without anyone to look after them. There were no relatives to whom they could turn and he knew that the neighbours would not want to help. Such forced separations were very common. How could the children be expected to discover the whereabouts of their father? Yet he was not allowed to do anything to contact them.

When he arrived at Likdam, he had been without news of them for several months. Visitors who lived in his neighbourhood were told about his problem. Eventually, he received news that the children had left school and the girl had started selling *gado-gado*, an Indonesian vegetable dish served with peanut sauce, in the streets. Her takings from the day's trade would bring in just enough to buy ingredients for the next day and they would eat whatever was left over themselves. But they were living far away and could not afford the bus fare to visit their father. He knew he might soon be transferred to Salemba where visiting regulations were far worse than at Likdam. As the days wore on, he grew more and more uneasy.

Then one day, during the Muslim festival Lebaran, when the number of visits always soared, someone made a special effort to bring the children to the camp. He couldn't believe his ears when his name was called. As he walked to the gate, the girl rushed towards him and collapsed in his arms, weeping. He carried her to a mat and tried to comfort her but she sat in front of him with her face buried in his lap, sobbing her heart out. And we, who watched, sobbed with her.

For some tapols, the loss of contact with loved ones had a terrible effect on their state of mind. Mrs K. was arrested when she came to Likdam to visit her husband. He had been taken into custody on suspicion of having contact with the underground in Jakarta. The army assumed she might know about his activities and the people who visited him at home, so they took this unsuspecting woman in and refused to allow her to return home.

As soon as she was taken into custody, he was transferred to Kalong to prevent them from coming into contact with each other. Mrs K. was interrogated for about an hour and we all thought that she would soon be allowed to go home, but we were wrong. When she left home on the day of her arrest, she had no idea that she would not be returning nor did her neighbours or relatives think that anything like this would occur. Nothing happened after the first interrogation, but she never doubted at first that she would soon be released.

After she had been with us for several weeks, it finally dawned on her that she was not going to be released soon so she started trying to make contact with her family. She had no children and asked some of the detainees to get their visiting relatives to help make contact with a brother or other relatives. Nothing worked. Each time someone came with bad news for her, she became more and more distressed and her physical condition began to deteriorate. After a while, she was obviously very ill indeed. She refused to eat because of a feeling of guilt about not being able to contribute any food to her food group. She developed a high temperature and became very sensitive to light, noise, sound and smell. Everything was offensive to her, including all our efforts to comfort her. She rarely spoke to anyone and would lie still on her mat, hardly ever moving. She grew weaker by the day and only stirred herself to go to the toilet, which she did frequently.

Adil was told about her state of health. For some time, he ignored the reports, but one day he came to our room in one of his more benevolent moods. He stood at the door, gazing down at her with a smile that extended no further than his moustache.

'Well, Mrs K.', he said, 'we'll have you taken to hospital. You'd like that, wouldn't you?'

His visit cheered her up no end. For the first time after months of neglect, someone in authority had shown some interest in her. But Adil didn't keep his word and after a few days of waiting, she deteriorated further. One day, as she was standing in line to go to the toilet, she collapsed and had to be carried back to our room. She relieved herself on the floor, passing out thick clots of blood. She had developed an intestinal lesion, apparently because of months of mental stress. This time, Adil was forced to act, not wanting another tragic death on his hands. Semi-conscious, she was rushed to hospital and remained there for two months. She was discharged and returned to Likdam looking much better. But the months of anguish and illness had left her in a state of shock and she was now resigned to her fate. She lost all interest in her family problems and behaved as if nothing in the world mattered to her but survival. After some time, she was transferred to the women's prison in Bukit Duri; in 1971, they moved her to the long-term detention camp in Plantungan, Central Java, where she spent several more years in detention. I have no idea what happened to her husband.

The case of Salim was a different kind of tragedy. A young lad in his early twenties, we could see, the moment he arrived at Likdam, that he was in a state of deep depression. He would sit on the floor most of the day, hugging his knees and staring into space. He was given a place in the corridor near the bathroom.

Every time one of us passed him on the way to the bathroom, we would say 'Cheer up, brother. Don't daydream. You'll make yourself ill.'

But words had no effect on him. He didn't seem to hear anything anyone said.

Then one day, a detainee escaped. This was a rare occurrence for a number of reasons. Security at all detention centres was very tight. But more important was the fact that punishment for breaches of prison discipline was meted out collectively, so there was a reluctance to do anything that would call forth retribution on others. On top of this was the fact that the army and its intel network held society in its grip and it would be difficult for an escapee to merge into the crowd without trace. No one can survive long in Indonesia without an identity card and any newcomer to a residential area needs to produce a certificate from her or his former place of residence endorsing the move. This meant that, unless a prisoner had made careful preparations with people outside, he or she was sooner or later bound to be caught.

News of the escape plunged the camp into deep gloom, prisoners and guards alike. The man had fled early in the morning before Adil arrived and everyone knew that all hell would break loose once he turned up. As I sat, with everyone else, waiting, I again sensed the humiliation of being at the mercy of a thug like Adil. I remember trying to break the tension by humming, singing, praying, telling stories, anything, but no one responded, so I gave up.

When Adil arrived and was told about the escape, he came down to the compound in a filthy temper, with a thick wooden stick in his hand and started beating the prisoners who slept in the same part of the corridor as the man who had fled, accusing them of being responsible. Salim was sitting in that part of the corridor and got a terrible swipe on the head. Something snapped in him and for the rest of the day he talked agitatedly to the men around him. At last, he began to reveal what it was that was troubling him. He was obsessed by the fear of someone chasing him. Then he began to talk about his parents and a younger sister who had been killed in the massacres in Central Java in 1965. He had seen them being put to death and had managed to escape. Now, he could not forgive himself for surviving and he lived in dread of an awful act of revenge. He was driven by a terrible sense of guilt.

As the day wore on, he grew more and more agitated and said he wanted to go and speak to Adil, but the men tried to dissuade him. After a night of tension for the men who tried to restrain Salim, he shook himself free and rushed up to Adil's office early next morning. At first, the officers took it as a huge joke, treating him like a madman. But then, as he became more violent, they began to beat him until they had him rolling on the floor in pain. They kicked him out of the office and he rolled down the steps into the yard, covered in dust. We soon realized that he had lost his senses.

From then on, for weeks, he was completely unmanageable. He had to be fed, washed and dragged to the toilet. He became so violent that he could not be left unguarded for a moment. It would take five or six men to bath him each day. No one had the slightest idea how to treat him, not even the two doctors in our midst. In desperation, the men who were trying to cope decided that they could only handle him by tying him firmly to a board, to prevent him from doing harm to himself or to others. No one saw this as anything but cruel, but who were we to criticize men who lived under the continuous strain of keeping him under control?

All the soldiers including Adil knew very well what was going on. Occasionally, an officer would come down into the compound, stare at Salim, listen to his ravings, then grin and mumble something about a 'loony communist' before returning to the office with a shrug of the shoulders.

Then one day, as the crisis over Salim was at its height, we were suddenly all ordered to get ready to move to another camp. No explanation. Just an order to move and be quick about it. Within seconds, the camp was in turmoil. We had been told to take everything, clothes, mats, pots and pans, stoves, everything. In all the commotion, Salim was left to his own devices. He happened to be in one of his more lethargic moods. He lay flat on his back, arms and legs flung in all directions, soaked in his own urine, while the rest of us rushed round, helter-skelter, as if he wasn't there. No one had a moment to spare for this demented colleague.

As it turned out, this was a false alarm and we were not all transferred; those who stayed behind quickly returned to the old routine of looking after Salim. Gradually, his behaviour returned to something approaching normal, thanks largely to the arrival at the camp of a detainee who had a way of sitting with him for hours at a stretch, singing him Javanese songs, telling him stories from Javanese folklore and cracking jokes. The compassion of this man restored Salim's mental health and he regained a degree of self-control, although he was still very disturbed. Sometimes, in the middle of a conversation, he would stiffen up and a look of dread would return to his eyes.

Then one day Salim was summoned to the office. We hoped this might be the prelude to his release or that he might be sent away for medical treatment. Up in the office, he was asked several questions which, in his present frame of mind, he was able to answer coherently.

On the following day, it was the turn for a number of tapols to be transferred to Salemba Prison. To our utter amazement, when the officer came down to read out the names, Salim was on the list. The previous day's questioning had been nothing more than a check-up to decide whether he was sane enough to be sent to prison.

CHAPTER 12

How I Secured Bud's
Release in 1967

Towards the end of 1969, not long after Salim was moved to Salemba, my own feeling of having settled down in Likdam received a severe jolt. It all started when I was taking a rather leisurely shower one morning, all on my own for a change. Suddenly I could hear people shouting my name.

'Ibu Carmel, you're wanted in the office.'

Damn them! Fancy calling me at a moment like this!

'Ibu Carmel, where are you? They're waiting for you at the office. Hurry up!'

Hurry up? How the hell can I? They'll have to wait till my hair dries.

'Please tell whoever it is to wait', I shouted back. 'I'm soaking wet from head to foot.'

It was early in the morning and I was in the bathroom, washing my hair, washing my clothes and having a shower. They couldn't have chosen a worse moment to call me.

'They can't wait. You must hurry up.' This time it was one of my room-mates at the bathroom door, knocking frantically as she spoke.

'They're taking you off somewhere, so we've started packing your things. You're to take all your belongings.'

Taking me off? Where? What's going to happen now? The news shook me and I quickly dried myself and began to get dressed, with water streaming down my shoulders. As people knocked and shouted, my heart began to pound. I didn't stop to rub my hair, which was very long and took an age to dry. The next moment, I was rushing along the corridor to my room, carrying a bundle of wet clothes in my arms. There was a flurry of excitement in the room. They had already wrapped up my belongings in my mat.

'Who's come for me?' I asked. 'Where am I being taken? Off to prison?'

Not surprisingly, no one knew. A guard standing by the office door kept shouting my name. One of my room-mates was kneeling on the floor tying my things up with a sash (we were not allowed to have string, for fear we might commit suicide) as I stuffed my wet clothes and towel into a plastic bag.

'Is it only me?' I asked.

'No, Dr Warno's been called as well.'

Dr Warno? Why him and me? The only thing we had in common was that we were both members of the HSI.

Moments later I was standing in the office with a bundle of belongings at my feet. I must have looked a sight. I was wearing a pair of faded thong sandals and a dress that was too large for me. My hair was still very wet. The mat holding my things had many holes in it so things were bulging out. Dr Warno was there already, looking tidier than me, standing awkwardly to attention, with a ghastly grey pallor on his face. He was one of those who found prison life extremely hard to bear. There was talk about his wife having deserted him. We had become very good friends at Likdam; he found great pleasure in trying out his English in conversations with me.

With no word of explanation, we were hustled into a waiting jeep by an officer I had never seen before. As we drove away, he sat in front of us, straight-faced, not even bothering to say 'I don't know' when we asked where we were going. I could see from the look on his face that Dr Warno was very shocked by this unexpected move.

The sudden upheaval had also shaken me profoundly and I was feeling very scared indeed. I could hardly speak, so we both sat looking through the flaps, trying to work out where we were being driven.

It was a short drive and we drew up in front of the headquarters of the Military Police Corps (CPM). This was a building that I was very familiar with. I had visited it often during Bud's second period of arrest. We were surely not going to be held here. Something else was about to happen. Release? Surely not.

We were ordered into the lobby and our bundles were thrown into a corner. A few minutes later, I was escorted upstairs and taken into an office. Now I was alone and had no idea what had happened to Dr Warno. I sat down on a comfortable couch and realized that I had been in this very office before, several times, two years ago, when I was trying to get Bud released. In those days, I was a free woman, treated – here in this office – with a certain degree of respect. But now things were different.

These moments on my own calmed me down and I enjoyed the luxury of sitting on a couch. The relative pleasantness of my surroundings strengthened the belief that, perhaps, this was the prelude to release. I had recently heard a rumour that Major Sukotjo, the officer in overall charge of Likdam, had recommended that Dr Warno and I should be released. Perhaps this was it.

As I was enjoying the thought, an officer came into the office and took me into a large room with long lines of benches and tables, like a lecture hall. Dr Warno was already seated at one end of a bench and I was told to sit at the other end. ' . . . and don't talk to each other', came the order.

We sat in silence with armed guards arrayed behind us, about ten metres apart. After half an hour or so, several other prisoners were brought in and told to sit on the benches, each many metres apart. I knew some of them by sight from reports in the papers. One I recognized as a former cabinet minister, another was Sukatno, General Secretary of the youth organization Pemuda Rakjat. Another man I recognized was someone high up at the PKI secretariat. This was quite a distinguished group of tapols, which set me wondering what on earth I was doing here. I began to feel more apprehensive than ever.

Another hour or so passed, waiting. Occasionally, an officer would enter the hall and walk to the other end, with a sheaf of papers in his arms, but no one said a word to us. Then I saw Atjep, and my heart sank. Was I going to be interrogated by him again? The waiting and the suspense began to wear me down. Was I going to be taken back to Satgas-Pusat? Anything but that! I suddenly felt a longing for Likdam and the friends there. That awful place had become like home to me.

Dr Warno was the first to be called away and was gone for half an hour. When he returned, he looked greyer than ever. I tried to catch his eye to get a hint of what was going on. He looked at me, lifted a finger, made a sign as if to cut his throat and pointed in the direction of the room where he had been interrogated. What was he trying to tell me? Had he been beaten up by Atjep? I could get nothing more out of him in sign language.

Then it was my turn. As I went back into the room where I had first been taken, I saw Atjep sitting in one corner, fiddling with a tape recorder. On the other side of the room, sitting at a desk, was an officer I immediately recognized. He was Lieutenant-Colonel Abdulrahman of the CPM, whom I had often been to see in 1967 when Bud was still in prison. I remembered him as one of the very few army officers I had ever met who spoke to me with a degree of politeness and respect. His presence in the room calmed me greatly as I sat facing Atjep, with a small microphone in front of me on the table, waiting for the interrogation to begin.

As the questioning proceeded, it became apparent that Atjep was trying to get me to admit that I had drafted a document called *Deklarasi Ekonomi*, the Economic Declaration or DEKON as it came to be known. This had been made public by Sukarno in March 1964. It was a preposterous charge and I flatly denied it. Atjep had an exaggerated idea of my position as a government official in the days before the October 1965 events. I had been appointed to run the economic secretariat of Dr Subandrio, who was Foreign Minister as well as Deputy Prime Minister, but I was not in a position to have any influence on the decision-making process. My role had been confined to writing memoranda that some members of Government probably read but no one ever acted upon.

I got the job in April 1965 because of my work at the Foreign Ministry as an economics researcher. Dr Subandrio asked me to take charge of an under-staffed economics office he had just set up, apparently hoping to use some of my ideas. (He never did.) It was Dr Subandrio's intention to create order out of the chaos afflicting the economy, in the belief that he could succeed where others had failed. Atjep wanted me to admit that I had got the job on the recommendation of the PKI and had been instrumental in steering Sukarno government policies in a leftward direction. He was taking a different tack now from his earlier line when we first met across the interrogator's table at Satgas-Pusat. Then, he accused me of wreaking havoc by my constant criticism of Sukarno's policies; now, he was trying to prove that I was responsible for those policies. He couldn't have it both ways.

Now, I was being asked to accept responsibility for DEKON. As the inquisition proceeded, Atjep did his best to trip me up by his volley of questions but he had no thugs behind him, leering and threatening in the background. Abdulrahman said nothing at all as the session continued and it occurred to me that he was there to exercise some restraint on Atjep. I had heard that some officers had serious misgivings about the methods employed by Atjep, not necessarily prompted by concern over maltreatment. Personal rivalries may have had something to do with it.

After this went on for some time, Atjep was called away for a few minutes. I was left alone with Abdulrahman.

'You were called in for interrogation several years ago. Why didn't you tell us then about your connections with the PKI?' he asked me.

'Why should I have done that? I would only have been asking for trouble.'

He paused for a moment. 'Of course, legally, you have every right not to tell us anything about yourself.' I was amazed to hear an officer talking about my legal rights. Then he went on: 'But you might have made things easier for yourself if you had told us then.'

'Do you really think so?' I said. 'Wouldn't it have meant my being arrested in 1965 instead of three years later?'

I don't know how he took this as, before he could reply, Atjep was back and continued with the interrogation. After questioning me further about DEKON, he brought the session to an end with a cynical sneer and dark threats about 'not having finished' with me. But the interrogation had gone quite well for me and I wasn't much impressed by his threats. Indeed, nothing more happened. This was to be the last time I was interrogated by Atjep.

Back in the hall, I was told to sit down again and wait. By this time it was early afternoon. There were many other tapols in the hall and each one was called away for long periods of time. We remained seated there until well past midnight, without getting any food or drink. I had never realized that sitting upright on a bench for hours without moving could be so tiring. My bones ached horribly.

In the far corner of the hall was a door leading to a room where officers involved in the interrogations were working. They came and went from time to time; whenever the door opened, I could hear the strains of music on a radio. It was too indistinct for me to hear what was being played but I knew it was classical music. As I strained my ears to listen, tears came to my eyes. I was suddenly struck by the cultural barrenness of my life. It seemed as if I would never again be able to listen to a Beethoven symphony.

Meeting Lieutenant-Colonel Abdulrahman had reminded me of my earlier visits to the CPM headquarters in 1967. The last visit I made was to thank him for his help in securing Bud's release in December that year. It may seem strange to thank someone for the restoration of freedom but I did feel grateful and I felt that he had behaved so much better than the others I had met. The whole episode gave me plenty of experience of how the system of detention worked in practice – capricious, unpredictable, all depending on the whims of men who held the reins of power.

Bud was first arrested in October 1965 and after being interrogated by the Jakarta interrogation team and waiting for them to make up their minds about him, the team ordered his release in March 1966. Thirteen days later, a soldier from the CPM came to the house and rearrested him. As usual there was no arrest warrant and the soldier was not in the slightest bit interested when Bud showed him his release document. On the morning after he was rearrested, I went to the CPM office with a basket of food and was assured that it would be passed on to him. Twenty-four hours later, Bud was back in Salemba Prison where he had spent most of his first six months in jail.

My first move was to contact the chairman of the Jakarta interrogation team to find out what had happened. He was puzzled and told me he had no idea why Bud had been rearrested.

'Would the team be interrogating Bud again?' I asked.

'I don't see how we can do that', he replied. 'We've already cleared your husband and his case is no longer in our hands.'

When I asked which authority was now responsible, he said he didn't know. From then on, I started doing the rounds of various military commands to find out who was now in charge of Bud's 'case'. I went to Kopkamtib, but they told me they knew nothing. Instead, I found myself involved in a three-hour interrogation about my work with Dr Subandrio when he was still Deputy Prime Minister. Some time later I went to the central interrogation team but they too said they knew nothing.

Each of these approaches took weeks; at first, I would be told to 'come back next week', or whenever, to get an answer to my inquiry. I could well understand why so many prisoners' wives gave up trying to do anything to get their husbands released. The process was time-consuming, humiliating and invariably frustrating. Perhaps it was a bit easier for me as a foreigner, not because they seemed to be slightly more respectful but because I was less timid and submissive than most Indonesian women.

Meanwhile, Bud languished in prison. He was not interrogated and no one was prepared to admit that he was any concern of theirs. In order to get anywhere, you had to be 'someone's' prisoner. Being 'no one's' prisoner meant that nobody was prepared to release him.

Then I had a bright idea. I would go to the CPM headquarters to find out who had ordered his arrest in the first place. Here, I was told that there was no record of his having been arrested.

'But that's ridiculous', I said. 'He was brought straight here and spent 24 hours in this building. I know this because I came here the morning after he was arrested to bring him a basket of food.'

They still wouldn't believe me so I pointed out to them the room where I had seen him being taken to write something. The officer I was speaking to then went into a huddle with his superiors and came back to say the words I had heard so often.

'Come back in a week's time. We may have some news for you.'

A week later, I was taken upstairs to meet Lieutenant-Colonel Abdulrahman. His first words, to my amazement, were to thank me for drawing their attention to Bud's case. Yes, I was quite right, the CPM had arrested Bud, he said, and he actually apologized because nothing had happened for a whole year. A whole year in detention through someone's negligence and all I was getting was an apology! But I had become so used to injustice that I felt grateful for his words and began to feel more hopeful.

The interview with Abdulrahman revealed to me that he did not know who had ordered Bud's arrest. He even asked me if I could identify the arresting soldier who had come to the house. This was ridiculous. I would never have been able to recognize the man a year after the arrest. The soldier bore no insignia on his uniform, no name-tag and produced no papers. Abdulrahman didn't press the point but promised to look into the matter immediately.

'Please feel free to come and see me any time about your husband. You are the detainee's wife and you have every right to do what you can to get his case settled.'

What a relief to hear words like this! My encounters with the military on Bud's behalf had gone on for nearly two years, since his very first arrest. But why are such words of encouragement not addressed to all those tens of thousands of women who have learned through bitter experience not to waste their time traipsing round military offices asking for action on a husband in detention?

From this time on, I visited the CPM headquarters about once a month, never more frequently, because I knew that, with the best will in the world, things would never happen quickly. One thing all this taught me was patience. Occasionally, the CPM would allow me to meet Bud and actually brought him from Salemba Prison for a short meeting. This was a real concession as prison rules excluded any meetings like this.

Then the CPM started interrogating him, but it dawned on me that they were not going to be in a position to take any decision. This could only happen higher up. Sooner or later, I would have to decide where to go from here. The main problem was to find out who had ordered his second arrest. It had become clear to me that this was the only person who could order his release. I went to see a general with whom Bud had had some business connections. This was General Ali Murtopo, by now an extremely powerful man. For the first fifteen years or so of Suharto's rule, Murtopo was Suharto's right-hand man. Murtopo had needed Bud's help to get a licence to ship goods abroad (smuggled goods, mind you!) so you could say that he owed Bud a favour.

From my conversation with Murtopo and from other inquiries, I discovered that, a few days after Bud's release in March 1966, a former colleague from the Ministry of Sea Communications where Bud used to work had seen him walking in the street. Bud had always been quite a controversial figure at the ministry, a tough negotiator with foreign shipping companies, trying to defend the country's national shipping industry. Apparently this chance sighting on the street had led people to believe that Bud would try to regain his job (nothing could have been further from the truth), so moves began at the ministry to get him back behind bars. By whatever means never became clear, but the problem was placed in the hands of Brigadier-General Sumitro, who was then assistant to the army chief-of-staff. He was the man who had ordered Bud's arrest.

Although I was now quite sure that this had happened, the CPM officers would not confirm anything. All they would say was that a 'high-level signature' was needed to release Bud. It occurred to me that the only way forward was to go and see the General himself. When I mentioned this to Abdulrahman, he tried to dissuade me. He wouldn't confirm whether my hunch was correct; all he would say was that he thought I would be wasting my time.

I thought things over for several days and finally decided to have a try. This was not an easy thing to do. It would mean going to the army high command, which could mean courting disaster. By this time, however, I had come to think that I was immune from arrest and, having got so far, it would be stupid to give up now. But would I, a dismissed government employee, be able to penetrate the inner recesses of the army high command?

On the day of my adventure, I left home quite early, after saying goodbye to Mbah, Bud's mother, who was staying with us at the time. I would have preferred not to tell her where I was going so as not to raise her hopes, but she knew all about my previous attempts on Bud's behalf so I explained that this was the make-or-break moment. She saw me off as I called a becak, giving me encouragement in her gentle-mannered way. Off I went to army headquarters.

The slow journey, as the becak-driver pedalled his way through the heavy traffic, gave me plenty of time to rehearse my words over and over again. When I arrived, I went to the reception desk and asked to see General Sumitro, half expecting to be told to leave. But the soldier on duty found nothing unusual in my request and gave me a security slip to fill in. I was then passed on to another security desk, then another. More forms to fill in and periods of waiting for I don't know who or what. Finally, after being directed to yet another security desk some way off, I found myself in the ante-room of General Sumitro's office. The General, I was told, was at a meeting and I would have to wait. The people at the office probably did not realize that I was a detainee's wife as I had stated on the forms that my business was 'purely personal'. Now it seemed that the General was prepared to meet me, and that was all that mattered. I was pretty certain that all my inquiries over the months had filtered through to him and he knew my purpose in coming.

After yet more waiting – it was nearly midday by now – the General came into the ante-room and, looking in my direction, said briskly 'Mrs Budiardjo? Come this way.'

I followed him into his office and, after he motioned me with his head, sat down in front of his desk. I found myself sitting in a large office before an enormous desk that didn't have a single sheet of paper on it. In front of me was an ornate ink-and-pen stand, a box of expensive cigars and one or two very elaborate pieces of office equipment. Along the side of the room behind me were several large windows looking out onto a magnificent view of Merdeka Square.

I said nothing as I waited for Sumitro to sit down. He was a short, fat man, bulging and fleshy. His cheeks and chin were so heavy that he didn't seem to have any neck; there was so much fat around his eyes that he seemed to be peering through a mask with a great deal of difficulty. He staggered rather than walked to his chair, leaning heavily on the arms as he eased himself in.

Just as I was about to speak, he waved his hand to silence me. 'Wait a minute', he said.

He picked up a phone behind him on a shelf, panting slightly from the exertion of having to get up from his chair, and started dialling. At first try, he got the wrong number, then nothing at all second time round. This was annoying him. Then, finally, he made the connection and I realized that he was calling the CPM. The first officer he asked for was not around, so he got someone else on the phone.

'About Sukendro (an intelligence officer who had been arrested some months ago), you needn't keep him under house arrest any more . . . . Yes, that's right, he's free from today. Now, about Budiardjo. Yes, the Budiardjo case. Release him . . . . What? No, no need for him to report. Just release him.'

So that was all. It was as simple as that. As the clipped phrases came out, I watched and listened. It was incredible. I would never have thought it possible. Here it was, before my very eyes. The power of one man over the fate of others. Just like that.

I should have been overjoyed at the success of my mission but I was stunned. I hadn't spoken a word. So this was how, twenty months ago, he had picked up a phone, dialled the CPM's number and barked the order 'Arrest Budiardjo'.

He put down the phone, turned round and said 'That's what you wanted, isn't it?'

I could only mumble an inaudible 'Yes'.

'It'll take a few days to arrange. Go home and wait. That's all.'

I don't remember now whether I said 'Thank you'; if I did, I certainly didn't mean it. He had consigned Bud to prison for more than twenty months and left him there as 'nobody's prisoner'. He was so confident of his power, so arrogant, that he had no qualms about showing me how the system worked, with not the slightest regard for law or procedures. He probably even enjoyed showing me how powerful he was.

As soon as I got home, I rushed to the phone and rang Abdulrahman. Strangely enough, our lines crossed as he was just making a call to tell me that Bud was going to be released.

'I know', I said.

'How's it possible? I've only just been instructed to let him go.'

'I was in the room when General Sumitro phoned the CPM.' I could hear him whistle with amazement as he congratulated me for my success.

Ten days later, Bud returned home for the second time. We thought that this time it would be for good.

CHAPTER 13

My Case: The Plot Thickens

Not long after Atjep interrogated me about my role in drafting DEKON, an officer, a major in the intelligence corps, came to Likdam and summoned me for a chat, not for interrogation. He told me things were not going well for me.

'Some members of the PSI are insisting that you should stay in detention.' The Major was watching me closely to see how I would react.

The Partai Sosialis Indonesia is a small social democratic party with a membership composed mainly of intellectuals. It was banned by Sukarno in 1960 for allegedly supporting a regional rebellion. Suharto did not lift the ban after coming to power but many of its members worked closely with the Suharto regime.

The Major went on: 'They say you were one of the architects of the PKI's campaign to have their party banned. You shouldn't take their opposition to your release lightly as they now hold positions of great influence in the Government.'

I could hardly believe my ears. I was well aware at the time that many PSI intellectuals had quite considerable influence but it had never occurred to me that these people would conspire against my release.

'Why do you think they are so hostile to you?' he asked.

What could I say to that? I had been interrogated many times already but no one had hinted that I was suspected of inciting hatred for the PSI.

'These people have an exaggerated idea of my influence in the former government, or for that matter, in the PKI', I told him. 'Perhaps they are getting their own back because I once issued a statement as chair of the HSI Economists' Section, criticizing the Indonesian Association of Economists for not taking action against Professor Sumitro after he openly sided with the rebellion in West Sumatra.'

One of the PSI's leading members and doyen of the economists who ran the economics faculty at the University of Indonesia, Professor Sumitro, fled Jakarta in May 1957 to join forces with the rebel movement in West Sumatra, later settling in Singapore after the rebellion was crushed.

The Major listened attentively but made no comment.

Then he told me about a series of articles in a leading newspaper, *Indonesia Raya*, remonstrating with some of the technocrats now in commanding positions in the state economic sector, accusing them of intellectual prostitution. The paper described them as 'all-weather men', ready to adjust to any regime as long as they could get good positions.

'They mentioned some people who have stuck to their principles, refusing to prostitute themselves. You were one of them', he said, looking at me intensely. Was I supposed to take this as a compliment? Maybe, but I couldn't help thinking that the Major was telling me, in so many words, that I should expect no leniency from my captors because I was seen as someone who would never compromise with the present regime.

Many years later, browsing through correspondence with members of my family in London about the prospects of my release, I found a letter sent in mid-1969 to my brother Ben by Herb Feith, the Australian academic. He mentioned press articles about Bud and me which alleged that we both deserved to stay where we were, in prison. Bud was accused in *Harian Kami* on 14 April 1969 of being at the centre of a 'communist cell' at the Ministry of Sea Communications. Another article, a few weeks later – Herb didn't know the exact date – alleged that I had participated in a communist-inspired attack on the leading economists at the University of Indonesia in 1964.

Since October 1965, I had been the target of some pretty vicious personal attacks in the Indonesian press. The only one I saw myself was an article entitled 'Mrs C. Budiardjo, economic trouble-maker' which was published in October or November 1965 in *Mertju Suar*, a newspaper that published some of the more malicious attacks on alleged communists. I was accused of deliberately causing economic chaos by writing articles critical of the Sukarno government. Still worse, I was said to be a British intelligence agent who had started trying to infiltrate into Indonesia after the first Indonesian diplomatic mission was opened in London. The scheme had been conceived by me with the help of Dr Subandrio, in 1949 or 1950, when he was head of the Indonesian diplomatic mission in London. My marriage to Budiardjo was just a ploy to acquire Indonesian citizenship and my decision to renounce British nationality was a trick to deceive the Indonesian authorities. Whoever wrote the article clearly had access to an intelligence file on me, weaving grotesque falsehoods around a few facts that could only have been known to anyone who had dug deep for information about my early years in Indonesia. The allegation that I had started scheming more than fifteen years ago with Dr Subandrio was clearly intended to implicate me in his later activities in the intelligence service. By 1965, besides being First Deputy Prime Minister and Foreign Minister, Subandrio was also head of the state intelligence agency, the BPI. It was as if I had been an agent of his – and of the British – for all these years.

I kept the article in my files, but it was confiscated, along with all my other papers, at the time of my arrest. I have been unable to find a library abroad that stocks back issues of *Mertju Suar*. I was angered by the pack of lies and felt that I had a right of reply. I showed the article to several ministers I knew, including Dr Subandrio, but their only advice to me was to ignore it. What else could they say? They knew as well as I did that the press was under tight military censorship and no newspaper would dare publish a rebuttal from me.

It was not until the Major came to see me in Likdam that I realized that the public attacks on me had continued and were having a very negative impact on my chances of release.

In the last ten years or so of the Sukarno regime, I became embroiled in a great deal of controversy over the state of the economy. In 1956 I obtained a master's degree in economics at the University of Indonesia, specializing in international economic relations. In those days, I had a very busy life, combining study with holding a job at the Foreign Ministry, doing a fair amount of translation work for the PKI, and bringing up a family. None of this would have been possible without the help of servants and the support of Bud's sister, Par, who often came to stay with us for months at a stretch.

After graduating, I applied for a teaching job at the University of Indonesia economics faculty. I heard nothing for months. Then one day, an American professor at the faculty, Don Blake, told me in confidence that my chances of getting the job were nil. He and I had become good friends, sharing many political views. At the time, the faculty had a partnership with the University of California and most of the professors were American. The links with the US Embassy were close. Don told me that the US Embassy was aware of my PKI connections and knew that I helped the party to produce *Review of Indonesia*, an English-language bulletin that published party documents and speeches. No way would the embassy give the go-ahead for me to get a teaching job at the faculty, he said.

This incident showed me for the first time that I already had plenty of enemies. The PSI had a very strong grip on the faculty. Professor Sumitro had been dean for many years, so I doubt whether the Indonesian staff would have liked to have me on the staff either. The Indonesian economists groomed at the faculty and later at Berkeley

University, California, were now the technocrats in charge of the Indonesian economy, the Berkeley Mafia, as they came to be known. In the years before 1965, they had developed a close relationship with the army and in particular with the army command school where Suharto studied after his dismissal as commander of the divisional command in Central Java in 1958.

I took Don's advice and looked elsewhere for a job. I got a lectureship at the Pajajaran State University economics faculty in Bandung and taught there for a number of years. In the early 1960s I got a job teaching economics at Res Publica University, which was run by BAPERKI, an organization for ethnic Chinese that was close to the PKI. I later became dean of its economics faculty, but held the post for only a couple of months. The 1965 upheavals led to the closure of the university and the outlawing of BAPERKI. Gangs of anti-communist youths staged a violent attack on the university premises, burning books and causing widespread damage.

The other strand of my life was my job at the Foreign Ministry, where I spent much of my time producing policy memoranda about foreign trade problems, the exchange mechanism and commodity markets. I also gave a course in international economic relations at the foreign ministry academy, concentrating, as I recollect, on the workings of international financial institutions set up at Bretton Woods in 1945, the IMF and the World Bank. This all seemed interesting and worthwhile at the time, though I doubt whether anyone took much notice of what I was proposing. Although people treated me with a certain amount of respect, I was aware that some of my office colleagues saw me as a 'lefty' who was not to be trusted.

Out of frustration at getting nowhere with all my ideas about the country's economic crisis, I hit upon the idea of writing articles in the press, a kind of lay person's guide to the country's economic woes, inflation, balance of payments deficits and the like. These were published by Antara, where I had once worked, and were reproduced by a number of newspapers in Jakarta and in the regions. The articles began to create quite a stir. I enjoyed my work as columnist and teacher far more than my work at the ministry. But I was well aware that I was being watched. Admiral Sudomo, who was then, like Bud, an Assistant Minister at the Ministry of Sea Communications, often mentioned the latest of my articles to Bud and complimented him for having 'such a clever little wife'. For whatever reason, he kept an eye on what I was writing. He was the man who, in the early 1970s, took over as commander of Kopkamtib, and served Suharto loyally in key positions in the regime's repressive apparatus for many years.

In 1964, I was invited to chair the economics section of the HSI. This was a period of acute conflict over the running of the economy. In late 1962, the Kennedy administration had intervened in the Dutch–Indonesian dispute over the territory of West Papua, backing Jakarta against The Hague. The western half of the island of New Guinea had been under Dutch tutelage but was not included in the territory ceded by the Dutch to the Indonesian Republic in 1949. After the Kennedy intervention, West Papua was handed over to Indonesia without consulting the West Papuan people. This led to a marked improvement in relations between Jakarta and Washington. During this thaw, the International Monetary Fund sent a mission to Indonesia to advise the Government on a stabilization programme, as the condition for obtaining foreign aid. Senior members of the Indonesian Government supported the US-backed package offered by the IMF while the PKI and others were fiercely critical. The *Deklarasi Ekonomi* issued in April 1964 by Sukarno represented a middle course between these two contending policies. While leaning heavily in the direction of a free market economy and the lifting of price controls, it made certain concessions to the left, especially by rejecting devaluation of the currency and offering ideas that contradicted the basic tenets of the IMF's stabilization policy.

However, a month later, on 26 May 1964, the government announced a package of measures which were in effect the first instalment of the IMF-endorsed stabilization programme, contradicting much of what DEKON had said. We in the HSI decided to mount a campaign against these measures and held a seminar in late 1964 criticizing the policy. A book reproducing the papers and conclusions of that meeting was published a year later, just before October 1965. The book was delivered to my home from the printers, but, before we had a chance to distribute copies, the entire stock was confiscated during one of the first raids on my house by troops after the events of 1 October. I well remember, some weeks later, sitting one day in an army office, making some inquiry or other about Bud. I rested my elbow on a pile of parcels to my left and realized to my astonishment that these were the packets containing our HSI book. I bitterly resented this theft but could do nothing to retrieve a single copy. Indeed, I don't possess a single copy of any of my writings from that pre-1965 period. Everything was confiscated. After 30 years, I still feel a great deal of pain and anger when I think how all these writings of mine were seized, leaving me with nothing.

Being close to Subandrio was obviously a black mark against me in the eyes of military intelligence. In the pre-1965 days, I was occasionally called in by Dr Subandrio for advice on speeches that he was drafting and I visited the Subandrios' home fairly frequently; I knew his wife, Hurustiati, quite well as we worked closely together in an Association of Women Graduates. In March 1966, Dr Subandrio was arrested along with more than a dozen ministers and he went on trial soon after. His trial was simply a way for Suharto to get at President Sukarno, a trial by proxy as many commentators later called it. Suharto knew very well that it would be strategically destabilizing to put Sukarno on trial. The charges against Dr Subandrio were all related to his activities in the performance of his duties as Foreign Minister, carrying out the policies of the Government. Subandrio had been the target of a shrill campaign of vilification by pro-army demonstrators in the months preceding his arrest and trial.

Army intelligence were well aware of my links with Dr Subandrio. On one occasion early in 1966 while Subandrio was still Foreign Minister, I was summoned to military police headquarters to answer questions about rumours that Subandrio had fled the country. There was no truth to the rumours, nor did I have any idea of his movements as I had been dismissed from the ministry many months earlier and had all but severed any connection with him.

During the months I worked on Subandrio's economic affairs secretariat, a battle royal was raging between him and the army's special command on economic policy, known as KOTOE. The contending sides were hopelessly unequal. KOTOE had a bevy of technocrats capable of drafting government decrees and regulations, whereas Subandrio just had me, assisted by a typist and an errand boy. I hadn't the first idea about how to draft a government decree. If Subandrio had other advisers, they were not known to me. We were outmanoeuvred every time. Even in those final days of the Sukarno era when the PKI was, according to Suharto and his allies, on the threshold of power, the army already held sway in major sectors of the state administration.

I knew then that the KOTOE officers were deeply suspicious of me. One incident sticks out in my memory. I was normally invited to attend meetings of officials to discuss aspects of economic policy, around a huge table where many of those present were ministers or officers from the army. I often felt uncomfortable at these gatherings. I was often the only woman present and I sometimes had to sit listening to smutty, sexist jokes.

One day, as I arrived to attend one of these meetings, a messenger was waiting for me at the door.

'Ibu Carmel, I have been asked to inform you that your presence is not wanted. Please leave the premises', he whispered, rather embarrassed by this unpleasant duty.

Later I learned that a senior army officer on their economics team had been infuriated by an article I wrote about government plans to increase the price of petrol. Alleging that I had used privileged information as my source, he insisted that I could no longer be trusted to attend these strategy meetings. I was also excluded from meetings at the foreign ministry at which the IMF's stabilization programme was discussed.

When the Major came to Likdam to warn me of the machinations of PSI technocrats to keep me behind bars, I was not yet able to piece together all the strands of the regime's 'case' against me. Others who faced lesser accusations fared much worse than I did, but he made things sound pretty grim for me. In the end, it was my being British that came to the rescue. However, in those days at Likdam, the eventual outcome was too far into the future for me even to imagine how I would be extricated from this predicament.

CHAPTER 14

Tari and Anto Leave for London

It was well past midnight when Dr Warno and I returned to Likdam, with our bundles just as we had packed them that morning. There had been no intention to move us anywhere. If we had known, we could have been spared a lot of anxiety.

The whole camp was in a deep slumber when we entered. There was only one soldier awake, standing on guard; the others were asleep on tables in the guardhouse. The grey night threw a shadowy gloom over the compound, partly concealing the disorderly appearance of the camp, the endless lines of washing, clothes and towels, the mugs, cans and tin plates stacked everywhere, on ledges, on top of wooden partitions and round a tap that jutted up from the ground in the corner of the yard. Many of the men were sleeping on thin mats in the stony courtyard and we had to pick our way round them to get back to our rooms. The corridors were so packed with bodies that I could not help waking some people up as I tiptoed to my room.

All my room-mates woke up when I crept in and gave me a warm welcome back. We had feared we might never meet again. I felt so relieved to be back. We whispered to each other for some time before settling down to sleep; they were all anxious to know about the day I had spent at the CPM. My experiences were the subject of lively discussions for several days, but as the interest died down it was back to the old routine.

A few weeks later, in March 1969, something happened that brought me hope and contact with the outside world. I was not in the habit of spending time watching the comings and goings at the office. There were plenty of others who did that and the arrival of anyone out of the ordinary would prompt speculation about new developments afoot. One day, when a white woman arrived and went to the office, the news went round that it must be a visitor for Ibu Carmel. I took no notice at first, but, as it turned out, they were right.

I was called to the office to meet a short, rather stocky, smartly dressed woman who introduced herself with a slight smile on her face. This was

Mary Sorongan, an Australian, the representative in Jakarta of the World Council of Churches. I was shaking like a leaf when I entered the office. She came to the point quickly and told me that she had received instructions from her head office in Geneva to arrange for Tari and Anto to go to London where they would be cared for by my family. She was very business-like, confining herself to the matter for which she had been authorized to meet me.

'I need your consent', she said, 'before starting with the preparations.'

My consent! I could have hugged her with delight but took the cue from her behaviour and restrained myself.

'Yes, it sounds like a good idea', I said, 'but I can't give my consent until I've spoken to my husband and I also need to know what the children think.'

Although I quickly grasped the opportunity offered by Mary, I had my misgivings about whether this was the right thing to do. Tari was seventeen at the time and Anto was twelve. How would they adjust to living in England? How would my family cope with looking after them? Would they have to make the journey to England all alone?

I had not met Bud since he was transferred to Salemba Prison six months earlier. Mary turned to Major Sukotjo, the senior officer in charge at Likdam, who was present to oversee this rather unusual encounter. There were five officers within hearing distance of our meeting; the military command must have thought that something unpredictable might occur.

'Well, Major. Mrs Budiardjo will have to meet her husband before I can go ahead. Can that be arranged very soon, please?'

It was wonderful to see how she treated the Major, bossing him around. But Sukotjo was delighted to have this foreign woman visit the office. He was a notorious womanizer, very corrupt and a show-off. He usually came to work in his brand new Mercedes and always wore a uniform cut from the best cloth. Besides his army job, he was manager of a young women's pop group and his wife carried on a profitable business in expensive jewellery. There was plenty of gossip about his many affairs, but the dreadful thing about him was that he took advantage of women tapols. I was told about several women who had been released on the understanding that they would bestow sexual favours on him. Mary's involvement in my case opened up new vistas for him and he was to cause her much embarrassment during her many visits to Likdam.

He immediately agreed to arrange a meeting with Bud. Two days later, I was driven to Salemba Prison. It was a brief meeting, only ten minutes, in the presence of several guards and officials. In the old days, when Bud was in prison and I was on the outside, our rare meetings would take place divided by a wire grid. Now that we were both insiders, we could sit side by side on a bench. As I sat in the office waiting for Bud to come, I glanced at a wall chart showing the number of deaths in the prison. For several months up to the day of my visit, the death rate was one prisoner a day, in a prison that accommodated about 2,000 men.

I was very excited to be bringing him such good news. I had never considered the idea of sending Tari and Anto to London on their own. Our plans for a shift to London had always been made on the assumption that we would move as a family.

Bud was astonished to see me and thrilled about the news. There was clearly no doubt in his mind that this was the best possible solution.

'Why don't they make arrangements for you to leave as well?' He had always thought that I would be released much sooner than him. I explained that this was a move by friends – at the time I did not know who – and it would be best to tackle our problems one by one. The main thing at present was to send the children away so that they could start living a more normal life. Other things could follow later.

Being Jewish, it seemed a bit odd for the WCC to intervene on behalf of my family, but this was a gesture of solidarity that I really appreciated. An English friend, Ingrid Palmer, who I had become acquainted with when she was doing research in Indonesia, had been trying to think of ways she could help us and wrote to the Council, suggesting that they take this initiative. Mary, who was married to an Indonesian, had been representing the WCC in Indonesia for some years.

When Tari and Anto came to visit me later that week, I broke the news that they may soon be leaving for London. Anto was so shocked that he collapsed and wept in my lap for several minutes. Tari didn't break down though she told me later that she had felt like crying and only managed to control herself when she saw Anto break down. But it was obvious that the news pained her a great deal.

'We can't go off and leave you both like this', she said. 'Who will look after you? Who will be around to try and work for your release?'

This was typical of the way she had behaved ever since our arrest: cool, practical and always keenly aware of her responsibilities.

'Both of us will feel much better not having to worry about you two', I replied. Once they were abroad, I said, she would surely be able to do more about our release, and, as for looking after us, Auntie Par would be able to handle that. I tried to sound optimistic, though I had little idea what she would be able to do abroad.

So, the decision was taken and preparations for their departure began immediately.

It was a great relief for both of us to know that Tari and Anto would soon be safely in London. All the burden of handling the household finances, contacting the military about our release prospects and dealing with attempts by the army to take over our house was being borne by Tari. Par, whose husband, Mudjajin, was also in prison in faraway Semarang, was wonderful at running the household but shied away from having any dealings with the military. What Tari lacked in experience, she made up for in sheer guts and determination. Anto was too young to help her much though he was already showing quite a flair for finding ways of earning a bit of cash.

Earning money was their main preoccupation. There was no regular income coming in except for the rent paid by an American company which had contracted to use two rooms at the back of the house. There were a few back payments for work I had done as a translator of ofiicial documents, but that soon ran out. Tari made some money selling yoghurt and had sold a few of our valuables. They sent food to both of us three times a week, which was a terrible strain on their resources. Visiting us meant making long journeys by bus in two quite difficult directions. But Tari made a point of hiding from me the financial and other difficulties they faced. Anto and Tari were both attending Catholic schools where fees were high but the heads had agreed to waive payment.

In addition to trying to earn money, Tari had to go to the Jakarta military command once a month to renew the permit to visit me at Likdam and she made frequent applications – mostly unsuccessful – to visit Bud. For this, she had to take a day off school and often had to cope with sexual harassment from the soldiers she encountered. This even happened with that wretched Sukotjo in charge of Likdam. On one occasion when she went to see him to ask about my release prospects, she had to dodge round a table, towards the end of the interview, to escape his advances. She later told me how she managed to slip out of the door just as he was trying to grab hold of her.

Another problem was the house. It was a large, attractive corner house located in Jakarta's élite Menteng district. Many of our neighbours were ministers, ex-ministers, generals or ambassadors. We had obtained our tenancy permit in the late 1950s. The house used to belong to a Dutch insurance company that was nationalized in 1957. Thanks to stringent rent controls, the monthly payment was small, and fell in real terms because of the inflation. Until 1965, tenancy laws placed us in a strong position against eviction, but soon after 1965 the army decided to take over the house. Many 'involved' families suffered the same fate. In our case, we managed to hang on to the property for much longer than most.

One reason for the delay was that we always reported suspicious developments to Ali Sadikin, Governor of Jakarta. Sadikin, a retired marine corps lieutenant-general, was Minister of Sea Communications in the early 1960s and was Bud's boss until his arrest. The Marine Corps, the KKO, was often at loggerheads with the army and when he became Governor, Sadikin strongly opposed military interference in the allocation of housing. Sadikin had no qualms about our visiting him and always did what he could to help. On one occasion, he took our complaints further, writing to the army asking them to stop interfering.

In fact, only two days before our arrest in September 1968, we had a visit from an army officer who asked Bud whether we would be willing to surrender the house to the army. Bud told him that it was not ours to hand over, but if the army wanted it they would have to provide us with alternative accommodation.

There were several officers vying with each other to grab the property, each seeking the necessary backing and scheming to prevent others from pouncing. The state company that owned the property also wanted us to move out and was trying to find alternative accommodation in a kampung, hoping to sell the property to a foreign company for a huge profit. All these manoeuvres had been going on for years.

Shortly after our arrest, the Jakarta military command issued an order proclaiming that 'no one may take over the house as it is under army control'. The order was sealed onto the front door, but on the inside of the door was another seal from the Governor saying that his office had control over the property!

From then on, the house was under constant military guard. Three soldiers were detailed to guard the property night and day, making a great nuisance of themselves, lolling around in the drive, cooking tea in our kitchen and treating the place as if it was theirs. Par, Tari and Anto tried to establish a rapport with the soldiers. Some were well-meaning fellows who didn't like doing the dirty work for senior officers who would one day take possession, but their constant presence was a nagging irritation and made friends even more reluctant to visit the family. The only people who came regardless of all this were some of Tari's school friends, her boyfriend Bobby, and a Filipino post-graduate student from Cornell University, Joel Rocamora, and his American wife Nancy, who both kept in regular contact with Tari and Anto.

When Mary first set about getting permission to meet me, she had difficulty convincing the military that the World Council of Churches was a respectable organization. When she turned up at the Jakarta military command with her letter of authorization, they kept her waiting for hours. There must be something suspicous about an international group that wanted to get involved with the children of tapols. They were worried about dealing with what might turn out to be an 'international communist conspiracy'. So she was asked to come back in a week's time. The army would first have to check up on the credentials of the WCC at the Foreign Ministry. After investigation, the reply came: No, it was not a communist front but a genuine Christian organization with worldwide connections. On her next visit to the army, the red carpet was out. She was ushered into the office of the Deputy Chief-of-Staff, chuckling at being treated like a queen.

Mary lost no time arranging for Tari and Anto's departure. Once Bud and I had given our joint consent, Mary arranged a meeting between herself, Bud, Tari, Anto and me, when the two of us would sign a document authorizing her to take charge of the arrangements for the children. When she heard that the Salemba commander had only allowed Bud and me to spend ten minutes together, she insisted that this time he be brought to Likdam. She even persuaded Sukotjo to agree to let us spend several hours together, after signing the letter. This was the last time the four of us met together in Indonesia. We were allowed to meet in the privacy of a derelict brick enclosure, sitting round a disused well. We sat on rickety, bug-infested chairs and enjoyed the pleasure of just being together. As we chatted about the future, Tari and Anto fed Bud with thick slices of bread, butter and jam.

After this, Mary visited me frequently to report on her progress, always bringing large packets of food. To get passports for Tari and Anto, she needed clearance from the army, tax clearance as well as documents from their schools and from the education authorities. All this red tape exasperated her but I never saw her more angry than when she came one day and told me she would need to obtain 'certificates of non-involvement in the G30S/PKI' from the military for the two of them.

'Tari was only fourteen in 1965 and Anto was only nine', she said, throwing up her hands in disgust. 'What's come over these people?'

Not long after Mary made contact, Sukotjo allowed me to receive other foreign visitors. Joel and Nancy Rocamora were the first to start visiting me. Joel was a student of Benedict Anderson, who lectured on Indonesian politics and culture at Cornell University in the US. As soon as Ben heard of my arrest, he asked Joel to visit our home and keep an eye on the family. Until Mary came into the picture, Joel used to visit me at the camp with Tari, posing as her boyfriend. Later, he and Nancy started visiting me officially, with special permission from Sukotjo. After they left Indonesia, they passed me on like a relay baton to other couples, all American, who would visit, bring food, books and other things, making life much easier for me and others with whom I shared these gifts. John Newmann, who was one of the last in this relay, worked for Ford Foundation. He became a very close friend and, many years later, became part of the solidarity group we set up in the US for Indonesian political prisoners. Unlike the family visits which all took place on mats in the dusty yard, I was allowed to receive my foreign visitors in the office, seated on chairs at a table.

As the day of Tari and Anto's departure drew near in June 1969, I requested permission for Bud and me to go home on the evening before they left. This ought not to have been a problem as the house was well guarded already. Major Sukotjo agreed to ask his superiors. He seemed only too willing to make a special effort for me and anyway, he had his eye on an Australian woman who was Mary's assistant and sometimes came to Likdam when Mary was busy.

It was late in the evening of the day before Tari and Anto's departure. I watched the minutes go by, wondering whether I would be able to see the children for the last time. When I had almost given up hope of seeing them again, Sukotjo turned up and called me to the office. He had come straight from the home of the Deputy Chief-of-Staff.

'I'm sorry, Ibu Carmel. Your husband will not be allowed to go home tonight. And as for you, I must have a written assurance that you will not commit suicide while you are at home.'

'Commit suicide? Why on earth should I do a thing like that?'

'That's not the point.' I could see that he was deadly serious. 'It hasn't been easy to convince the Chief-of-Staff to allow you home tonight. If I don't get an assurance from you about this, I won't be able to take you home.'

So I gave him the assurance he needed. I had long given up trying to understand what these people were on about. After I had promised to be a good girl and not do myself in, he led me to his jeep and drove me home. On the way, he told me he had been to the house to check up on the situation earlier that day and had met our Filipino friend Joel and his wife.

'As there wasn't any male member of your family present', Sukotjo went on, 'I told him I would hold him responsible if you tried to kill yourself.'

'What did he say?' I asked.

'He didn't seem to mind at all.'

After driving for a few minutes in silence, Sukotjo began again: 'Your family in London must love your children very much to have gone to all this trouble to take them to London.'

'Not more than most families love their grandchildren or nieces and nephews. What they don't understand is how children can be left at home without their parents, without any income, without social security from the state. In most civilized countries, such things would not be allowed to happen.'

But this did not satisfy him. 'What amazes me is that your family want to have anything to do with someone like you, a communist in prison.'

'What you don't seem to understand is that people in other countries don't shun others just because of their political affiliations, especially members of their own family.'

Then he began to mumble about 'all these foreigners, Americans of all people' who kept coming to see me. He had expressed his surprise in the past about what he called this 'white-skinned solidarity'.

'Are they all communists?'

'No, of course not', I said.

He nodded as I spoke but kept his thoughts to himself.

When I arrived home, I found the house full of guests, mostly Tari's friends. Bud's younger brother Wandi was also there.

It was just as well, I thought, that there were plenty of guests as this would keep the emotions in check. And it was heart-warming to see that they were getting such a good send-off. I was allowed to spend only a short time at the house and after tearful goodbyes, I was driven back to the camp, feeling very lonely and bereft.

Tari and Anto had been allowed to have their farewell meeting with Bud several days before their departure. A soldier at the prison took a photograph of the three of them, standing happily together. This is the only photo we have of our prison days.

When they left the next day, there were many friends to see them off, together with Par and her children. Anto was perplexed at first because Wandi was nowhere to be seen. He didn't appear until after they arrived in the departure lounge. Because in the air force, he had managed to get through immigration so as to be with them after they had said their farewells to everyone else.

The trip to London was long and tiring. They first made a short stopover in Singapore where they boarded a charter plane to Rotterdam. As Anto later told me, 'We seemed to stop at every place on earth'. From Rotterdam they took a plane to Southend, on the south coast, where they were welcomed by my sister Miriam and my niece Nina and her husband Gary. Yet more travelling by road for a couple of hours before they arrived home, tired and weary.

———————

After Tari and Anto left, I was in a state of depression for days. To ease things a bit, Sukotjo allowed me to take to my room some books that Mary had brought for me. When she asked for permission to bring me books, Sukotjo said this would be all right, as long as they were books about religion. I remember her bringing me a small packet of books and putting them on the table one by one, saying 'This one's about the Christian religion, this one's about Islam, this one's about Catholicism . . . .' In fact, they were nothing of the kind.

At first, the books were kept in the office and I was only allowed to have them one at a time. But with Sukotjo feeling sorry for me, he allowed me to have them all in my room. This little library was very welcome to many of the other tapols. Another of Sukotjo's concessions was to allow me to correspond with Tari and Anto.

Sukotjo also wanted to give me something to do and asked me to teach him English with some other officers. These lessons were a waste of time and didn't go on for long because Sukotjo was too lazy to study anything and didn't like other officers to see how poor his English was.

All these special privileges infuriated Adil and he did what he could to countermand Sukotjo's orders. The contrast between the two men could hardly have been greater. They were both thugs but Sukotjo was more urbane and fancied himself as an upwardly mobile socialite. My presence at the camp delighted him because it was giving him access to foreigners. He would do anything (almost) to please them. He was at heart a playboy. Adil, on the other hand, was the gruff sergeant-major type who regarded all of Sukotjo's favours as a serious lapse of army discipline. They were both corrupt, though Sukotjo's projects were on a much grander scale and more sophisticated. Adil treated us with severity. He hated our guts and regarded us as infidels and criminals, always insisting on strict adherence to army discipline and rules. Sukotjo was more flexible and even a bit of a sentimentalist. He showed preference for some prisoners, especially women, but men as well when he thought this might advance him in some way. He even seemed to show sympathy for our plight. In actual fact, he cared little about what happened to any of us. All that mattered to him was promoting his own prospects, socially, financially and professionally.

Sukotjo's privileges turned Adil against me and he went out of his way to pick on me. He would sometimes come down to my room and take all my books away because I was 'having a bad influence' on the other prisoners. He often stopped me from writing to London and, since he was the officer in charge of day-to-day affairs, his word carried more weight than Sukotjo's. He did allow me to receive letters from Tari but said they would all have to be read first by an officer to make sure they contained nothing subversive. There was no one, however, who could read English well enough to understand what Tari was writing; her letters were always hand-written, very long and quite difficult to read. Whenever a letter arrived, I would be called to the office to wait while it was checked. On one occasion, I was sitting opposite a second lieutenant who was skimming through about five pages of text. Suddenly he became agitated; he had found something important.

'What's all this about China?' he asked.

Was Tari passing on some dangerous political information? If so, this was a serious matter. In those days, China was seen by the army as Indonesia's worst enemy because it had allegedly supported the Untung coup attempt.

I read the sentence and translated it into Indonesian for him: 'On Friday, Sid took me out and we went to a Chinese restaurant. The food was delicious.'

He looked a bit sheepish, took the letter back and read on till the end, then gave it to me with a shrug. After that, the censors didn't raise any more problems about Tari's letters.

CHAPTER 15

Another Transfer, Another Camp

'It beats me to understand how you manage to survive in a place like this', said Mary one day, as we were sitting alone in Sukotjo's office. Whenever she came to visit me, which was pretty often, especially after Tari and Anto had left and I was missing them so much, she never failed to remark on the squalor of the camp and questioned me closely about the food we were given. On her very first visit to Likdam, I had told her about the vermin that infested the place, spiders, ants, mosquitoes, cockroaches and rats, but it was the bugs that really troubled me. However, there was another side to life there down in the compound.

'You can get used to almost anything, if you try', I said. 'Anyway, there are a lot of fine people down there and life can be very interesting, even in a place like this.'

I really felt that way. Detention had caused me a great deal of suffering, anger and frustration. There were times when I felt desperately hungry and when I hated the lack of privacy. I could never get used to sleeping on the floor without a mattress or with the light on. I never had a pillow but always rested my head on a small pile of clothes, which made them look as if they had been ironed. I was very angry at the way my family had been torn apart and the way Tari and Anto had been forced to deal with difficult problems so early in life. These were the personal things that aggravated me constantly, on top of the terrible injustices and the horrors I witnessed.

Yet, despite all this, or perhaps because of it, I often considered myself privileged to be living through such an experience. There were times when I was able to detach myself from the person in detention and almost relish her good fortune. There were moments, usually when some particularly brutal or moving incident occurred in my presence, when I would think to myself 'Now remember this. You may get a chance one day to tell the story.'

Mary was, like me, a foreign woman married to an Indonesian. She had lived in Indonesia just as long as I had, if not longer, but had lived in a different milieu, keeping close links with the foreign community, living like an expatriate; I doubt whether she had learnt to speak Indonesian properly. I had never fostered such ties, I never met anyone from the British community, had only ever visited the British embassy a couple of times – to renounce my British nationality – and had immersed myself in the life of my adopted country. I had given up British nationality without any regrets, believing at the time that Indonesia would be my home for the rest of my life. Most of my close friends were Indonesian, along with a few other foreign women who, like me, were married to Indonesians and had no links with the expatriate community. I had assimilated very well into Indonesian society and I am sure that this made it easier for me to come to terms with life as a detainee.

Every time Mary came to Likdam, crossing the courtyard to reach the office, she was acutely aware that we were lacking many basic necessities. One day, she asked me to draw up a list of things the other detainees needed most desperately. She had access to relief funds from the Church World Service, she told me, and would be able to send in some supplies. It didn't take long to prepare a list: towels, vests and underpants for the men, underwear for the women, vitamin pills, disinfectant, medicated talcum powder for the many people suffering from skin disorders, aspirins, toilet soap and washing soap, toothpaste and toothbrushes.

A few weeks later, word went round that several wooden cases had arrived and were being carried into the office. Everyone knew about the list I had compiled and we guessed that Mary had kept her word. There was an air of excitement. It wasn't just that supplies of much-needed goods had arrived, but that someone had taken an interest in us. We saw Judy, Mary's assistant, go to the office, speak briefly to an officer, then leave. It was the month of May and all family visits had been suspended. May was the month of two dangerous anniversaries – Labour Day and the anniversary of the PKI's birth on 23 May 1920 – so the army was on special alert. The military don't like anniversaries of the wrong type. So, when Judy went to the office and asked for me, she was told we could not meet.

I expected to be summoned to the office about the goods and started thinking about how we should handle the distribution. As the hours dragged on, I heard nothing. Then some of the tapols who were watching the goings-on at the office more attentively than usual began to report that officers were going home with their brief-cases and pockets bulging. A tapol who was on duty to clean up the office spotted wrapping paper for ladies' underwear and the discarded packaging of toothpaste in the wastepaper baskets that afternoon. Then someone else saw empty packing cases being thrown into the boot of a car that had drawn up close to the office door. Our hopes of getting any of Mary's gifts were dwindling fast. By nightfall, all the officers had left and there was still no sign of anything being handed on to us.

The next day, Dr Warno, who was the camp RT at the time, was called to the office. A few minutes later, he came to my room carrying a few things in his arms: nine bars of soap, seven tubes of toothpaste, a tin of medicated talcum power, two bottles of vitamin pills and a tin of disinfectant.

'Pak Adil told me to give you these things', he said. 'They've been donated to us by someone but he didn't say who. He said he would leave it to you to distribute them to people in need.'

I looked at the things Dr Warno put down on my mat and gasped. Was this all they had left us? After a quick calculation, I worked out the value of the things we received: Rp. 1,750. Mary told me later she had sent us goods worth Rp. 65,000. She was horrified to hear what they had done and blamed herself for sending in so much at once. She should have sent the things in small batches, along with the food she sometimes sent me. But she had assumed that the goods would be handed over to me straight away, reducing the chances of corruption. She thought that her cordial relations with Sukotjo meant that he would be anxious to make a good impression on her.

Joel Rocamora had become a regular visitor to Likdam. He was doing research on the Indonesian National Party, the PNI, and when he met Sukotjo on the night before Tari and Anto's departure, he told him about the research project and thought up the idea of submitting some questions to him. Later, he spent a long time chatting with Sukotjo in his office, which pleased the Major no end. Having his views sought on a research project for a US university was really something he would be able to boast about. After the interview, I was given a chance to spend some time with Joel in the office. As we sat chatting, just the two of us, in Sukotjo's office, I suddenly heard the cries and groans of a tapol being beaten in the next room.

I froze with horror and asked Joel 'Did you hear that?'

'No, what was it?'

'Someone's being beaten in the next room. An interrogation is in progress. Can't you hear?'

But Joel had heard nothing. The cries and groans were not loud or piercing but they were distinct enough for my ears, which had become attuned to the special sounds emanating from a torture chamber. I also knew who was being interrogated. It was a young boy who had been beaten savagely for several days running. Each day, he returned to the compound with a bleeding nose or some other injury. Friends would treat and dress his wounds and patch him up for the next bout. The boy had difficulty expressing himself and behaved rather like an overgrown schoolboy. It was obvious that he was having a bad time with the interrogators simply because he infuriated them by his inability to answer their questions coherently. It was sickening to see how they took advantage of his vulnerability.

By the time Sukotjo returned, the cries had stopped but I was still feeling very upset. He came and joined us at the table.

'They're beating someone outside. Can't you do anything to stop it?' I asked.

He looked at me in his rather patronizing way and said, in a reassuring tone of voice 'Don't worry, Ibu Carmel. He'll be all right. He won't die. We have strict orders not to kill anyone.'

I knew that Sukotjo was one of several officers at the Jakarta military command who took exception to Atjep's methods of interrogation and the goings-on at Kalong. We had heard that he managed to have photographs taken, using a concealed device, during the interrogation of naked women by Atjep's thugs. These were later used in an attempt to curb Atjep's methods. The 'more humane' officers were probably motivated in part by professional jealousy. And now Sukotjo was trying to assure me that he was different, that it was all right to torture, as long as it was kept within bounds.

When Joel left, we had to pass through the room where the beatings had taken place. The boy was still there. I'm sure Sukotjo had slipped out to tell the interrogators to go easy while there was a visitor present. As we walked past him, the boy sat motionless, under orders not to say anything. On the other side of the table sat his tormentor who followed us both with his eyes. Joel left the camp and I returned to my room. Almost immediately, the boy's cries again filled the air, this time more piercing than before.

Three years later, Joel was arrested and held as a political prisoner in the Philippines after the introduction of martial law under Ferdinand Marcos, in September 1972. When I heard the news of his arrest, I wondered whether he would remember that incident in Likdam.

As for my own 'case', things proceeded very slowly at Likdam. It took nearly a year before the questioning was completed. Everyone here was supposed to be questioned so as to determine our classification, but they seemed to be in no hurry to deal with me. Strange as it may seem, although it was very stressful or frightening to be interrogated or questioned, we would get very impatient if nothing happened.

Adil himself took charge of my 'case'. From the start, we got bogged down over the question of my nationality. After checking my name he asked his second question.

'What's your nationality?'

'Indonesian.'

'Prove it', he replied.

'Well, I'm married to an Indonesian. Isn't that proof enough?'

'No, it isn't', he said in his usual gruff manner.

Adil obviously knew a thing or two about nationality laws in Indonesia. He was in the habit of interrogating people of Chinese or Indian origin, mostly traders who owned businesses in the nearby market, Pasar Baru. Picking up a Chinese businessman provided a welcome source of income for army officers. Even though Likdam was now used solely for political prisoners, the unit occasionally rounded up a few shopkeepers who were given a very rough time in the office. They would be ordered to join us in the compound for several days until they were willing to pay up in order to purge their alleged offences.

Adil was accustomed to handling these cases himself and he knew that all Chinese who held Indonesian nationality were in possession of a document certifying this. In April 1955, a treaty had been concluded between Indonesia and China providing for the elimination of dual nationality. There are several million people of Chinese descent in Indonesia. The aim of the agreement and subsequent legislation in Indonesia was to compel all overseas Chinese to make a choice between Indonesian and Chinese nationality.

It had never occurred to me to apply for a document certifying my Indonesian nationality. When I joined the staff of the Indonesian Foreign Ministry in 1954, the Foreign Minister, Sunario, more or less made it a condition that I should only have Indonesian nationality. The treaty with China had been signed but Indonesia's new nationality legislation had not yet been enacted. He told me that once the new legislation came into force, unlike in the UK, it would be impossible for me to have two nationalities. I had no problems about giving up British nationality as I had no intention of ever returning to Britain to live. So off I went to the British Embassy to inform them of my intention to renounce British nationality. I was told that this would not be possible unless I could produce evidence that I held another nationality because, under British law, a person cannot renounce British nationality if this renders her stateless.

The only way I could comply was to seek a declaratory statement from a court confirming that I held Indonesian nationality by virtue of my marriage to an Indonesian citizen. I obtained this without difficulty, delivered it to the embassy and was then allowed to renounce British nationality. However, this procedure was of no interest to Adil and he repeated the question.

'I have a statement from a court of law which certifies that I am an Indonesian national because of my marriage. Would you like to see that?'

No sooner were the words out of my mouth than I realized that I had made a mistake. If he was having doubts about whether I was Indonesian, why should I try to assure him that I was?

Adil was not interested in my offer, probably thinking that I was trying to be awkward. He terminated the session and told me that the interrogation would not continue until I could give a satisfactory answer about my nationality. He summoned me several more times but we never went beyond the first two questions.

Eventually, he must have been instructed to stop making a fuss about my nationality. His superiors must have realized that if I was having difficulty proving that I was Indonesian, they might have an international problem on their hands if the British claimed me as 'theirs', with the possibility of intervention from London. After several months' delay, he summoned me one day and, without even asking me question number two, he wrote 'Indonesian' on the paper in front of him. From this time on, I never told anyone that I was Indonesian, saying instead that I wasn't sure what I was.

With this confusion out of the way, the sessions with Adil proceeded rather uneventfully. He covered much the same ground as Atjep at Satgas-Pusat: my membership of the HSI, my articles in the press criticizing the Sukarno government's economic policies, my work as a translator for the PKI's international affairs department, my job as an economics adviser to Dr Subandrio, and my circle of friends. After the interrogation report was completed, that was the end of the matter as far as my 'case' was concerned and life went on much as usual. No one bothered to tell me whether I now had a classification.

In August 1969, Mary brought a very special guest to visit me, Stefanie Grant of Amnesty International. She had told Sukotjo that Stefanie and I were 'old friends' and I picked up the cue from the way Mary behaved that I had to pretend to welcome someone I knew. We chatted for quite a while about how I was and whether I was in need of anything. I had no idea that Stefanie was on a mission to Indonesia together with Sean McBride, a member of Amnesty's governing council and also Secretary General of the International Commission of Jurists in Geneva. This was Amnesty's first official mission to Jakarta and it played a big part in establishing Indonesia as one of the major campaigning issues for the organization, the country with possibly the largest number of political prisoners worldwide.

Not long afterwards, about a dozen women were transferred to the women's prison, Bukit Duri, the first time this had happened since my arrival in Likdam. Among those transferred was my good friend Nuriah and others whom I had first got to know in Satgas-Pusat. Their departure distressed me greatly and I felt as if I had lost all my best friends in one blow. I was also puzzled about my own prospects. Could I now assume that I might soon be released?

———————————

In December 1969, a team of interrogators from the air force came to question me about Mrs Suryadarma, the wife of a former air force chief-of-staff, whom they suspected of being a PKI plant. She had been appointed Rector of Res Publica University where I taught economics. I had no idea what they were trying to pin on her. She had been a close ally of Sukarno's and highly respected in the left-wing movement. Her husband had retired as air force chief several years earlier. The force was suspected of harbouring too many pro-Sukarno officers and had therefore been drastically purged after the Suharto Coup. But Mrs Suryadarma had a political persona of her own.

This session was conducted by a young lawyer who had been with the air force legal department for several years. He was quite frank with me: they were seeking information about Mrs Suryadarma in order to construct a case against her, in preparation for her arrest. Usually, I thought to myself, things went the other way round – arrest someone first, construct the case later.

The difference was that she had been a prominent figure in her own right and also the wife of a senior air force officer, so the army needed to tread carefully.

My new interrogator seemed to want to impress me with his knowledge of world affairs and sometimes allowed the dialogue to turn to other subjects. He told me he had read in *Newsweek* about student upheavals during 1968 in many western countries and said he saw the anti-Sukarno student demonstrations in Indonesia in 1966 as part of that global movement of students. What a load of rubbish! Soon after the

Suharto Coup, thousands of students were mobilized by the army to hold demonstrations on the streets, taking as their targets the politicians Suharto needed to discredit. They spearheaded the demand calling on Sukarno – who still held nominal power – to outlaw the PKI. It was also alleged at the time that the student demonstrators had been funded by the CIA. The students operated in close allegiance with Kostrad, Suharto's special strategic force, and played a role in helping to topple Sukarno and establish a military regime. Their 'radicalism' had nothing to do with the spirit of 1968.

Then he talked about human rights and tried to convince me that the government respected the rule of law.

'At one end of our legal system stands the prosecution', he said, expansively. 'It's my task as a lawyer to prepare the case for the prosecution, to be argued in a court of law. The court stands in the middle, weighing the arguments and passing down its verdict. You, Ibu Carmel, stand at the other end.'

'That sounds fine', I said, 'but if I am at the defence end, why can't I have a lawyer?'

'Because you're not the accused. You're only a witness and you don't need a lawyer.'

'Well, if I'm only a witness, why have I been arrested?' I might have scored a point but I doubt whether I shook his confidence in the system.

It was while this discussion was going on that a burly lieutenant came into the room with an order for me to be transferred. It was Sukotjo who broke the news to me. He knew that it would unsettle me so he softened the blow by telling me I was going somewhere where I would be given a special task, to teach English to a group of officers.

Once the transfer order had been received, things moved fast. The session with the air force fellow was immediately terminated. Nothing was allowed to stand in the way of a transfer. After hasty farewells from my room-mates, I was on my way to my new detention camp, the headquarters of the Special Intelligence Task Force of the Jakarta military command, Satgas-Jaya, the regional equivalent of the unit that had arrested Bud and me back in September 1968. This unit was soon to take over from Likdam and Kalong, in charge of the arrest, detention and interrogation of all political detainees in the Jakarta region. Lower-level military commands still had powers to arrest people but it was the task of Satgas-Jaya to decide who would be held indefinitely and transferred to prison as 'A' or 'B' category prisoners. Here too I was to witness a constant flow of tapols arriving from other units, waiting their turn to be interrogated, then sent to Salemba Prison.

Shortly after my transfer, Likdam was wound up; Kalong continued to function but was now subordinated to Satgas-Jaya. My new 'home' was accommodated in the former office of China's Hsinhua News Agency. The building had been attacked by pro-army gangs because of China's alleged support for the Untung 'coup attempt'. Tit-for-tat raids on diplomatic premises in Jakarta and Beijing had led to the severance of diplomatic relations with China in 1966. This was the building where Bud and I had been taken, on our way to Satgas-Pusat fifteen months ago.

The building was set well back from the main road and there were no signs outside to indicate what was going on inside. In front was a long, well-kept garden with a lawn, beds of flowers and neatly trimmed bushes and trees. This was a far cry from the squalor of Likdam. The building was clean and freshly painted. No prisoners could be seen in the front part of the premises. It could easily have been mistaken for the residence of a wealthy family. The lieutenant who had brought me here, a man called Situmorang, showed me to my room facing the garden, on the right of the main building. He told me I would be sharing the room with a woman who, until my arrival, had had no room of her own but had spent the daylight hours sitting in a corridor and going into an office at night to sleep.

The room had no furniture, but a divan was moved in for my benefit. It was almost as if they were preparing a hotel room for a special guest! When I lay down to sleep on the divan, I was soon covered with bug bites. I grabbed my mat and went down onto the floor to sleep. The next day, I had the divan removed; I wanted none of that.

The next day, I was taken to meet the unit commander, Lieutenant-Colonel Prijo Subagio. He came across as a decent sort of chap who went out of his way to show concern for my welfare. There was a huge chart covering one of the longer walls in his office. It was an organizational chart of the PKI. Lines linked up little boxes horizontally and vertically, representing the committees, commissions and departments of the Party's central secretariat. Some boxes had names in them, others were still empty.

Until his appointment to head this unit, Prijo Subagio had been a field officer, a commander of the special commandos, the red berets, the notorious RPKAD which was involved in both combat and intelligence operations. He had spent some time on a mission to Cambodia to train troops of the Lon Nol Government. Before that, in the late 1950s, he had been on operations against the Dar'ul Islam in West Java. Now his battle-ground was intelligence, to mop up PKI 'remnants', filling in the boxes on the wall.

When I entered his office, he invited me to be seated. After a few pleasantries – Was I in good health? How were the children? – he said 'I hope you will be comfortable here. Mrs Sorongan came to see me about you. She seemed to be very concerned about your being in Likdam. I hope you will find things more pleasant here.'

So that was it. Some army officers were getting worried about my foreign connections, worried that I could become a source of embarrassment. I heard later that Mary exploded with rage when she met him, and asked him what they thought they were doing 'keeping an English woman in a rat-hole like that'. She had spoken in English and he may not have understood everything she said but it was enough. I felt uncomfortable about appearing to these people as a complaining foreigner, less able to cope with conditions than my Indonesian fellow-prisoners. It was also amusing to see them going out of their way to accommodate foreigners. It was Mary's decision to play this card and she had never consulted me. It would have been foolish of me to forgo a move that might advance my chances of release. Things were so weighted against tapols that there was little else to hope for. Anyway, I hardly had a say in the matter.

Prijo Subagio asked me whether I would mind teaching him and a few other officers English. It was all so polite, so unlike anything I had experienced before.

'I can't possibly do it if I don't have access to books, paper and writing materials', I replied.

'That's no problem', he replied. 'Just say what you need and it will be yours.' I asked for paper and pens and a supply of English-language newspapers.

The next day, a soldier came to my room and handed me a packet.

'From the commander, for Ibu Carmel', he said. Prijo Subagio had sent me paper, pencils, a ruler and six brand-new notebooks. Later I was to get copies of the Singapore daily, *The Straits Times*. When I next met Prijo Subagio, I asked him what the notebooks were for. Were they intended for the students or just for me?

'They're all for you', he replied.

'Thank you. That's very kind of you. But why so many? How many groups will I have to teach?'

'Only one. You can use the other five for your own needs. I would have thought that someone like you would want to write your memoirs, so why not start now?'

Was this a challenge? Or a provocation? Or was he trying to make sure that he would get a good write-up? I could not tell. What he was suggesting contradicted all the prison regulations that had been drummed into us. I was suspicious of his intentions and decided not to write anything on those gleaming white pages, however tempting they were. It was just as well because what later happened meant that I would never have been able to keep them and take them out of the country. In my innermost thoughts, however, I did accept the challenge. So you, Lieutenant-Colonel Prijo Subagio, are in part responsible for my decision to write this book.

CHAPTER 16

An Experiment in Being Nice

Satgas-Jaya looked clean and tidy. It was run by a commander who wanted his unit to be efficient, effective and humane. Lieutenant-Colonel Prijo Subagio had not been in intelligence work long and had come to it with a determination to establish a new tradition. Treating prisoners like human beings would be one of his guiding principles; curbing the worst excesses of interrogation techniques would be another. He wanted to change the relationship between intelligence officers and their communist collaborators, keeping them more firmly under control than at Kalong.

He would also create an efficient bureaucracy with good documentation so that interrogation reports were filed away in orderly fashion. The interrogation process would be speeded up and decisions about a prisoner's future would be taken more quickly. Improvements were needed because documents were often mislaid and decisions delayed for months or even years. Satgas-Jaya would be bright and pleasant to behold, full of contented prisoners and efficient, hard-working officers. His men would be warned not to play around with women prisoners for this lowered the tone of the unit, compromised its reliability and damaged its reputation.

When I was at Satgas-Jaya, Prijo Subagio was hard at work putting his experiment into practice. My presence fitted neatly into his plans because it gave him an opportunity to show foreigners – not only me but those with whom I was now in contact – that intelligence officers could be decent chaps.

He tried hard to make a good impression on me. He took a keen interest in the lessons I gave and allowed me to use whatever facilities I needed. I was required to give English lessons every evening. Prijo Subagio joined the class himself, as well as a group of cadets, recently graduated from the armed forces academy AMN. He asked me to use reading texts dealing with world affairs because he also wanted his cadets to have a better understanding of international developments. It was quite a change for me to be able to read *The Straits Times* every day. He insisted that, during the lessons, my pupils should treat me not as a prisoner but with the respect owed to a teacher.

I was paid for the lessons, something unheard-of for a political prisoner, and allowed other privileges as well. I was permitted to have a radio in my room with no one around to check up on what I listened to. I got the most pleasure from it every Sunday evening, listening to a programme of classical music on a station called El Bahar. One of the presenter's favourites was Chopin's Second Piano Concerto, a work I was unfamiliar with. To this day, whenever I hear that work, it reminds me of my time at Satgas-Jaya.

For a few weeks, Bud was 'on loan' to the unit, so Prijo Subagio allowed us to meet every day and have our meals together though not to share a room or spend the night together. He even permitted us to hold a family celebration for our twentieth wedding anniversary in February 1970 and joined us for the occasion. I realized that I was part of his grand experiment and considered myself lucky not to be doing anything that compromised me politically. I felt that if I played along with his scheme of things, it might improve my chances of release.

Like Atjep and Suroso at Kalong, he too needed to win over collaborators from the PKI. His methods were more subtle, offering likely recruits certain privileges like going home for the weekend and eventually allowing them to go home every night so that their activities at Satgas-Jaya became like a nine-to-five office job.

How did Prijo Subagio's 'humane experiment' fit in with the army's strategy towards the political prisoners? It was now nearly 1970. The many waves of mass arrests that had started in October 1965 were largely over. The main problem now was what to do with the many tens of thousands of 'B' category prisoners who would not be released but who could not be tried. The army's 'Final Solution' was to banish them to the infamous labour camp on Buru Island. This started in 1969. Sweeps against communist suspects would no longer occur on the same scale as previously. In other words, the army were at the tail end of the operation to wipe out the PKI. They could now afford to clean up their act and remove officers who had 'gone too far' in their atrocities against prisoners. They could now afford to adopt a 'more humane' strategy, leaving the fundamental injustices intact.

There was a yawning gap in Satgas-Jaya between what was visible to the visitor and the reality experienced by the majority of tapols. Beyond the well-tended garden were two freshly painted bamboo blinds pulled down to the ground during the day to hide the male tapols staying in overcrowded rooms, lying side by side on the floor and under strict instructions to keep quiet whenever visitors were on the premises. Nor would visitors ever know about the tiny cells that had been constructed behind the main office, where tapols who refused to tell the interrogators what they wanted to know were kept in solitary confinement for days, weeks or even months.

There were four of these cells with solid black doors, close together like a row of lavatories. The floor space was about five foot six inches long and two foot six inches wide. There were no windows or lights inside, not even bars on the doors to let in some light and fresh air, only a small hatch at the foot of the door through which food and drink was passed. The walls were of brick and the floors were of stone. Tapols kept there were allowed out twice a day, in the morning and the evening, to wash and go to the toilet. For the rest of the time, they remained in those terrifying cells, sitting or lying down, often with nothing more than a thin cotton sarong to protect them from the cold, damp floor.

On my way to the bathroom and toilet every day, I had to pass the cells. At first, I dreaded the thought of going anywhere near them but I managed to overcome my horror and realized that I could help the men inside. I was one of the few people in the camp with freedom of movement so I got into the habit of going past the cells as often as I could, whistling, singing or coughing as I approached. When there was no guard around, I would linger a few minutes and ask the men how they were and whether they needed anything. I rarely discovered the names of the men inside. I also passed them food and drink, vitamin pills and other medicines when they were ill.

Sometimes a grateful voice would say 'Please come by as often as you can'.

It was obvious that they felt comforted having someone around whom they could call on when they were in trouble though there were some who never responded to my offers of help.

When I was transferred to Satgas-Jaya, the cells had just been built. The first person to be put inside was Nizar, a PKI leader who had taken over the leadership of the Jakarta clandestine movement after Sudisman and others were arrested. The moment they put him inside, he started a hunger strike and kept it up until they took him out and transferred him to Salemba Prison. Another man given the 'cell-treatment' was a young prisoner whom I had seen at Likdam. He did not strike me as being a particularly strong-minded prisoner; on the contrary, he hardly seemed to know what was going on. Several days after he was put in a cell, we suddenly heard a frightful din. He was beating on the door.

'Let me out! I'm choking!'

When the guards eventually let him out and put him in another room, he sat panting and looking about him furtively. Later, when a guard came to check on his condition, he rushed out of the door, ran round to the back and started banging with his fists on the door of the cell he had just vacated. He was dragged back to the other room, sobbing and shaking.

The 'cell-treatment' was supposed to reflect a more subtle approach, relying on psychological rather than physical pressure. Yet there was plenty of the latter at Prijo Subagio's 'humane' detention centre. The door of my room was only two metres from the window of one of the interrogation rooms so I often saw or heard interrogations in progress. On one occasion, a soldier was being questioned. There was always a steady trickle of soldiers among the detainees. It was well known that the PKI had many supporters in the armed forces before 1965 and Sukarno had a big following there too.

The victim this time was a second-lieutenant who was given a severe beating for a couple of hours. I caught a glimpse of Prijo Subagio in the room as I passed the window and saw him aiming blows at the poor fellow, who was standing stripped to the waist, not murmuring a sound. Later that afternoon, I was sitting outside my room not far from a sub-lieutenant who was on guard duty. He looked crestfallen and suddenly began to talk about the morning's events.

'Poor devil. Fancy beating him like that. It could easily have been me, couldn't it?' Although he was looking in my direction as he spoke, the guard seemed to be thinking aloud, hardly aware of my presence.

'That's what can happen to the little guy whose only crime is that he carries out the orders of his superiors. Suppose my commander ordered me to deliver a truckload of weapons and ammunition somewhere and it turns out to be supplies for people who are against the Government. I couldn't refuse to carry out the order, could I? How am I to know what it's all about. Even so, I could one day be picked up and bashed about for doing what I was ordered to. They could keep me in clink for years.'

My room was separated from the rooms where most of the tapols were kept. I was only allowed to mix with a few of the men. I missed the communal life at Likdam and felt dreadfully lonely during my first few weeks at Satgas-Jaya.

For most of the time I was there, I shared the room with Is, a young woman who had been arrested along with her husband about a year ago. She had been a rather prominent member of the women's organization, Gerwani, in East Java. She had a beautiful face and a well-trained soprano voice. She was now pregnant from a liaison with an officer at Kalong and had recently been transferred to Satgas-Jaya where she was to remain under Prijo Subagio's supervision until the baby was born. She spoke frequently about her new boyfriend and was hoping to settle down with him after her release, either as his mistress or his second wife. Even so, she wanted to retain the confidence of her husband who was now in Salemba Prison. She had been allowed to spend a few nights out of camp with him soon after she realized she was pregnant so that she might later be able to convince him that he was the father.

Is always kept her eyes and ears open and knew a lot about what was going on. She told me about the death of a tapol named Ismojo, who had committed suicide shortly before my arrival there. We had heard about this suicide at Likdam and were inclined not to believe it, but the things I subsequently heard and saw convinced me that it was true.

Is was the last person to see Ismojo alive. He was locked up in one of the rooms upstairs, away from the other male prisoners. Late one afternoon, as dusk was falling, she was strolling in the garden, singing, when she looked up and saw Ismojo gazing at her through the window. He smiled at her, nodded and gently waved his hand, as if to say 'That's beautiful. Please go on singing.'

She smiled back and continued with her song. Then he disappeared from view. A quarter of an hour later, a guard went through the garden carrying an evening meal for Ismojo. When he unlocked the door upstairs, he found Ismojo hanging from the iron casement of a side window. He had hanged himself with a thick cord of embroidery silks which his wife had given him. Is was sure he must have been alive when the guard found him because it was so soon after she had seen him alive, but no one dared to cut him down until a senior officer arrived at the scene to take charge.

The room where Ismojo had killed himself was left empty for several weeks and was only put to use again for our English lessons. When I first went in, I spotted a few inches of the embroidery silk still hanging down. No one had bothered to remove it.

Later I became a participant in a sequel to Ismojo's death. About two months after my transfer to Satgas-Jaya, I suddenly heard a lot of noise and chatter in the garden. I went out and saw a guard talking in an agitated voice to a group of people. He had just rushed out of an empty room and swore that he had heard a voice inside and seen a soldier's tunic, moving, on the wall. Everyone agreed that this must have been Ismojo's spirit coming back to haunt us. While the topic was being heatedly discussed, somebody suddenly realized that it was exactly one hundred days since Ismojo's death, a day observed by Muslims for commemorative prayers and a *selamatan* at which certain kinds of delicacies should be consumed. Everyone agreed that we had been given a warning and should immediately hold a *selamatan* for the dead man's soul.

That evening, after dusk prayers had been said, including a special prayer for Ismojo, straw mats were laid out in the porch in front of the main building. Those of us who were permitted to move about, together with any officers and interrogators who happened to be around, as well as the guards who were on duty that day, sat on the mats; we chewed nuts, ate light refreshments and sipped tea, talking in subdued voices. After half an hour or so, we dispersed. The mats were rolled up and there was a feeling that we had helped to placate the spirit of the dead man for whom the horrors of political detention had been beyond endurance.

I had moved to Satgas-Jaya just before Christmas 1969, so Mary decided to follow up her success by asking for me to be allowed to spend Christmas with her and her husband Andrew. This was agreed and I spent the first day out of camp, with two soldiers as my escorts. As I sat among friends who had gathered at Mary's place to welcome me, I was in a daze. In the evening, Mary and Andrew took me and my escorts to a Chinese restaurant for dinner. What a change it was, sitting at a well-laid table eating exquisite Chinese food, after having got used to eating all my frugal meals on the floor.

After dinner, I was taken back to Satgas-Jaya punctually. Prijo Subagio had been worried that I might abscond with a passport that Mary was concealing up her sleeve. When I returned as pre-arranged, he was immediately informed by phone that everything had gone according to plan. He asked the officer who phoned to tell me that he was delighted.

Not long after this, he told me I would be allowed to spend every other weekend with the Sorongans, though he would not allow me to return to my own home. He felt that I would be safer with the Sorongans. Like Mary, Andrew was connected with the Protestant Church. He was manager of the guest house of the Indonesian Council of Churches. The guest house was on the same road as our house, just a few doors down on the other side of the street, but I didn't go near the place. The commander probably thought he could rely on Mary and Andrew not to do anything that would compromise the Church. His reluctance to allow me to go home may also have been because of the continuing row between several senior army officers over occupancy of the house. People from the rival groups frequently turned up at the house to make sure that the others had not yet taken possession and if one of them had seen me there, this might have put Prijo's experiment in jeopardy.

The weekends I spent at the guest house were delicious moments of respite from detention, camp and soldiers. I spent most of the time wallowing in the comforts of the spacious and well-furnished guest house. But it was not easy for me to get used to the pleasure of sleeping between clean sheets on a mattress in a cool, well-ventilated room, free of mosquitoes and bed bugs. The first two weekends at the guest house were very unsettling. Far from falling asleep the moment my head hit the pillow, I was quite unable to sleep. I had a large room with a fan on the ceiling above the bed. I tried everything to combat sleeplessness – reading, turning off the fan, even keeping the light on as we had to do in the detention camp – but nothing worked. I began to worry that these weekends off would be no good for me if I couldn't get a good night's sleep. When the third weekend came round, I was more settled mentally to the change and slept well from then on.

The time at Satgas-Jaya dragged on without anything happening about my case, but things clearly could not continue like this. It was now nearly five months since I had been transferred from Likdam in December 1969. This was supposed to be a transit camp. It was one matter for prisoners who had turned collaborator and were helping the army with their intelligence work to stay there indefinitely. It was quite another matter to keep someone there indefinitely as the commander's English teacher. Prijo Subagio had to be careful that nothing should stand in the way of his chances of promotion and rumours were now circulating that I was giving him English money for the privilege of staying at this unit. A decision about my status would have to be taken fairly soon.

I knew that there was a huge row going on about what to do with me. Some officers thought that, in prison, I would continue to be a source of embarrassment because of my foreign connections. They had gone far beyond Mary and the Council of Churches. After Joel and his wife Nancy left Indonesia, other couples started to visit me at Likdam. And as each couple left, they passed me on to another couple. I was profoundly touched by the hand of friendship offered by people I had never met before. After my transfer to Satgas-Jaya, American and then Australian couples kept up the 'relay', bringing me food and taking a keen interest in my personal welfare. For most of the time there, my 'foster parents' were John and Mary Newmann, who spared no effort to help me. John visited me as regularly as he could and showered me with gifts. He also kept in contact with Tari and Anto in London. His affection, interest and support was a great comfort and a reminder to the authorities that foreign friends with contacts like the Ford Foundation were following my fortunes closely.

Other officers at the Jakarta military command, and also at army headquarters, were flatly opposed to my being released. Although I now knew what some of my former professional adversaries were doing to keep me inside, I found it difficult to understand why the army wanted to hold on to me. There could never be any question of my going on trial. There was nothing to prove that I had been involved in the 1965 events nor could anyone produce evidence that I had been part of the underground movement.

In an effort to reach a final decision on my 'case', I was interrogated all over again. My interrogator this time was a former prisoner, an economist. The interrogations proceeded without any particular problems and covered much the same ground as before. This time, I was given more opportunity to express my views, though whether this helped or hindered my chances of release is hard to say. With hindsight, I would say that in cases like this, the less said the better.

This time, I was the one to raise the question of my nationality. I said I had reason to believe that the formalities for adopting Indonesian citizenship had not been complied with, which might invalidate my renunciation of British nationality in 1954. I gave as the reason the fact that I had never registered my marriage to Bud in Prague after moving to Indonesia. The interrogator seemed interested and promised to investigate.

While I was waiting for the results of this latest round of interrogation, I received some very disturbing news from London. My eldest sister Lebah was gravely ill, though I didn't know at the time that she was dying of cancer. After their arrival in London, Tari had moved in with Lebah and Anto went to stay with her daughter Nina at a nearby flat. Nina and her family later moved to a small house but it would be difficult for both Anto and Tari to live there. Now that Lebah was so ill, other accommodation would have to be found.

The only solution was for Tari and Anto to set up house on their own. My sister Miriam, who worked as a casting director for the film industry, had an office in a flat in central London, off Piccadilly. Outside office hours, the flat was vacant and Miriam decided to let them use it as their home. But the financial consequences were serious; there simply wasn't enough money in London to provide them with a regular income. I had been able to deposit money in a London bank before my arrest, in preparation for what I thought would be our move to London after Bud was released in 1967. But the money soon ran out.

I decided to go and put a proposition to Prijo Subagio. If he really wanted to be nice, here was his chance.

Of course, he said, he could well understand the desire of a parent to look after her children but what did I think he could do about it?

'You already allow me out at weekends. Why not allow me out for a few hours every day? I could return every evening to spend the night at Satgas-Jaya. I can easily find pupils and earn enough to keep the two of them in London.'

It sounded a bit odd but not so very different from what other prisoners were being allowed to do. If they were allowed to go home at night and report for duty every day, why couldn't I do it the other way round. If the army were not going to free me, the least they could do, I argued, was to let me earn money to send to London.

Prijo Subagio said he thought this might work but it would be for his superiors to decide. Several weeks later, I was told that a recommendation for my release was under consideration. The soft-liners had apparently gained the upper hand. I was told that the terms of my 'release' would be strict. Satgas-Jaya would need to know at all times what I was doing and where I was living, and I would be under constant surveillance. Perhaps there was an element of using me as a bait should members of the underground try to contact me. But I never for a moment believed that I would be putting others at risk because I had had no contact with people working underground and they surely would not have taken the risk of contacting me. I was too well known for that.

In May I was told that I would be allowed to leave the detention centre. By this time I had spent 21 months in detention. I was greatly relieved, even though I did not believe that my case had been settled one way or the other. The conditions made it sound like a temporary arrangement, a kind of 'leave of absence' from detention.

I left Satgas-Jaya on 23 May 1970 and immediately began to set myself up as a full-time English teacher.

CHAPTER 17

Leave of Absence

A single advertisement in a Jakarta newspaper, placed the morning after I left Satgas-Jaya, resulted in enough inquiries to fill a timetable for six hours a day, five days a week. I trebled my fee, charging $5 an hour for single pupils and more for pairs or larger groups. Some said they couldn't afford the rate, but I was amazed to see how many were willing to pay for one hour the equivalent of the monthly wage for a middle-ranking civil servant and double the wage of a primary school teacher. There were several civil servants ready to cough up, as well as an army officer and his wife. They must have been living on perks and other extras.

I insisted on being paid at the beginning of each month for a month's teaching. Within a few days of my release, I was able to send £80 to London as my first contribution to Tari and Anto's upkeep. Although the money I was earning was quite modest, I felt as if I had struck gold. I had no training as an English teacher and had to be quite innovative in the methods I used. Being English as distinct from American or Australian gave me the edge over others who taught English, far outweighing my lack of experience and skills.

Every time I collected fees from my pupils and took the money to the bank for transfer to London I wondered whether I would be around long enough to complete the lessons for which I had been paid. Little did these trusting souls realize that I could disappear in a puff of smoke, leaving them with no way of getting their money back. It was the first – and last – time in my life that I lived solely in order to make as much money as I could.

I took lodgings in an expensive boarding house which cost me the equivalent of two days' teaching. I had a large, pleasantly furnished room and was exceptionally well fed by my Menadonese landlady. I put on more than a stone in my first month outside prison. Most of my lessons were held in Andrew's guest house, an arrangement that had been sanctioned by Satgas-Jaya. He put at my disposal a large, well-shaded terrace where my pupils and I sat undisturbed.

During those few months, I lived in greater comfort than I had enjoyed in my eighteen years in Indonesia yet I now felt acutely that Indonesia had lost all its attraction for me. Bud was in prison and I could not visit him; nor was I in a position to do anything about getting him released. Tari and Anto were thousands of miles away. The only person in Bud's family who stayed in touch with me was Par. No friends visited me because of the risks and I was bereft of the communal life that had made detention endurable. There was nothing I could do, politically. There were no professional openings in research or teaching and no publication would have dared to publish anything by me, even under a pseudonym. I was living on borrowed time and knew that there was no future for me here.

I did not tell any of my pupils that I had just left a detention centre for political prisoners, for that would have scared them all away. Superficially, I had now become part of a society that lived, behaved and spoke as if nothing was amiss. Who, looking at me, fairly well dressed, in keeping with my chosen profession, could have guessed at the problems and sorrows I had to contend with? Having myself berated others for being ignorant or unconcerned about the fate of so many of their compatriots, I was now giving the same impression to those with whom I interacted. Appearances give a very warped view of a society that lives in the grip of fear.

By the time I left Satgas-Jaya, Par and her three children had moved. The family was ordered to quit the house in Tengku Umar in January 1970 and they were living in a small house in the suburb of Tebet. Having had to put up with soldiers trampling all over the place, it was a relief for them to move to a house that was too small and remote to arouse anyone's envy. The final stages of the move had been handled with an unusual amount of decorum. This was largely because Tari had made persistent efforts to keep Bud's former boss, the Governor of Jakarta, Ali Sadikin, interested in our housing problem. So many other tapols' families I knew had lost their homes without a cent in compensation. What usually happened was that an officer would install himself in the house, take it over room by room, and leave the occupants with no alternative but to get out and find alternative accommodation. Prisoners' families could not expect to achieve anything by going to court. In those days there were no legal aid institutes willing to provide legal services to the families of tapols for a civil action to reclaim property.

The order to quit the house was delivered by the municipal housing department and we were actually paid compensation for the loss of our tenancy. Par used this cash to purchase the house in Tebet. The house in

Tengku Umar was immediately occupied by an army officer who worked at the State Secretariat. I decided that it would not be practical for me to live at the house in Tebet because of its remoteness from the centre of town. Quite likely, Satgas-Jaya would not have approved anyway.

I noticed many changes in the Jakarta I returned to after my twenty months in detention. It was fast becoming a Western-type metropolis, showing signs of large-scale foreign investment, greatly encouraged by the foreign investment law introduced in 1967. Along the main roads were multistorey blocks of office space for the new businesses that were taking advantage of the economic policies of Suharto's New Order. Several four-star hotels had also been built to cater for visiting businessmen, along with casinos, massage saloons, sauna baths and night-clubs to cater for the country's new élite. Some of the main roads had been widened and street stalls and vendors regarded as an 'eyesore' had been removed to give the city a face-lift.

For the vast majority of Jakarta's five million inhabitants, the new policy had brought little improvement. They still lived in conditions of overcrowding, lacking hygiene and social facilities and with widespread unemployment. Under the New Order, the gap between rich and poor had widened.

On my way to Andrew's home every day, I passed a group of homeless families who had squatted along a road close to the guest house. There were several women dressed in rags with babies strapped to their sides, cooking rice in a tin can over a makeshift fireplace. Older children, obviously undernourished, stood by, watching their mothers at work, with expressionless faces. Just metres away was a street in which ministers, generals and ambassadors lived. One day as I was sitting on the terrace waiting for my five-dollar-an-hour pupils, I heard a commotion in the side turning where the families had set up home.

'Off with you! We've had enough of you lot fouling up the place.'

Then I heard their tin cans being kicked violently across the road, babies wailing and women protesting in high-pitched voices. Soldiers from the local command had been given the order to clean the street of waifs and strays. After all, this was Menteng, one of the classiest districts in Jakarta.

It was here that the lawyer, Yap Thiam Hien, was able to come and see me to chat about my case. He was a good friend of the Sorongans and a member of the central board of the Indonesian Council of Churches. I had no idea that, within days of my arrest in 1968, he had been asked by the family in London to act on my behalf. He discussed my nationality status with me and said that my failure to register our marriage which had taken place in Prague meant that it had no legitimacy in Indonesia. This, he thought, would render my renunciation of British nationality invalid.

It was during this 'leave of absence' from Satgas-Jaya that I first heard about the Greek artist Mikis Theodorakis. I read about a concert he had given at the Royal Albert Hall in London which turned into a rousing demonstration of protest against the colonels' regime in Greece. I read too that he had been released as a result of international pressure. It made me wonder what was being done to support Indonesia's tapols. Was Indonesia a 'far-away' country of little importance to the West? Didn't people realize that we had a generals' regime every bit as awful as the colonels' regime in Greece? Were people applying different standards to countries in Europe and Asia?

It was during my brief period outside, too, that an event occurred which caused me to reflect on the role of Sukarno, Indonesia's first President. I knew that he had been under house arrest for years and the press occasionally reported that he was under interrogation. He had been cast into almost total oblivion.

Sukarno had been removed from power by Suharto in a series of moves that chipped away at his position. On 2 October 1965, Suharto took control of the armed forces against the President's wishes; on 13 March 1966, three generals, acting on Suharto's behalf, forced the President to sign away his powers to General Suharto. In 1967, Suharto became Acting President and a year later he was appointed President.

Sukarno's history is not unlike that of many first generation nationalist leaders in the countries of the Third World. Before the Pacific War he stood in the forefront of the nationalist struggle against Dutch colonialism and spent several years in detention. During the Japanese occupation, he collaborated with the Japanese invaders, hoping to win their support for *merdeka* (freedom). At the end of the Pacific War, he proclaimed independence along with Mohammad Hatta on 17 August 1945 and became the country's first President. After the transfer of sovereignty in December 1949, Sukarno was head of state in a parliamentary democracy until, egged on by the army, he installed the system of 'guided democracy' in 1957, which allowed him to exert almost dictatorial powers. Throughout this period he enjoyed the support of the PKI which gave him a mass base for his role as national leader. However, he became increasingly reliant on the armed forces whose role in government and the economy grew enormously during the last six years of his presidency.

Sukarno was a populist who enjoyed enormous popularity everywhere in the country. His guiding political creed was the preservation of national unity, binding together what he considered to be the three main ideologies in Indonesia, nationalism, religion and Communism, symbolized in the acronym NASAKOM. He made valiant efforts against great odds to hold these three elements together and preached the idea of national unity the length and breadth of the country. As a powerful orator, he drew huge crowds and enjoyed people's affections. He had an idiom and style that appealed to villagers and town-dwellers alike. During the final years of his presidency, he tried to maintain a balance between the two great contending political forces, the armed forces and the communists. He believed that he could keep the armed forces in tow, by supplying them with plenty of weaponry from the Soviet Union and the Eastern bloc. Although the armed forces, anti-communist leadership harboured deep misgivings about him, there were plenty of generals and middle-ranking officers who were Sukarnoists. It was this fact that compelled Suharto to take a gradualist approach in ousting him from power. Many people, including members of the armed forces, who were arrested after 1965 stood accused of being Sukarnoists.

Personally, Sukarno was a vain man with a shamelessly licentious private life, who took advantage of his Islamic faith to have more than one wife. His populism had everything to do with mobilizing the masses around political slogans and nothing to do with solving the country's deepening economic crisis. By 1965, he had become known as The Great Leader of the Revolution, Father of the Nation and President for Life. One of his greatest follies was to build status symbols, like the phallic National Monument in the centre of Jakarta, crowned with gold.

Following the events of 1 October 1965, the army began to discredit him, claiming that he had been 'involved' in the coup attempt which, they had initially said, was aimed at deposing Sukarno. In other words, he was being accused of involvement in a coup attempt against himself. After he formally surrendered presidential powers to Suharto in 1966, his fall from grace gathered pace. After 1967, he lost his freedom of movement and was not allowed to receive visits from any but his closest relatives.

In mid-June 1970, it was announced that the former President was critically ill at the central military hospital in Jakarta. Even as he lay on his deathbed, there was strict control of visitors. His only sister later complained that she had been refused permission to see him. The last people to visit him were his Japanese wife, Dewi Sukarno, and their daughter whom he had never met. They reached him only after a frantic tussle with the authorities over permission to enter the country.

When his death was reported on the radio on Sunday, 20 June, the news spread like wildfire. Everyone spoke about it, but only in whispers, for who could tell what the official reaction would be? To be safe, people tried to hide their sorrow.

When all the lodgers at the guest house where I was staying sat down to lunch on that day, the talk was all about Sukarno – how he had died, his brief encounter with Dewi, the tragedy of his isolation. Gradually, the conversation turned to his role as President and his outstanding political contribution. There was one man at the dinner table who remained silent, my landlady's nephew, a soldier who often visited her when he was on leave. In his presence, the others seemed to be holding back. Suddenly, the landlady, a good-natured woman with an unshakable faith in God and always with a warm, motherly smile on her face, jumped up from her chair at the end of the table.

'I don't care who hears me say it but I think Sukarno was a great man. I think he did great things for this country. It's a terrible shame that he should have died in such sad circumstances.' Having said her piece, she sat down again, looking steadily at her nephew.

Her spontaneous outburst seemed to symbolize the pent-up feelings of millions of people and the sense of grief that swept the country in the next few days. Once Suharto had announced that Sukarno would be buried with full honours and declared a week's mourning for the man he had deposed, people began to express their sense of loss openly. Tens of thousands of people filed past his body as it lay in state in Jakarta. Suharto was unable to treat his predecessor in death in the despicable way he had treated him in life, so he officiated at the ceremony at which Sukarno's body was placed on a bier for transportation to East Java. It was interred alongside his mother's grave in Blitar. For many miles along the road from the airport to Blitar, hundreds of thousands of people lined the route to pay tribute. Many were peasants who had walked from miles around, the same path they had probably trekked years before to hear him arouse the passions of the masses, when he was still their Great Leader.

For two months after leaving Satgas-Jaya, things went smoothly for me. If any pupil dropped out, there were others to fill the gap. I never went to Salemba Prison to take food parcels for Bud, but left it to Par. It would have been unwise to mingle with the prisoners' relatives as they might have wanted to visit me, which could have been dangerous. But there was one woman whom I had known from the time when I went to

Salemba during Bud's first and second arrests. She visited me and told me she was in dire straits: no regular income, no financial support from relatives, living on the proceeds from the sale of home-made cakes or selling nick-nacks to other tapols' wives. She had no qualifications and was unable to find a job because she could not get a 'non-involvement certificate'. Could I help her? She was not asking for money. What she wanted was ideas about how to get a job, whom to contact, what to do.

'You should try to get qualifications of some sort', I told her. 'Anything. Hairdressing, dressmaking, typing, shorthand. Then you'll have a better chance of finding a job.'

'What's the use? Everything costs money and I have none. It's as much as I can do to keep my daughter at school, to give her a litre of rice for her teacher every month and buy medicine when she falls ill.'

I suggested that she come to visit me once a week and I would give her English lessons. I would get her a place in a typing school run by friends of mine where she could learn English shorthand and typing, and I would pay her fees. She had a fairly good knowledge of English already and would probably qualify fairly quickly. She took up my suggestions. She was almost the only person to visit me at my lodgings and I began to look forward to her visits. She often walked the long distance to my place as she couldn't afford the fare and would bring me a packet of home-made biscuits, as her way of saying thank you.

I took advantage of these days outside to send a detailed account to Tari of my marriage and nationality status, as I understood it. I told her that my release was probably not permanent and anything could happen. If I were rearrested, she should take it that my release prospects were very bleak. My only hope would then lie in discovering a technical flaw in my renunciation of British nationality.

From time to time, an intelligence officer from Satgas-Jaya visited me, dressed in plain clothes and posing as someone coming to inquire about lessons. This was how the unit kept a check on me, reminding me constantly that I was being watched. Then one day, rather unusually, he came to see me on a Saturday and told me to be sure to be home the following Monday at about twelve noon as someone would be coming to visit me. Who? Why? He refused to say. I had a presentiment of trouble but tried to push it out of my mind. If something was going to happen, I was powerless to prevent it.

At the stated time on Monday, I was at home teaching two new pupils. It was the beginning of the month, 3 August, and the two girls paid me the month's fee at the start of the lesson. Halfway through the lesson, an army jeep drew up in the drive just outside my room. When two heavily armed soldiers alighted, I knew that the worst was about to happen. It was like a replay of my arrest nearly two years earlier – the lesson, two women pupils. Although I had told myself to be mentally prepared, I was shaken when it happened. As I rose to go out and speak to the men, my legs shook under me.

'Come along with us, Ibu Carmel.'

'Where to? On whose orders?'

'We don't know. Please come without making a fuss.'

Then I saw another soldier alight, a man I recognized from Satgas-Jaya.

'Are you taking me back to Satgas?'

'No. If you must know, we are taking you straight to Bukit Duri Prison. Hurry up, we've no time to waste.'

I returned to the room and told the girls I would have to cut the lesson short. I returned their money and said they could come another time if they wanted to. What a hope! They gathered their belongings and hastily departed, pretending that they had seen and heard nothing. I bundled a few things together in the wicker basket I had brought from Satgas-Jaya and left a few instructions with a servant to get a message to Par so that she could pass the news on to Tari and Anto. Minutes later, we were speeding through Jakarta on the way to Salemba Prison, our first call on the way to Bukit Duri. At Salemba, my particulars were recorded on a large prisoner's card. I felt desolate and helpless, hating the system that had me in its grip. The tears began to flow. The men at the office in Salemba knew me, so I asked them to tell Bud what had happened, though to be sure not to tell him about the tears.

From there I was driven through the backstreets to Bukit Duri Prison which was situated on the banks of one of Jakarta's murkiest rivers. It was located just off a main road, in a place overcrowded with stalls, street-vendors and pedicabs waiting for passengers. Soon I was in the prison office and met the commander, a lieutenant named Rompis, whom I knew from former days when he was on guard duty at Salemba.

'So here you are, Ibu Carmel. You've made it at last! I've been told so many times that you'd be coming here, I stopped believing it.'

I managed to put on a faint smile for his jokey welcome. A woman tapol on duty in the office came out and took my basket, held me by the arm and guided me across a small yard to a barbed wire enclosure where a large number of women were hanging around, waiting. They had heard that someone would be coming and were eager to see who it was. As I entered the enclosure, the women surged round and followed me into a block, along a corridor with cells on both sides and into a large cell at the end. As I walked along, friendly hands stretched out to touch my arms or press my shoulders, welcoming me with encouraging words.

'Take heart. Cheer up. Things aren't all that bad here.'

Soon I was sitting on a stone platform in my cell, surrounded by women and young girls – behind me, kneeling down in front of me, their hands on my shoulders or in my lap. Others kept coming in to say hello, people I knew, people I had never met. Someone put a cup of tea into my hand and told me to drink. It would make me feel better, she said.

I was unable to say anything, but sat looking at all those friendly faces, sipping tea, shedding tears which just wouldn't stop.

CHAPTER 18

Bukit Duri Prison

My cell was one of the larger ones in the three blocks occupied by about 150 women tapols. It had a very high ceiling with two tiny barred windows near the top. There were four other women in the cell, all in their early twenties and all newcomers. One woman had a baby boy, five of us and the baby living in a cell intended for three.

There was no furniture, not even a cot for the baby, just a few scruffy mats and piles of neatly folded clothing belonging to each of the women, alongside their basket or suitcase. The space allotted to each prisoner was marked out by their mats.

More than half the cell was taken up by a sloping stone platform about seven feet wide and eight feet long. This was occupied by my four cell-mates and the baby. In the corner occupied by the mother and baby, things were in disarray as the baby was constantly moving around, shifting the mat out of place and crawling perilously close to the edge of the platform.

In the place facing the cell door was a narrow stone bunk with a space underneath which had been allotted to me. One of the women had been using it until my arrival, but she insisted on giving it up for me.

'It will be easier for you to sleep on your own', she said.

This was typical of the consideration often shown to me, the only foreign-born woman in the prison. However hard things were for everyone else, they always assumed that it was just a little bit harder for me to bear. But I found the 'single bed' given to me very difficult to get used to; several times on the first night I fell off in my sleep because it was too narrow.

During my first hours in Bukit Duri, I was too stunned to respond to anything or anyone. My basket of clothes had been pushed under my bunk but I did nothing to prepare for the night.

We were given nothing at all apart from space to sleep. We were not even supplied with blankets or a mat to cover the floor or bunk space allotted to us. Very soon, women were coming in to see me; someone brought me a straw mat to sleep on, someone else brought several sacks to put under the mat for protection from the cold, and other women produced a pillow, a mug and a plate. The mat and pillow were gifts from the Indonesian Council of Churches the previous Christmas. The other things were on loan until I got supplies from home.

When I asked them not to bother themselves so much with my comfort, one woman said 'This place is cold and damp. The sun never penetrates and you'll get very cold unless you take great care. We don't want you falling ill the moment you arrive.'

Then someone appeared with a small portion of vegetables and a slice of meat.

'Sorry, it's not much. The last visiting day was on Saturday and I don't have much left, but you're welcome to it.' Someone else brought me half a bun and a cup of milk, and from another woman I got a few biscuits.

Through my tears I recognized several women who came to say hello, to ask how I was, where Tari and Anto were, and to hear about what was happening outside. Some grasped my hands or stroked my shoulders, others were a bit shy of a foreigner, wondering how I had got mixed up in all this.

Life inside was cut off from the world outside, with no access to newspapers (which were strictly forbidden) or the radio. A new arrival, especially one who had come from outside and not from one of the detention camps, was greeted like a breath of fresh air, possibly bringing news of events that might indicate whether things were getting better or worse for us.

On that first day, I hardly took anything in as my fellow-prisoners told me about life in prison. I would have to pick things up as I went along, when the shock of my sudden plunge from the limited freedom and comfort I had enjoyed outside, to prison frugality and isolation had worn off.

Someone offered to show me the toilet, but I didn't want to go. It was as if going to the toilet would make this real. I was clinging to the hope that it might be just a bad dream.

In the afternoon, there was a choir rehearsal for Christian women which I was invited to attend. The rehearsal took place sitting along the edge of a drain in the yard outside. I don't remember what hymn they were practising but, whatever it was, it gave me no consolation.

In the evening, Muslim prisoners gathered together for communal prayers along the corridor. The rest of us were required to remain in our cells while this was going on. After prayers, there was a session of Muslim religious instruction which non-Muslims were also not allowed to attend. No cross-fertilization was allowed, no sharing of religious beliefs. Everyone was required to keep to her own faith. Under Suharto's New Order, everyone is required to have a religion, though the number of faiths permitted is limited to five. According to the regulations, you have to be a Muslim or a Protestant Christian or a Catholic or a Buddhist or a Hindu. There is no place for anything else. What would the authorities have thought if I had declared myself a Jew or, still worse, an atheist? The easy way out for me was to join the Protestants, which had its advantages, not least meeting the ministers and other prison visitors who came to see us from time to time.

On one occasion, a Muslim prisoner, a schoolteacher who knew a lot about hymn singing, started taking choir rehearsals while the regular conductor was incommunicado for some misdemeanour. When our soldier-warders found out, she was severely reprimanded and the two tapols in charge of the 'spiritual welfare' of Christians and Muslims were warned never to allow such a serious breach of discipline to occur again.

We had our *pembina mental*, literally 'mental guides', soldiers who came to the prison from time to time to give religious instruction to their respective flocks. For these men, religious observance had nothing to do with personal devotion, still less with a search for the truth. Religion for them was a question of duty performed in blind faith. Furthermore, on the orders of the Jakarta military command, conversions from one religion to another were not only discouraged, they were strictly forbidden.

After the Muslim rituals were over, there was a last, hurried visit to the toilets, then back to the cells to be locked in for the night. The heavy door of the cell was closed with a thud and I heard the outside padlock being locked. The whole prison was wrapped in silence. I stretched myself out on my bunk and stared at the bare electric light hanging from the ceiling which would stay on all night. Among the clothes I had grabbed when I was rearrested was a black bra. I took it out and used it to cover my eyes to block out the light. I wore this 'blindfold' every night during my time at Bukit Duri.

On that first night I was unable to sleep for a long time, exhausted by emotion and tears. It was not till this moment that the full enormity of my situation hit me. Although transfer to Bukit Duri had always been a possibility, when it actually happened I felt terrible. All the confusion over the past two years about what might happen to me had lulled me into thinking that I might never land up in jail. Now, I felt, this was a turning-point, all hopes were shattered. Somehow I would have to survive this blow and come to terms with a long period of detention here in Bukit Duri. I was very worried about what would happen once the news of my re-arrest reached Tari and Anto in London. What would happen once supplies of cash dried up just as suddenly as they had begun?

The next day, Tuesday, was 'visiting' day, *hari bezoek,* when relatives could bring food for women inside but no visiting was allowed. Here too, as at Likdam, food could be delivered three times a week, on Tuesdays, Thursdays and Saturdays. I knew Par would not come as it would take time for her to hear about my re-arrest and then get permission to 'visit' me.

Late that afternoon, long after food parcels had stopped being delivered to other tapols, a woman came hurrying to my room, carrying a huge basket of fruit.

'A white-skinned gentleman brought this for you', she said. 'He said he tried to get permission to meet you but was refused.'

I knew immediately that it was John Newmann. I had no idea who had told him of the move, but I was deeply touched by his thoughtfulness. It meant so much to me to know that friends outside knew where I was and were trying to make contact.

Some of the prisoners in Bukit Duri had lost all contact with their families long ago; they had no way of finding out where they were or even whether they were still alive. Take Sri S. She and her husband were arrested at the same time and had no option but to leave their five children alone at home. The oldest was in her early teens, the youngest not yet at school. A few days after their arrest, the older children found out where they had been taken and went to see them. They were bewildered and at a loss to know what to do. There was hardly any money in the house and no relatives nearby to whom they could turn, so Sri told them to leave home that very evening, take the train to Surabaya in East Java – nearly 700 kilometres away – and go and stay with their grandmother. Since then, the children had never visited her again. Maybe they had sent her letters but she never received them. So here she was, with no idea about the whereabouts or fate of her five children. Sri, a gentle, soft-spoken woman, never made any display of her anxiety, but it is not difficult to imagine the anguish she went through every day.

We were allowed out of our cells each day from dawn to dusk, unless disciplinary measures were in force. We spent most of the time sitting in each other's cells. For most of the day, it was far too hot to sit out in the yard where there was no shade except for one tree in the far corner.

Bukit Duri was said to be the best-built prison in Jakarta, constructed during colonial days for male Dutch prisoners. In the centre, there was a large hall and offices. The wings on both sides consisted of two long rows of cells at right angles. We tapols occupied one whole wing, the other was for women who had been convicted on criminal charges. There was absolutely no contact between us. Our wing was under army control, theirs was run by the Prisons' Department of the Justice Ministry.

Harsh as things were for the women who had been convicted, there was a world of difference between their conditions and ours. They were allowed to receive visits, we were not. They were supplied with prison clothes and some basic needs, we got nothing. Our food was prepared in different kitchens. A large kitchen with reasonably good cooking facilities was used for our sisters on the other side. The tapols who had to cook for us had to make do with a derelict hovel and stoves that often broke down. During the fifteen months I spent in Bukit Duri, I hardly ever got a glimpse of the women on the other side. The only contact was when one of our women was punished by being sent to the other wing and held there incommunicado.

There were two sizes of cells. The smaller ones were very small and built to accommodate one person while the larger ones were supposed to hold three people. In our wing, all the cells were overcrowded: there were three women in the smaller ones and five women in the larger ones. It was stictly forbidden to have only two women in a cell because this might encourage sexual liaisons, or so I was told.

As I wandered through the block on my first full day, I was struck by the rhythm of life the women had created for themselves. Everywhere I saw women sitting cross-legged on the platforms, the bunks or the floor, hard at work doing embroidery, crocheting or knitting, making tablecloths, handkerchiefs, pullovers, baby clothes and shawls. I was surprised to see them so hard at work as I had heard that in Salemba Prison inactivity was a major problem.

'What do you do with all these things?' I asked.

'We sell them to buy more material to make other things and use the money to buy soap, sugar and other essentials which they don't supply in prison.'

'Do you sell the stuff through the office?'

'Heavens no. Any money that fell into their hands would go straight into their own pockets. We sell things with the help of relatives who come here regularly with food.'

They told me about one occasion when someone outside wanted to pay a prisoner Rp. 6,000 for tablecloths he had received through the prison commander's office. The commander said he would have to deduct Rp. 3,000 to defray his own 'expenses'. So the man decided that, to make sure the women got the full amount, he would give the commander an extra Rp. 3,000, but the commander pocketed the lot.

It wasn't long before I got drawn into the activity. I started off trying my hand at embroidery but soon discovered that I was far too slow to make it worth while. So I turned to knitting, a favourite pastime of mine in my early youth, and was soon impressing everyone with the speed at which I could make things. I was also something of a curiosity because the English way of holding knitting needles is different from what women in Indonesia are used to, having learnt to knit from Dutch women.

We were only allowed to do needlework during daylight hours and had to hand everything in before the evening meal. Knitting needles, crochet hooks, needles, pins and scissors were considered by the authorities as being 'too dangerous' to be kept in our cells at night. They said they were afraid we might commit suicide.

As a high-speed knitter, working ten or twelve hours a day, I could earn Rp. 30 a day, the equivalent of 8 cents, quite a drop from the $5 an hour I had been making before my re-arrest. I slogged away, turning out cardigans and jumpers by the dozen to supply myself with a few essentials and lighten the burden on Par.

The money earned from all this handicraft made conditions at Bukit Duri a little better than at Salemba, but the improvements had come only a year or so ago.

'You should have seen the state we were in before we started selling things like we do now', one woman told me. 'We were dressed in rags and many of us were seriously undernourished, not much better than Belsen victims.'

This was under the former commander who grabbed as much as he could from the women. When Rompis, the present commander, took over, they told me, things improved.

'The former commander's wife insisted on selling our things herself and buying the materials we needed. She kept most of the proceeds. As for the commander, he pocketed the money for our rations and even supplied us with mouldy food.'

She told me about an incident that I was often to hear about throughout the time I spent in Bukit Duri. Rotten cabbage had been served for several days running so when the commander came to inspect the blocks, he was greeted by the sound of bleating.

'I don't know who it was who started it but everyone took it up. All he could hear from every cell was ba-aa, ba-aa. No one said a word, but he understood the message. He was livid. He rushed back to the office and instructed the soldier on duty to have us all locked up in our cells.

'A few days later, we were summoned to a special roll-call. He ranted on, scolding us and saying it wasn't his fault that we had been given rotten food. He said things would soon get even worse as the Jakarta military command was about to stop allocating money for anything other than rice. Soon, he warned, we would only be receiving rice twice a day and nothing more.

'"So what do you have to say to that", he said, as he strutted up and down in front of us. "You made enough noise the other day. Now. let me hear you speak."

'There was complete silence for a few moments. Then Ibu Salawati stepped forward. . . .'

(I was soon to share a cell with Ibu Salawati and got to know her very well but long before that, I heard a great deal about this remarkable woman.)

'"Let me make one thing clear before saying what I have to say. I am speaking only for myself and I alone take full responsibility. I am not speaking on anyone's behalf.

'"I was imprisoned many times under the Dutch, many times they maltreated me and held me unjustly for my beliefs. Yet never, in all my experience, did the Dutch, bad as they were, supply their prisoners with nothing more than rice. Never! Now, go back to your bosses and tell them that. I have nothing more to say."

'With that, she stepped back into line again.

'The commander looked very uncomfortable. He said nothing and ordered us back to our cells. From then on, the food improved a bit but it wasn't until he was replaced by Rompis that we were allowed to take control of the sale of our products and conditions became a bit less intolerable.'

In some ways the atmosphere in Bukit Duri was more relaxed than in the interrogation and detention camps where I had spent the first two years of my imprisonment. Generally speaking, interrogations did not take place here, though sometimes tapols would be taken 'on loan' to be interrogated elsewhere. Another reason why we could be more relaxed in prison was that although there was always an undercurrent of frustration, nobody now expected anything dramatic to happen. Being in prison was the end of the story for the foreseeable future.

However, there were rare occasions when hope of release was rekindled. When I entered Bukit Duri in August 1970, a group of women had been led to believe that they were category 'C' prisoners, scheduled for release. In the latter part of 1969, nine months before I arrived in the prison, 50 women had had their personal details checked;

their fingerprints were taken and they were photographed. It was hinted to them by some officers that they were soon to be released and some even started sending their belongings home.

Not long after, a dozen of the women were released. It had all been very secretive. They were taken from their cells in the middle of the night and ordered not to make a sound. They tiptoed to the prison hall where they waited till morning for some officers to release them. A month later, another group was released in the same way. By this time, about half the group had gone home, leaving the others confident that their turn would come soon. But the days turned to weeks and the weeks to months and now, nearly a year later, they had given up all hope of being released. They were never told what happened to stop the process in its tracks. Later, there were rumours that gossip about lesbianism in the prison had reached the ears of the authorities, but whether this was the reason for the change in policy was never explained.

No further releases took place and these women were later transferred to a long-term detention camp in Central Java where they were held for many more years. This could only mean that they had been reclassified into the 'B' category.

A few days after my arrival in Bukit Duri, I was sitting in the yard when I saw a group of women come out of a door at the far end of the wing, carrying their mugs and plates to the washroom. Several of them were very young. One in particular caught my eye. She was quite tall and well built, and she walked with a very graceful step. She must have been about the same age as Tari.

'How long has she been here?' I asked someone sitting nearby.

'Nearly five years, like the rest of us.'

She was still under twenty and had been arrested in her early teens. Her resemblance to Tari shook me. I suddenly thought that it could have been my daughter walking across the yard.

A few moments later, I saw her return and go back through the door. I made up my mind to follow her and find out who she was. I got up and started to walk towards the door but another woman was quickly on her feet. She grabbed at my arm and pulled me back.

'Ibu Carmel, where do you think you're going? We're not allowed in there. That's Block C. The women there aren't allowed to mingle with women in the other blocks. Please come back. The guards can easily see you from the office.'

This was my first encounter with Block C where the women with 'heavy' cases were held. They included leading members of the women's organization Gerwani, some tapols who had been involved in underground work and a number of young girls whom everyone else called *anak-anak*, the 'children'. They were children when they were arrested in 1965 and the name had stuck. These young women had been arrested because they were at the Lubang Buaya training ground on the fateful night of 1 October 1965. I got to know them quite well during my stay there.

Having been cautioned that the block was out of bounds for the rest of us, I was determined to get into the block. I chose a moment when the guard on duty was well out of sight. As I neared the entrance, I bent down and crawled in on all fours.

All the cells in Block C were small, intended for one person, with a single stone bunk, like the one I slept on. The cells were five feet wide and less than nine feet long. Each one was occupied by three women. One slept on the bunk and the other two slept at right angles on the floor. I was later to spend some time in one of these cells. Because of my height, it was not possible for me to sleep on the floor. You had to be very short to sleep across the width of the cell, with your feet going under the bunk. If the one sleeping lengthwise on the floor was too tall, it would be difficult to open the cell door.

In Block C, I found most of the women sitting in their cells with the doors open, or along the corridor, all busy doing needlework. At the far end were three cells with the doors locked, each of which was inhabited by three women who spent most of the day locked up, stifled by the heat. They were 'in special isolation'. Some of these women who were treated as 'extra heavy cases' had been caught during the army's operation against the underground. Others were isolated simply because of who they were, not for anything they had done. There were two Mrs Aidits in these cells. One was Dr Sutanti Aidit, the wife of D. N. Aidit, the Chairman of the PKI who was murdered by the army in November 1965. Dr Sutanti had not been involved in any underground work and had gone into hiding for a year after her husband disappeared. She was a member of Gerwani and used to run a very busy medical practice in one of the poorer districts of Jakarta. Her sister-in-law, the wife of Aidit's younger brother, was my good friend Nuriah from Satgas-Pusat who had been such a comfort on the first day of my arrest; she too was now in special isolation, within the isolation block.

Another of these isolation cases was the wife of the man who owned the well at Lubang Buaya into which the bodies of the murdered generals had been dumped. This connection alone seems to have been enough reason for her to be treated as a 'heavy' case. She was frail-looking and highly strung. She would sometimes go into convulsions of laughter for no apparent reason; at other times, she would weep uncontrollably. She had not the slightest idea about the political events that had plunged her into this dreadful situation.

Another prisoner in isolation was Dr Sumiarsih Carabopeka, a cheerful woman, short and rather fat. The striking thing about Sumiarsih was her very positive attitude towards life, always smiling, except when she talked about all the injustices under army rule. When I recognized her, I greeted her through the bars of the cell door. She was wearing a sarong draped round her body below the armpits, in an attempt to keep cool. It was her firm conviction that the best form of resistance for a prisoner was to keep healthy. She strongly believed that 'to survive is to win'. When officers came round on an inspection tour and asked her how she was, she would always reply 'I'm fine, thank you, very fine. I've done nothing wrong, so why should I brood and make myself ill?'

After my first visit, I often crept into Block C to chat with the women there. There was a feeling of warmth and friendship and nobody was troubled by thoughts about release. They had no reason to expect anything to happen. I also liked sitting among the 'children', listening to their stories and telling them about countries where people could not be put into prison for years on end without trial.

———————

My presence at Bukit Duri was regarded as a golden opportunity for the prisoners to have some English lessons. Very soon, people were pressing me to start.

'How should we go about it?' I asked. Although I knew how Adil at Likdam had treated 'organized activity', I wondered whether here in prison I might be given permission to hold regular clases. After all, there was regular Muslim instruction every evening.

'Never. They'll never give us permission to organize anything. No, we'll have to do it in our own way.'

The lessons started spontaneously one evening as we were sitting out in the courtyard, just before dusk. I began to tell some women clustered around me the English words for several objects in the yard and put the words into sentences. More women gathered round, wanting to listen and to try and pronounce the words. The next evening, they asked for more and the dusk lessons soon became part of the routine.

We took the necessary precautions to make sure the guard would not find us in a compromising situation. There was a well-run warning system, with one or two women always keeping watch near the barbed wire along the far end of the yard. Whenever they saw a guard leaving the office and walking towards our compound, they would come into the blocks humming a tune which we all knew to be the sign of trouble. There was a strict understanding among us that the moment the song was heard, all unauthorized activities had to stop immediately.

The group that gathered round me for these lessons soon grew too large to keep the noise down so we decided to shift the location inside, into a large corner space between Blocks A and B. I graded my pupils into beginners and more advanced and began to plan my lessons carefully. It was not simply that the women could pick up a bit of English. Far more important was the fact that this activity kept people's minds busy and the lessons helped to improve morale among the tapols. Every day I would hear women repeating the question-and-answer sentences I had taught the night before. My pupils were eager, serious and very attentive, and the attendance record was excellent. What more could a teacher want? I was probably the one who enjoyed the lessons the most and benefited from this very gratifying activity.

Even inside the building we had to be on the alert so as not to be discovered by a guard. Whenever the signal was heard, we would all quickly disperse. On one occasion it didn't quite work. I was concentrating hard on some objects I had collected for the lesson and had my back to the class, writing something on a blackboard with a (strictly forbidden) piece of chalk. When I turned round, everyone had vanished and I was standing there alone with the chalk in my hand, surrounded by my bits and pieces. I hadn't heard the tune and there was no time for me to disappear before the guard came wandering down the block. Fortunately, the soldier on duty that night was more decent than the others. He stood there gazing at me as I gazed back.

'Good evening, Pak', I mumbled, feeling very uncomfortable. He was good-natured enough to smile and continue his inspection tour without saying a word.

CHAPTER 19

In the Isolation Block

Bukit Duri was under the jurisdiction of Salemba, a very much larger prison exclusively for men. The commander was Lieutenant Rompis. I knew him from the days when I used to take food parcels to Bud in Salemba; in those days, Rompis was a prison guard. On one occasion when he was not on duty, we were told that he had gone off with a firing squad to execute the South Moluccan leader, Dr Soumokil.

He was capable of punishing prisoners with extreme cruelty. When a prisoner at Salemba was accused of stealing cassava root out of sheer hunger, Rompis forced him to eat so much of the root that he died of overeating. It is well known that when the intestines have been deprived of nourishment for some time, a sudden drastic intake of food can be fatal.

Rompis had joined the army under the Dutch when it was still known as KNIL, the Royal Netherlands East Indies Army. He had spent most of his military career guarding prisoners; prisoners had become part of his life. He didn't bother about what political crimes we were in for. As far as he was concerned, if we were in prison, it meant we must be guilty. But unlike most army officers I came across, he believed that prisoners should be given the chance to work for their living, which was why we could carry on with our needlework without much interference. There was in Rompis a peculiar blend of cruelty and caring; whatever mood he was in, we were always at his mercy.

Rompis only came to the prison during office hours. The office in control of our wing was in the far corner of the front court. This meant that anyone leaving the office to come to our compound for inspection had to walk about fifteen metres before reaching the entrance to our barbed-wired enclosure. This made it fairly easy for us to run an effective warning system.

There were three soldiers who took turns doing guard duty for a 48-hour stretch. For much of the day and all night, therefore, our wing was guarded by a single soldier. Security at the front entrance of the prison was in the hands of officials of the criminal prisoners' wing. The three soldiers who kept the roster going for the whole time I was at the prison were quite different from each other. One was a kindly looking man with a bushy moustache. I never saw him get angry with anyone. He was the one who had caught me red-handed, giving an English lesson. During his 48-hour watch, the atmosphere was more relaxed and he didn't seem to mind bending the rules in our favour. For instance, although there was a rule strictly forbidding prisoners from seeing, let alone keeping, family photographs (I could never fathom the reason for this), he would allow photos in. Because he was much the nicest of our guards, we tried not to take advantage of him for fear that he might get into trouble for being too lax.

Another of the guards was a strict disciplinarian and showed no flexibility at all. He would never allow his own judgement to guide him. He never permitted anything that was not explicitly allowed under the rules. He was a very ignorant man and sometimes came out with the most ridiculous statements. One of his classic remarks was his reply to a tapol who asked whether a new regulation he had just announced was temporary or permanent.

'Temporarily permanent', he replied.

The third guard was a vicious and cunning brute, with a quick, unpredictable temper and an arrogance that was difficult to take. In addition to doing regular guard duty, he was also our 'spiritual guide' in charge of the prison's 'spiritual enlightenment programme', an odd phrase that had something to do with the army's efforts to brainwash or indoctrinate us. At the heart of the indoctrination programme was the conviction that communists – and we were, after all, all communists – were by definition atheists and needed to be brought back to the path of religion. This man was responsible for seeing to it that we carried out our respective religious observances. He didn't seem to bother much about his own religious practices. We hardly ever saw him at prayer once a day, let alone the five times required of a good, practising Muslim.

Whenever he was on duty, he made it his business to inspect the blocks at dusk to check who was joining in communal evening prayers. A Muslim woman is not allowed to pray when she is menstruating and he took pleasure in checking up on the women who had 'taken the day off'.

'Indisposed', the women would say.

'Funny, so many of you indisposed at the same time', he would say, with a leer.

Conversion from one religion to another was forbidden. The only likely shift in religious adherence I noticed was that some Muslims began to show an interest in Christianity. It rarely happened the other way round. This was partly due to the fact that the Christian preachers who came to take services, including the army chaplains, were never vindictive. They spoke to us (I always attending the Protestant services) as sinners, not criminals. I remember one of the chaplains saying to us 'Here, but for the grace of God, go I'.

From what I heard, the Muslim ulemas who came to the prison treated the prisoners as infidels who deserved no mercy. This surely does not accord with the true message of Islam, but it is what came across to the tapols who attended their sermons.

Christianity had another appeal. The Church was the only source of material relief for prisoners and this counted for a great deal as we were so starved of the most basic needs.

On one occasion, our 'spiritual guide' decided that we all needed a systematic course of religious instruction. He hit upon the idea of delivering a sermon every afternoon for a week; we were all ordered to sit out in the yard and absorb his words of wisdom, relayed to us over a loudspeaker, while he sat reading his oration in the comfort of his office. As he could not keep an eye on us himself, he had a civilian employee sit at one end of the yard – under the tree for shade – to make sure that we all remained seated and listened attentively.

I spent most of the time during these lectures watching the ants crawl back and forth on the ground, the first time I could recollect when I really paid any attention to the behaviour pattern of those insects.

However, one afternoon as we were sitting listening – or not listening but letting our thoughts wander – the voice suddenly changed from exhortation to fury.

'. . . and learn to do God's will for otherwise . . . You bitches, pigs. What the hell do you think you're doing? Get the hell out of here!'

Shaken out of our lethargy by the unexpected outburst, we wondered what we had done to deserve such an ugly rebuke. After several moments of tension, the word went round that a couple of prisoners from the other wing, unaware of the solemnity of the occasion, had walked past the office chatting loudly to each other and had tripped over the wire connected to his microphone to the loudspeaker, jerking the thing out of his hand. Order was soon restored and the lecture continued, but the incident gave us something to laugh about for several days.

The army's programme of indoctrination for ex-PKI is a never-ending process. Although they devote considerable time and resources to transforming ex-PKI into decent, God-fearing Indonesian citizens, their underlying attitude is 'once a communist, always a communist'. They will never accept the fact – and it is a fact – that a large proportion of the members of the PKI and the associated mass organizations were devout Muslims or Christians, or adherents to other religious faiths.

Two months after I entered Bukit Duri, an incident occurred that resulted in a dramatic shake-up in the prison. One of the prisoners had succeeded in smuggling a letter out to her son with advice on how to arrange some rather pressing family affairs. She had committed the heinous crime of having been in possession of a piece of paper. The note was discovered and the boy was arrested, but at the time we had no idea that this had happened.

The day had started as usual, with early morning exercises in the yard, visits to the washroom and toilets, queuing for our daily supply of boiled water and then breakfast which, for most, meant eating yesterday's leftovers. As we were settling down to the day's needlework, our head of block suddenly came scurrying through the corridor, tense and very agitated.

'Sani Gondjo's here. He's in a filthy mood. Quick, put everything away.'

According to prison rules – which were broken every day with the tacit agreement of Rompis – needles, scissors and everything else we needed for our handiwork were strictly forbidden. In a trice everything was gathered together and hidden out of sight and we were ordered to close our cell doors. In our cell, we managed to conceal the various needles we had on the window ledge, up near the ceiling. This could only be done by one of the women standing on another woman's shoulders. She did it in such a hurry that some of our 'dangerous weapons' slipped out through the bars, and we were never able to retrieve them.

Sani Gondjo, Rompis's boss, was the commander of Salemba and had overall responsibility for our prison as well. He rarely came to see us, but when he did it was usually to reprimand and punish or impose a new set of rules. His very appearance always sent a shiver through the prison. I never found out whether he knew that we did needlework, but whenever he turned up the guards always insisted on clearing everything away so that Sani Gondjo would not see us handling anything sharp. As he approached our block, I simply could not bring myself to respond in the way expected of us. I was aware that these small acts of defiance achieved nothing and annoyed some of my fellow-prisoners but I couldn't demean myself by complying with bullying. As he swept into our block, my cell door was still open and I was sitting in full view, stirring a cup of coffee. He saw me from afar, and yelled down the corridor.

'Shut that door, you bitch!'

I got up slowly and did as I was told. I was to pay for this.

Soon, we were ordered out of our cells and ushered into the prison hall while the cells were thoroughly searched. We never found out whether anything clandestine, such as incriminating scraps of paper, was discovered. I later heard that some tapols had masticated and swallowed scraps of paper. After Sani Gondjo left we were ordered back to the blocks and told that we would now be confined to our blocks for the whole day and be allowed out only to take a bath and wash our eating utensils. No more exercises or saunters in the yard. This punishment was to last for several weeks. It was applied particularly harshly in Block C as the woman who had committed the 'offence' was from that block.

The other change affected me personally. Immediately after he left, I was ordered to gather my belongings together and move to Block C. Did this mean that I was now a 'heavy' case? An 'A' category prisoner? The very idea was absurd. The more logical explanation was that I was being punished.

In Block C, I shared a cell with Ibu Salawati and Ibu Abdulrachman Sundari, remarkable women from whom I was to learn a great deal.

Both my cell-mates were members of the PKI and both had been members of parliament. They had spent many years in political activism, going back to the days before the Pacific War and the Japanese occupation. But the contrast in the circumstances of their arrests, and their response to the events of October 1965, said a great deal about the confusion in the PKI's handling of the situation that confronted the Party immediately after Suharto's counter-strike against the Untung group of conspirators.

Ibu Salawati was now in her sixties. She was short and fairly stout, with rugged features and usually had a rather stern look on her wrinkled face. She was always dressed in clothes made from flour sacks or cheap calico, with trade marks usually showing down the legs of her slacks. She kept her more elegant clothes for church services. She was a devout Christian who knew her Bible inside out and often used biblical stories as examples to condemn the way we were being treated. One of her favourite biblical figures was Joseph, the man who, as a prisoner, had won his freedom by giving sound advice to Pharaoh.

Charlotte Salawati first became politically active in her early teens when she led a protest against discrimination at the local church in her birthplace, Sangir, a small island to the north of Minahasa. She objected to *inlanders* (natives) being obliged to sit in the back pews, leaving the front pews for the Dutch. She became a teacher, quite an achievement for a woman in those days, but the Dutch banned her from the profession because of her habit of advocating anti-colonialist views in the classroom. She then moved to Makassar (now Ujung Pandang) in South Sulawesi, trained to become a midwife and joined the nationalist party, the PNI.

After independence was proclaimed in August 1945, she supported the republican cause in South Sulawesi where a Dar'ul Islam movement under Kahar Muzzakar was waging an armed struggle against the government in Jakarta. After the transfer of sovereignty to the Republic in December 1949, she was elected Mayor of Makassar, the first woman ever to hold such a position in Indonesia. As Mayor, she helped the armed forces to quell the rebellion. On one occasion, she undertook a perilous trip through dangerous territory to deliver a message from the army, inviting the rebels to enter into negotiations. Makassar had become the centre of a heavy concentration of republican troops and many men who had done service there knew of her exploits and respected her for her courage. This was also where Suharto was first sent to take part in an operation to quell a rebellious, separatist movement, so he would certainly have had personal knowledge of the way she helped the army.

She did not join the PKI until the late 1950s. She told me that what had attracted her to the Party was its close ties with the common people. Although she had held high office, she never gave up her modest life-style. She refused to live in the Mayor's residence, travelled to work every day on a bike and continued to practise as a midwife in the poorest districts. When Aidit invited her to join the Party, she told him that she would not accept any interference from the Party with her religious convictions.

After being elected to parliament in 1955, she moved to Jakarta and became active in the women's organization Gerwani. In parliament, she became a member of the defence and security commission because of her experience with the army in Makassar.

'Imagine', she would often say, 'I represented the PKI on the defence commission, hob-nobbing all the time with these military types, yet when the events of October occurred, I knew absolutely nothing. You others would have had even less access than me to what was going on. Yet here we are, all accused of "being involved in the coup attempt".'

But she had plenty of criticism for the PKI leadership too.

'I've helped organize plenty of campaigns in my time, strikes, demonstrations and the rest. But there was one principle we never forgot: make sure that, if the movement fails and difficulties emerge, the number of victims should be kept as low as possible. But with this affair? God knows what they thought they were doing, but, still worse, they forgot this basic principle. Never before have there been so many victims because of the mistakes of a tiny handful of people.'

On the day the Untung Group launched its operation, and unaware that anything had happened, Ibu Salawati went to the Palace because she had a breakfast appointment with Sukarno. He wasn't there and a guard told her to return home immediately. Soon the Party leadership was in disarray. Its offices were being mobbed; its people were arrested and the homes of many activists were ransacked. Her own home was one of the first to be destroyed. She and four other PKI members of parliament whose homes had been rendered uninhabitable felt that the legitimate rights of their organizations should be defended. So they went to parliament to protest at what had happened to their homes and to seek protection. The five were given alternative accommodation in the parliament complex. Soon after they moved, the army swooped and arrested them all in a single operation.

Salawati remained in detention until the late 1970s. She was never tried. After her release, she lived for several years in the care of her son. She died in 1988. Of all the women I knew in prison, I always felt that she was the one whose life-story should be written. Maybe, one day those who knew her will be able to publish the story of this very remarkable woman.

On 1 October 1965, Ibu Sundari, unlike Salawati, did not fall into any trap. She too was a PKI member of parliament. Realizing that the PKI could not function legally any longer, she left the capital and went into hiding in a region where no one knew her.

Ibu Sundari was the daughter of a Javanese forestry official with a low-ranking job in the colonial administration. Her early years were spent living in a remote house on the edge of a dense forest. Her father's position secured her and her brothers and sisters the privilege of going to Dutch schools. After leaving school she worked for the postal service and got involved in anti-colonial activities. She was part of the organized underground resistance during the Japanese occupation and later joined one of the Marxist groups that subsequently merged to become the post-war PKI. During the period of armed struggle against the Dutch from 1945 to 1949, she joined one of the militia forces. She later became leader of the Semarang Working Women's Association, then a founding member of Gerwis, later renamed Gerwani.

After the transfer of sovereignty in December 1949, she was part of the PKI leadership in Central Java and later moved to Jakarta to work for the Party's organization department. This job took her to many parts of the country and made her familiar with Party organization in some of the most difficult places.

By October 1965, she was a candidate member of the central committee as well as a member of Parliament. After the Suharto crackdown in October 1965, she slipped out of the capital and went to Lampung in South Sumatra. There she joined forces with the local PKI leadership who had gone underground and began the slow and painstaking task of building an illegal organization. She was put in control and spent several years working underground in the most arduous circumstances. She moved around, disguised as a peasant woman, and had no difficulty mingling with the local population, many of whom were impoverished peasants from Central Java who, before the war, had been shipped off to South Sumatra as cheap labour by the colonial administration.

She escaped detection by shifting her headquarters frequently. For several months she suffered from a serious liver disorder and high blood pressure, but continued to lead the movement, sometimes being carried by stretcher from one place to another. Her comrades procured medicines for her and she eventually recovered. She gave me graphic descriptions of the policy documents they produced, copying out everything by hand, and the Marxist study courses held at night in the forest or sitting along irrigation canals by rice fields. In the end, the army got wind of their activities; some of her personal bodyguards were arrested and she was caught soon afterwards.

When the troops found her in 1969, this tiny woman was frail, very thin and haggard, dressed in the tattered clothes of a peasant. She always smiled when she described the look on the faces of the officers who arrested her, never imagining for a moment that the person they had been tracking down for months was a woman.

'Do you know', she told me, 'they beat me, punched and kicked me and battered me with their rifle butts to make me tell them who I was. I held out. I felt very strong despite all the brutality. But when they brought in one of my bodyguards and he identified me, I realized that he was the one who had betrayed me. Only then did my knees buckle under me and I felt my strength ebbing, helpless before my persecutors. That was the worst moment of all.'

For months she was held in a prison in Lampung, in a dark, windowless cell night and day, next to a cell that was used to accommodate dead or dying detainees.

'Sometimes the stench was unbearable', she said. The prisoners were grossly underfed and the death rate was very high.

'Whatever we suffer here in Jakarta', she would say, 'things are infinitely worse in places like Lampung. Prisoners there are being starved to death, deliberately and systematically.'

In 1970, she was transferred to Jakarta for further interrogation. She went on trial and was given a life sentence in October 1976, eight years after her arrest. The sentence was later commuted to twenty years but this was in addition to the eight years she served before her trial. She was eventually released in August 1989, seven years before schedule, because of pressure on her behalf by the Inter-Parliamentary Union. She was nearly 70 years old. She now lives in Jakarta with her daughter.

Despite frequent bouts of illness in Bukit Duri, Ibu Sundari was always cheerful, full of spirits, quick with jokes and pranks, a good listener and ready to offer advice to others.

Opposite our cell was Dr Sumiarsih Carapobeka, who was held in strict isolation. Sometimes during the day, the heavy, wooden cell door was left open, leaving only the bars closed, so I could sit on the floor and have a chat, ready to slip back into my own cell if there were warnings that a guard was approaching the block.

Meeting Dr Sumiarsih in prison had a special meaning for me as I had often wondered what happened to her after a devastating attack on her house early in October 1965, which was sensationally reported in the press.

The clamp-down by the army in the aftermath of the events of 1 October 1965 was harsh and extremely oppressive. Heavily armed troops were on guard everywhere or patrolling the streets in trucks. A dusk-to-dawn curfew was in force for weeks. The press, radio and television were under army control. More than a quarter of the country's newspapers – 46 out of 163 – had been shut down, and those that remained in operation stuck close to what the army told them to publish. Every day brought reports of more arrests, new decrees and commands. The military commander of Jakarta pronounced the PKI and all 'affiliated organizations' unlawful and all members were ordered to report to their local army unit.

How did the left respond to the dramatic turn-about in its political fortunes? The Party's instruction to activists was 'Carry on as usual. Go to work as if nothing has happened.'

In a situation in which the army controlled all the means of mass communication and the Party had lost everything, there was no way to counter the claims about 'communist treachery'. The PKI leadership seemed to have drawn the conclusion that the best way to contradict these lies was to keep going 'as normal'. By going into hiding or fleeing from the cities, the army's accusations of the PKI's guilt would be confirmed. But the army was not in a mood to allow any investigation of the facts, and the Party's instructions placed many members and sympathizers in a very exposed position. A huge communist party that had seemed to be nearing the peak of its power was suddenly forced to contend with a turn of events for which it was completely unprepared.

I went to work for about ten days after 1 October until I was told to stop coming because I was a member of the HSI. At the office, I had tried to behave normally, but many of my colleagues would have nothing to do with me while others were afraid to approach me for fear of being 'contaminated'.

At home, it was difficult to know what to do, with the constant worry that either of us could be arrested. In October, Bud was arrested after returning home from a mission to Japan on behalf of the ministry. Each day, as I made my way to the office or on my way home, I passed gangs of youths speeding along in trucks, shouting anti-communist slogans. They were on their way to attack one or other of the many offices of the PKI or other left-wing organizations. In a few short days, Jakarta had changed beyond recognition. Often when I returned home, I would find friends waiting for me with news of arrests or of buildings that had been mobbed. Once when I returned home, I found the words 'Death to the Peking pigs' scrawled on our garage gate.

Most evenings, friends would come, asking for help to find them a place to sleep. Could I put them up? Was it safe to stay here? It certainly wasn't, but we usually had no choice because the curfew was approaching. So they would stay overnight and leave the next morning, not knowing how they would spend the next day and night.

The evenings were long and fraught with fear. Our house was quite spacious yet the curfew made it feel claustrophobic. Nothing moved on the streets except for army trucks and jeeps. With nothing else to do, we would sit and watch the television until that became unbearable. How much could one take of military pronouncements, declarations of support for the army, denunciations of the PKI, shots of the bodies of the murdered generals, of bodies being exhumed, being borne on biers, of the funeral scenes, or of young women confessing to having mutilated their bodies? It was a spectacle stage-managed to provoke the most violent reaction – mobbing people's homes and, in the countryside, killing anyone suspected of being communists or communist sympathizers.

Then I started hearing about friends whose homes had been ransacked and occupied. Would this happen to us? While Bud was away in Japan, I had to cope with the problems alone and try to calm Mbah, who wandered from room to room, looking perplexed and seeking assurances from me. For several days running, Tari returned home from school to say that her school friends were treating her with suspicion. They knew she was a member of the left-wing youth organization, the IPPI, and this was enough to make her suspect. Some boasted that they had seen lists of PKI members whose homes were to be attacked. My name was said to be listed.

'Your Mum's going to catch it', they told her, 'so you'd better watch out.'

The atmosphere at school became so bad that she stopped going. She didn't start school again for several months, not until I was able to find a place for her in a Catholic girls' school, without explaining why she needed to change schools.

At first, I shrugged off the stories about our house having been targeted. Most attacks I had heard about occurred in the back streets or in the kampungs. Anyway, why should they pick on me?

Then one day, on my way home from work, a newspaper headline caught my eye: 'Communist woman doctor's house destroyed. She's the Lubang Buaya doctor!'

I saw a photo of Dr Sumiarsih and a photocopy of a letter. I bought the paper and was very distressed to read the story. I knew her well and had visited her clinic. She had recently been elected onto the executive board of the HSI.

Mobs had plundered her house, I read, destroying everything they could lay their hands on. They had ransacked her documents and allegedly discovered a letter from the local PKI branch secretary asking her to issue sick-leave certificates to people who would be going on a training course. Whether or not she had issued such certificates hardly seemed relevant. This was enough to label her the 'Lubang Buaya doctor'.

She was not at home at the time of the attack. Many years later, there in Block C, she told me what happened. She was on her way home when she noticed that her house was surrounded by a gang of youths. She turned back and went to seek refuge with a friend. She was left only with the clothes she was wearing. She had no alternative but to go underground.

The press reports about Dr Sumiarsih made me realize that the stories Tari had heard could well be true. When I got home, I discussed the problem with a friend who was staying with us at the time. We decided that it would be better for the children and me not to be at home as this could only provoke the attackers. We packed some things in suitcases and the three of us left home, along with Mba, to stay with Bud's youngest sister, Tar. Sri, our friend, offered to stay in the house to keep an eye on things.

Sure enough, a mob came the very next day; they invaded the house, searched the cupboards, swept our books off the bookshelves and ransacked our belongings. They were apparently looking for incriminating documents but found nothing. There were soldiers standing guard a few houses away, but they did not intervene. Luckily, a unit from the local police station came hurrying to the scene. A chauffeur from Bud's office happened to drive past the house soon after the attack started and he alerted the police. They cleared the house of the mobsters, sealed the doors and left my friend to tidy up the mess. We returned home a week or so later.

I often thought of Dr Sumiarsih, wondering what had happened to her and hoping that she had escaped arrest. Now we were together in prison with plenty of time to exchange experiences. Sumiarsih coped with prison life in a very positive way. Whatever the difficulties, she would always be ready with a solution. She had little patience with people who were forever complaining. There were few things, she used to say, that could not be turned to good use by a good dose of sterilization in boiling water. Resistance for her was making the best of what we had and never allowing our captors to wear us down. Her attitude in prison reminded me of the scenes I had witnessed in her very busy surgery, always packed with mothers and children from the most disadvantaged groups. Babies, many very poorly clothed, would be crawling around, or crying in their mothers' arms. No one was ever turned away, however long the queue, and she always treated her patients with kindness and respect.

Despite the sensational claims about her and the years she spent in isolation as a 'heavy' case, Dr Sumiarsih was never charged or tried. In 1971, she was transferred to a work-camp in Central Java and held there for many more years. Years later, in London, I saw a film about the camp made by a Dutch television crew in 1976. There were shots of Dr Sumiarsih examining a fellow-prisoner. She answered the cameraman's questions cautiously but emphatically, with a camp official standing by her side.

'The health of the prisoners here is reasonably good', she said, looking at the official out of the corner of her eye. Then she bent down over her patient.

'Don't you have a stethoscope?' the cameraman asked.

'No, I have to check her heartbeat with my bare ear', replied Dr Sumiarsih, pointing to her ear. She spoke with dignity, conveying much of what she would have liked to say by the strained look on her face.

In Bukit Duri, Dr Sumiarsih was never permitted to function as a doctor, but was held in the isolation block for as long I was at the prison.

Whatever the reasons for my transfer to Block C, where I spent about three months, I was glad of the opportunity to spend a great deal of time listening to the experiences of women whom I grew to love and respect.

CHAPTER 20

The Children

For me the most tragic victims among the prisoners in Bukit Duri were
the young women, some still in their teens when I entered Bukit Duri,
who had been arrested in late 1965 or soon after when they were little
more than children.

In the months before October 1965, Indonesia was caught up in a
wave of militancy to 'confront' the British Government and Teuku
Abdulrahman, the Prime Minister of Malaysia, for their decision to
incorporate the territories of North Borneo into the state of Malaysia,
against the wishes of the population. The Indonesian army sent troops to
the region and some fighting occurred across the border. Back home,
several of the political parties responded to President Sukarno's call to
mobilize for a possible confrontation by giving military training to their
youth. Each of the parties made their own arrangements with different
wings of the armed forces. The PKI's closest ally was the air force, so the
PKI's youth organization Pemuda Rakjat sent their members to the
Halim air base outside Jakarta. This was where the Lubang Buaya
training ground was located, the place from which the Untung Group
launched its coup attempt on 1 October. The presence of these young
people at the site of the crime was used by Suharto to incriminate the
PKI.

I got to know many of these young women, heard their stories and
listened also to what other women had to say about them. I deposited
accounts about them with Amnesty in London after my release, but,
having lost all contact and knowing nothing of their present
circumstances, I have decided not to identify them by name. For all I
know, they have tried, since their release, to conceal their prison
experience in order to survive in a society where prejudice against ex-
tapols is still kept alive by the regime.

W.H. was only fifteen at the time of her arrest in October 1965 when Suharto's troops captured the Halim air base. She was subjected to extremely violent torture during interrogations at Bukit Duri prison in the early days of her arrest. She became mentally deranged as the maltreatment persisted and would scream for hours on end, alone in her cell. Women who were in Bukit Duri at the time told me that they often heard her banging her head against the cell wall. On one occasion, Ibu Salawati told me, a prison guard was so alarmed by what he heard that he took Ibu Salawati to her cell to calm her down. She soothed W.H.'s shattered nerves with gentle persuasion and prayer.

Once the interrogation and torture had ended, W.H.'s condition improved slightly, but she often broke into spasms of laughter and could rarely relate to other women. On occasion, she would lose control, start breaking things and refuse to go to the toilet or take a bath. Although the prison authorities knew that she was mentally so unstable, they never allowed her to be taken anywhere for treatment. The guards rarely took any notice of her, though on one occasion, during one of her wilder fits, two of them carried her to a tub of cold water and plunged her in, head first.

W.H. was transferred to Plantungan, the women's labour camp in Central Java, in July 1971.

I never got to know the real name of 'Si Gendut', or 'Fatty' as she was called. Si Gendut was the youngest woman in Bukit Duri during my time there; she was only thirteen at the time of her arrest in October 1965. She was a rough-and-tumble, poorly educated girl, a high-spirited youngster who never wanted to be left out of anything. She wasn't a member of any of the left-wing youth organizations but when she saw other boys and girls leap onto a truck in the kampung where she lived a few days before 1 October, she cried until they let her on. The truck was taking Pemuda Rakjat members to Halim for a training course.

The women who remembered her when she first came to Bukit Duri recall her crying without stop for her mother. In prison, five years on, she had more or less adjusted to being a 'political prisoner' without any inkling of politics. I remember hearing someone sobbing one day and was told it was Si Gendut, still longing for her mother. She rarely had visits from home.

She too was transferred to Plantungan and I spotted her in a film of the camp by a Dutch television crew which I watched many years later in London.

N.D. was a little older than the other 'children', sixteen at the time of her arrest. N.D. was at Lubang Buaya on the fateful night but succeeded in fleeing before the assault on the base by Suharto troops. She managed to reach home, but was picked up two days later. Her father, now quite elderly, had been a communist all his life and had been exiled to Digul in West Papua in 1926 after an uprising against the Dutch in that year. He was arrested in 1965 and was being held in Tangerang Prison on the outskirts of Jakarta, where conditions were notoriously bad.

N.D., one of the youngest children in the family, was her father's favourite, but she showed no inclination, despite his encouragement, to follow in his footsteps and become a communist. She preferred to mix with her own gang of street kids and refused to join Pemuda Rakjat. But her father *did* succeed in convincing her to go with them on the training course in Lubang Buaya, playing on her enthusiasm for adventure.

In Bukit Duri, she often told us about her exploits on the streets and the cunning tricks she used to play on her father.

'Rah' was never in Lubang Buaya. She was sixteen when she was arrested at her home. She had just got married to a man not much older than herself who was a member of Pemuda Rakjat, and they had only recently moved to Jakarta from Central Java. She hadn't yet got round to joining the organization.

The troops who came for her took her straight to the local military command where she was beaten repeatedly but denied that she had ever been to Lubang Buaya. Her interrogators said that her husband had told them that she was there. She could not believe this and agreed to a confrontation with him. She was stupefied when he repeated his allegation in her presence, and couldn't find the words to contradict him. Six years later, when she told me how it had happened, she still could not contain her emotions.

After being transferred to Bukit Duri, she was again interrogated and tortured with cigarette burns, but still refused to confess to a lie. It took her years to get over her husband's betrayal, although when she started receiving news that he was constantly in a mood of deep depression her attitude changed. Realizing that he had been under terrible pressure at the time, her affection for him returned and she began to send him small tokens of her love. The rest of her family, however, still refused to have anything to do with him.

Rah shared a cell with a tapol who had been head of block for several years and she helped her, locking up the cells at night and unlocking them when someone needed to go to the toilet. She was a devout Muslim and had won recognition as an imam not long before I entered Bukit Duri, which meant that she could lead communal prayers; her Koranic incantations were a pleasure to hear. Rah was also a devotee of classical Javanese music, a very different type of song. Her voice could often be heard echoing through the prison after the cells had been locked up for the night.

S.J. was a shy girl, tall and handsome, who never had much to say. She was fourteen when she was arrested immediately after 'the event'. Her friend I.P. was more out-going and friendly and very fond of any of the small children who sometimes spent short periods in the prison with their mothers. They had both been at Lubang Buaya on 1 October. They suffered terribly at the hands of their tormentors during interrogation. They both made confessions about sex orgies and admitted that they had seen the kidnapped generals being roughly treated by soldiers of the Tjakrabirawa palace guard. The confessions were a godsend for the army in their plan to bring some of the Tjakrabirawa soldiers to court.

Two years later, in 1967, S.J. and I.P. were interrogated under less distressing circumstances and retracted much of what they had said earlier, only admitting that they had attended the training course at the air base. During a later interrogation, this time with P.R., a lawyer, a former member of the HSI, now serving as an army lawyer, he asked them to testify for the prosecution at the trial of a Tjakrabirawa officer. At first they refused because they didn't know the men but the interrogator started yelling at them and terrified them into signing a document agreeing to testify.

A few months later, they were collected from prison and taken, in an armoured vehicle, to the court. Later, they giggled as they told us how journalists waiting outside the courthouse were astonished to see a couple of young women step down from the grim-looking vehicle.

When they were summoned into the courtroom and asked whether they were willing to testify, they each told the judge that they had never agreed to do so.

'But you have signed this document', the judge said.

'Only because we were forced to', they each said in turn.

'Who by?' asked the judge.

'Him', they replied, turning and pointing to P.R., who was sitting next to the army prosecutor. The judge had no option but to dismiss them and, triumphant, they were driven back to prison.

Back in Bukit Duri, our commander, Lieutenant Rompis, was furious. He summoned us all to a roll-call and accused several of us, especially Ibu Salawati and another woman, of 'having put them up to it'. We were all confined to our cells for several days as punishment for the affair.

A few days later, an armoured vehicle again turned up to take the two girls to court where they were given a furious ticking-off by P.R. Several soldiers who were present in the room started to slap and punch them in the face.

Were they upset by what happened, I asked them after their return.

'Well, yes, it was all rather awful but we did get a couple of rides on an armoured vehicle. We wouldn't have missed that for anything!'

J.S. had been caught up in this mess by a most unfortunate sequence of events that had nothing to do with the Pemuda Rakjat, military training or anything remotely political. She was the daughter of a low-ranking member of the air force who lived at the Halim base. She had decided to get married to a man against the wishes of her family. Unfortunately for her, she decided to run away from home on the morning of 1 October. She took a bus to Bandung, but the bus was stopped on the way by troops looking for anyone who had fled from Lubang Buaya and all the passengers were ordered to get down. When asked where she was from, she told them she had come from Halim and was immediately arrested.

I well remembered the terrible reports that appeared in the press about her soon after 1 October. Photos of her standing in a cell were published, alongside a confession that she had 'served' dozens of soldiers on the night before the kidnaps. In another, she was shown with a fierce-looking man in uniform standing over her. According to the caption, she had confessed to having been involved in the murder of General Yani. A few weeks later, she allegedly confessed that Aidit had promised to give awards 'to anyone who masnaged to kill a genral'. According to *Mingguan Berita* in December 1965, she told her interrogators that 'women and men were to engage in free relationships as they already had received indoctrination that in Communism there are no differences between women and men'. (See Saskia Eleonora Wieringa, *The Politicization of Gender Relations in Indonesia* (1995), p. 316.) In fact, she had been brutally tortured, stripped naked and forced to sign confessions, which she only agreed to do after being told she would immediately be released if she signed.

I had never imagined that I would meet up with her in Bukit Duri. She was not one of 'the children', being in her mid-twenties. By the time I entered Bukit Duri, an uncle or cousin, who was himself a soldier and who knew perfectly well that the stories about her were pure fabrication, was working for her release. The family had known for years that everything being said about her was untrue but it had taken them a very long time to find the courage to take the matter up.

I saw this relative of hers one day at Satgas-Jaya. He was pointed out to me by a prisoner from Bukit Duri who had been transferred to the camp for a few weeks and who first told me all about J.S. Even with army connections, it took him more than a year to rescue J.S. from the predicament that her innocent flight from home had landed her in.

Everyone in Bukit Duri was greatly relieved when we heard that J.S. was going to be released.

There were twenty or so young women in Bukit Duri whom we always knew as 'the children'. They all spent up to fourteen years in detention, six in Bukit Duri and the rest in the Plantungan labour camp. Despite the serious charges levelled against them about what they were alleged to have done in Lubang Buaya, not one was ever brought to trial. The only political purpose served by their terrible sufferings was to incite mob violence during the massacres.

CHAPTER 21

Living and Dying in Bukit Duri

The fifteen months I spent in Bukit Duri were punctuated by harrowing incidents of separation, disappointment, meaningless suffering, heart-rending reunions and death.

Many of us had husbands in detention in other prisons in Jakarta or in other parts of the country. Quite a few were held in Salemba, which should have made it easy to arrange meetings, but this was not the case. We were not allowed to communicate with or even to know what was happening to our men in the other place. One woman's husband died in Salemba without her being told. She only heard of his death many months later when she asked for permission to send him a parcel of things she had bought from her meagre earnings.

'He's not there', she was told. 'He's not anywhere. He's gone.'

There was no apology, no explanation of how he had died. He was 'gone', and that was all.

There were twenty of us in Bukit Duri whose husbands were imprisoned in Salemba Prison. We tried several times to obtain permission to visit Salemba as a group. In August 1971, a year after I arrived in Bukit Duri, permission was granted and we were told to prepare for the meeting. We dressed ourselves in our best clothes and got a few things ready to take as gifts. Some of the women had to borrow a shawl or a pair of shoes, to look a bit less like the prisoners we were.

Soon after we arrived at the prison, the meetings began. We were divided into small groups and taken in turn to a meeting hall. My meeting with Bud was supervised by the chief security officer who not only listened to every word we said but took up much of the time – just twenty minutes – offering us 'fatherly advice'.

After eleven of us had met our husbands, the other meetings were abandoned. There were no explanations. Nine deeply disappointed women were given no reason for the sudden change of plan. We were simply told that there would be no further meetings and ordered back onto the trucks that had brought us from Bukit Duri, for the journey 'home'.

A year earlier, just before my arrival in Bukit Duri, meetings planned for another group had ended in fiasco. When the women arrived in Salemba, they were taken to a room to await their turns. The first woman to be called went to the meeting hall where she was told to wait. She sat there waiting for some time but nothing happened. It soon became evident that the guards responsible for fetching her husband were in a panic. Her excitement turned to anxiety. Someone had blundered. The guards were shouting at one another, blaming each other for the confusion. It was clear that her husband was no longer at the prison. Eventually, the guards, angry and exasperated, turned to all the women: 'The whole thing's off. You're all to go back. There won't be any meetings today.'

Not that day or any other day either. The women were given no explanations. News of what had really happened did not trickle out for several weeks. The husband who failed to appear had been transported to a remote hard-labour camp on Buru Island. His wife had not been told because it was against prison rules for her to know. Under the rules, she should not have been taken to Salemba. That was the only thing the guards were upset about, a breach of the secrecy that surrounded the transportation of thousands of prisoners to Buru.

The Buru Island forced labour penal colony for political prisoners was set up in 1969. Buru is a small island in the Malukan archipelago, far away to the east of Java. The island was covered by dense jungle. Communications with the rest of the country were almost non-existent, with only an occasional sea transport service between Namlea on the island and Ambon, the capital of Maluku, several hundred miles to the east.

In the words of the Attorney-General, Sugih Arto, who wrote the preface to a brochure published at the time by the Buru Resettlement Executive Authority, the purpose was not to 'isolate the tapols from the public but merely to provide them with a new means of living together with their families because it will only risk their own safety if they are to be returned to their original community'. In the very next paragraph, he contradicted the impression that they were being sent to Buru for their own protection. The penal colony, he wrote, was intended for prisoners who had played 'an important role in planning, supervising and carrying out . . . the G30S/PKI Movement; however, we do not have sufficient evidence to prosecute them. We consider it still to be a danger to our security to return them to the community; they are still like a thorn in the side of the community.'

Buru island was the chosen destination for tens of thousands of 'B' category prisoners, where the Suharto regime would carry out its Final Solution.

In Bukit Duri, we were told nothing about the transfers to Buru even though some of our men had been sent there months ago. When the existence of the colony was first publicly acknowledged in late 1969, some 2,500 men had already been banished to the island. The entire operation was shrouded in the utmost secrecy and it was to be many years before the true horror of Buru came to light. The ships used to transport the prisoners set sail from the virtually inaccessible Nusakembangan prison island, off Central Java, where the tapols had been held for weeks, living on minimal rations, deprived of the supplementary food that families were able to supply in Salemba and other prisons. Conditions on the vessels used to ship the men out were uniformly atrocious.

After arrival, the men were set to work to build barracks for their own accommodation and transform large tracts of jungle into rice fields. Conditions were primeval, disease was rampant and there were numerous fatal accidents. In the early stages, the men had to clear extensive savannah covered with *imperata* – a hard-stemmed, sharp-edged grass – with their bare hands. Many of the tapols suffered from malnutrition and the death-rate, particularly during the first years, was appalling.

The decision to establish the Buru project was taken by Kopkamtib, and the Attorney-General was appointed to manage it. This made it appear as though a civilian authority now had responsibility for the tapols, creating the impression that their cases had been resolved according to judicial criteria. In fact, this was indefinite detention without charge in a remote corner of the country, plus the additional burden of hard labour. The camp was supervised, managed and guarded by soldiers from the Military Police Corps who established a regime of great brutality. The men were forced to work twelve hours a day or more under the most arduous conditions. One foreign journalist, writing in *Newsweek* in February 1971, described the 'gruelling manual labour' as 'sheer physical punishment'. Punishment inflicted for 'indiscipline' was harsh in the extreme; prisoners were frequently beaten by their soldier-guards and subjected to other forms of cruelty. This was Indonesia's Devil's Island.

Although the regime clearly intended Buru to be the permanent resettlement for all male 'B' category prisoners, it became the target of worldwide condemnation. During the 1970s, the policy became a huge embarrassment to Suharto and gradually the Buru tapols were allowed to return to their homes.

Not long after I arrived at Bukit Duri, a cell-mate of mine suffered a disappointment of quite a different order. Her husband was a junior naval officer who had been tried and sentenced to six years in 1968 for giving refuge to Brigadier-General Supardjo, one of the 1 October 1965 conspirators. Although his wife was much younger than most of the women in Bukit Duri, everyone called her 'Ibu' (Mother), a title usually reserved for older women, simply because she was perceived by others as being from a higher social background, more Western educated in fact, than the rest of the women. I couldn't bring myself to address her as 'Ibu' – it seemed perverse for a woman as young as her – so I called her Nancy. We became good friends and I think she liked my preference for informality of address.

Nancy had no interest in anything political. She had been detained a year or so after her husband's conviction for reasons that were difficult to fathom. She was arrested when on a visit to the naval authorities to arrange for an appeal against her husband's conviction; she was also trying to get alternative housing for herself as she had been ordered to quit the house where she was living, in a naval complex in Tanjung Priok. She was transferred to Bukit Duri almost immediately; nobody seemed interested enough in her 'case' to bother to interrogate her. She had often asked to be questioned when interrogation teams visited the prison, in an attempt to get things moving. So there she was, uncharged, unconvicted, just waiting to be interrogated.

As her husband had been convicted, he had been transferred to Cipinang Prison and was therefore in the hands of the civilian authorities, not the military. This meant he enjoyed many facilities that she was denied. He was allowed regular visits by his family, but she was not. He was better off having been found guilty than poor Nancy whose case had not moved an inch in more than two years.

One day, quite unexpectedly, he was brought to Bukit Duri for a meeting with his wife. One of our friends spotted him as she passed the office on garbage duty. When she returned, she rushed to tell Nancy to get ready to meet her husband. What excitement there was! After rushing back to our cell to put on something decent, Nancy managed to get herself onto the next garbage corvée team which meant she could peep at him through the office window. By the time she got back, she was consumed with excitement. She waited to be called but nothing happened. After more than half an hour of high expectations, we were shocked to see him leave the office and be escorted out of the prison. There was to be no meeting. The few metres that separated them could not be crossed because the rules for Bukit Duri prisoners could not be bent to accommodate the rules for Cipinang prisoners. Nancy needed a lot of consoling after that terrible disappointment.

Sukarni's problems were different. Her husband wasn't in prison, he was dead. When I first met her, we were sitting on a bench just inside the entrance to Block A. She was rather sad looking and walked with a bit of a slouch, obviously worn down by worry. As we chatted, she asked me bashfully to try out her English. I began by asking her a few simple questions in English. Then came the rather obvious question, spoken with care to pronounce each word clearly: 'Where is your husband?'

'My husband is in Kalibata', she answered, saying the words with the same precision that I had used. Concentrating at first on the words, I missed the significance of what she had said. Then it dawned on me. In Kalibata? Did she mean the Kalibata national heroes' cemetery? She could see I was puzzled.

'Yes, Kalibata. You know what that is, don't you?'

'Yes, of course I do. But when?' I had stopped bothering about speaking English now.

'A few weeks after the events of 1965.' She said nothing more about him but sat looking at me with a sad smile. I was too embarrassed to ask any more questions. How could she be in prison, the widow of a man who had been given a hero's burial? Later, I was told that he was killed when a group of youths attacked the office of the veterans' organization. It was said that the youths were from Pemuda Rakyat, which made him eligible for a hero's burial in Kalibata.

As for Sukarni, she was picked up much later because she had held a minor position in the Gerwani. At the time of her arrest, Sukarni, now a single parent, had three small children to consider. She took the two smallest children into detention with her. The oldest, a boy, went to live with an uncle and she heard nothing about him. After spending some weeks in Bukit Duri, the two other children were moved into foster homes and Sukarni lost all contact with other members of her family.

One day, Sukarni was on garbage duty which meant spending a few moments outside the prison gate. She disliked this chore and usually traded it with others. On this occasion, just as she and the other tapols went out through the gate, she suddenly started shouting 'Toto, Toto! Look, there's Toto!'

Rompis, who was escorting the garbage team, shouted 'What are you yelling about, woman? For goodness sake, shut up!'

But she continued to scream. 'Look, Pak Rompis, over there! That's my son!'

Reacting swiftly this time, Rompis started running towards a small boy dressed in rags who was scavenging in the busy market street. As soon as he saw a soldier running towards him, the boy took to his heels. Street-vendors joined the chase, caught the boy who was by now screaming with fear, and handed him over to Rompis, who dragged him to the prison gate where Sukarni stood, weeping. It was Toto all right, a street urchin, barefoot, grimy from head to toe.

It took a while before the boy could be pacified enough to understand what had happened. Within moments, everyone was watching the scene – prisoners, guards, soldiers, the warders of the civil prison. There wasn't a dry eye among us at the sight of this heart-rending reunion.

A very dazed little boy followed his mother into the prison. She had soon washed him clean, thrown away his rags and dressed him in whatever she could find. Gradually, she was able to piece together what had happened since her arrest. He had stayed with the uncle for several years, but when the man remarried, the new wife made the boy's life a misery. Toto ran away and, by the time his mother found him, he had spent several weeks begging, scavenging and sleeping in railway sidings. He stayed at Bukit Duri for a few months until Rompis found him a foster home, with the help of the visiting priest. For as long as Sukarni remained in Bukit Duri, the boy was allowed to visit his mother twice a month, on Sundays, with the priest. I often saw him on those occasions, looking well cared for, rescued from a dreadful fate by an amazing stroke of luck.

———————————

Rogayah was brisk and efficient, always bustling with energy. Her eyes sparkled most of the time, though her face was sometimes clouded by nervous tension. She was in charge of the women who worked in the kitchen, doing their best to cook something edible from the meagre, poor-quality rations supplied by the army. Rogayah was a warm-hearted, motherly woman who never failed to defend the interests of the women who worked with her. The kitchen duty was particularly onerous. They had to cook for 150 people on two paraffin stoves, one of which was continually breaking down. The kitchen for the political prisoners was a ramshackle shed with a leaking roof and potholes. When an International Red Cross team came to inspect Bukit Duri to see the conditions of the tapols, the commander didn't dare let them see the place where our food was cooked but showed them the kitchen of the civil prison which was spacious, airy and relatively well equipped.

Rogayah was in her mid fifties. She had a large family of children ranging in age from their early twenties to below school age. She was a devout Muslim and skilled in Koranic chanting. Besides her kitchen duties, she also gave regular courses in religious affairs. We became good friends, chatting most of the time about nothing in particular. I found her company relaxing and uncomplicated. She was also very good at massage; her powerful fingers could get rid of a headache within minutes. I had headaches very often in Bukit Duri and appreciated her help. But the officers and guards took advantage of her skills; often, after a strenuous day's cooking, she was called to the office to give Rompis or one of the guards a 'complete overhaul'. Sometimes, they even took her home to massage their wives.

Her husband was very much older than her and going senile. It was quite beyond him to understand why she was in prison and he found her absence from home unbearable. Many a day, he would walk the many miles from their home to Bukit Duri and arrive at the prison gate in a state of great distress, to plead with the guards to allow him to meet Rogayah. Sometimes they would let them meet, but only through an iron grid. Each time it was the same: he pleaded with her to come home fast.

'What can I tell him?' she would say after these brief encounters. 'He doesn't understand that I can't go home until I am released. He'll die of a broken heart before they ever let me out.'

So what was her crime? A meaningless case, typical of so many of the women I met. Some time in the 1950s she was approached by a local Gerwani organizer to set up a group in her kampung. She organized a few social gatherings called *arisan*, a kind of mutual savings group. But she didn't keep this up for long because many of her neighbours who were devout Muslims were deeply hostile towards anything left-wing.

1965 came and went without disturbing her life. She had had no contact with Gerwani for many years and never for a moment felt obliged to report to the local military after the organization was outlawed. One day, her home was burgled and money that she held in trust for the canteen where she worked was stolen. The police suspected a man living in the neighbourhood, but he turned on her, telling the police of her past Gerwani connections. Instead of questioning him about the burglary, the police investigated her. Why had she failed to report herself? Why had she said nothing about her past connections with an outlawed organization? How had she been able to insinuate herself into a job in the canteen of a government department? There was more than enough reason to suspect her, so she was detained. When I last spoke to her on the day of my release, she had been in prison for four years.

It was while I was still in Block C that Ibu Rumini arrived in Bukit Duri. She was a thin woman in her late forties with a badly deformed face and a misshapen back, all of which made her look much older than her years. The gaunt shape of her chest and rounded shoulders were the clear signs of an asthmatic. Her restless eyes revealed that she had suffered a great deal of pain. She spoke with a thick Jakarta accent and her manner of speaking was that of the traders in Jakarta's street markets.

Not long after she arrived at the prison, her asthmatic attacks began and even though her cell was far removed from mine, two blocks away, I could hear her gasping for breath as she sat on her bunk. After spending several months in Block C, I was moved to Block B, then back to Block A where I shared a cell with Ibu Rumini and one other woman. By this time, she had had numerous attacks and was fast becoming a physical wreck. Everything about prison life seemed to bring on the attacks, the cold and damp of the cells, the tensions caused by a sudden visitation from officers at Salemba, the sudden imposition of new rules or orders for prisoners to move from one cell to another. Such events traumatize everyone, but for Ibu Rumini they were a thousand times worse. She was allergic to everything associated with prison life.

The time I spent in a cell with her was agonizing for all of us. Whenever an attack came on, she would sit day and night on the edge of her stone bunk, her feet resting on a wooden box, leaning heavily forward on her two hands and groaning with the pain of every single breath. When the strain on her hands became unbearable, she would turn round, lift her legs up in front of her and prop her head up against the cold wall, protecting it only with a thin pillow. She was unable to lie down during an attack.

'Aduh. The pain is unbearable. I'm going to die. I can't stand it any longer. This is the end.'

There was little we could do to relieve her agony. Even to approach her and wipe away the perspiration from her face would irritate her intensely. All we could do was to keep guard nearby, taking turns to stay up all night to make sure she didn't fall off her bunk.

Rompis and the guards knew all about her condition, and so did Sani Gondjo. I remember him coming to the block one day and standing at the door of our cell, watching her struggling for breath. He was in a magnanimous mood.

'If she gets too bad, send her to hospital', he said.

She was sent to hospital several times when she 'got too bad'. A few days of treatment away from the prison quickly restored her health and she returned looking much better, even having put on a little weight. But the attacks soon returned. After her third spell in hospital, the doctor discharged her. 'Ibu Rumini, be very careful. Your next attack may be the last', he warned.

What good was such advice to her? Everyone knew that the only thing that would save her life was release, but that was not possible. No allowance was made for ill-health; there was no such thing as release on compassionate grounds. They had a 'case' against her and she could not be freed until it had been 'resolved'.

So what was the case against her? She had been an activist, the treasurer or deputy secretary, I can't remember which, of a local Gerwani group. The group's activities had only recently come to the notice of the local military command and, since the most senior functionary was no longer in the area, she was detained as the next best thing. This did not happen until 1970, five years after 'the event'. Whatever they had against her was connected with the pre-1965 era, and for this she was now going through such agony.

When the final attack came, even some prisoners were becoming immune to her cries for pity. A female nurse was supposed to visit us daily, but she often failed to turn up and, when she did come, she was more interested in looking for embroidered tablecloths that she could sell. On the day that Ibu Rumini's condition deteriorated, the nurse had been on a visit early in the afternoon. We called her to the block because Ibu Rumini was writhing in pain on the floor of the cell.

'Put her back up on the bunk and make sure she doesn't fall down again. She'll be all right', the nurse said reassuringly. Two hours later, Ibu Rumini was dead. We had been unable to do anything to relieve her death agonies.

Silence fell as word spread that she had died. Each of the tapols allowed to move around the blocks came to pay their last respects to her emaciated body. Among us were women who were skilled in the treatment of the dead. They came and stretched out her body, straightened her limbs, combed her matted hair, placed coins on her eyes to keep them closed, and covered her body with a batik wrap.

We sat cross-legged in silence along the corridor outside the cell, stunned by this futile and tragic death. Prayers were said as we waited for her husband to come and collect the body. He arrived several hours later with a health orderly and a couple of tapols from Salemba Prison who placed her body on a bare plank of wood and carried her away.

CHAPTER 22

Plantungan Labour Camp, the Final Solution

Early in 1971, things at Bukit Duri took a turn for the worse. News began to circulate that a large number of tapols were due to be transferred to a detention camp in Central Java. We were not supposed to know about the transfer until it happened, but one or two of the guards couldn't keep a secret to save their lives. The first real sign that something was afoot came when a drastic rearrangement of cell accommodation was announced. Rumours abounded that, from now on, everyone accommodated in Block B was due for transfer.

I knew nothing until very much later about the place that had been selected. A former colony for lepers in a village called Plantungan, Central Java, had been taken over for women political prisoners who would become 'political lepers'. The special camp for women tapols, opened in April 1971, was located in a remote part of Central Java, surrounded by high mountains, the kind of location considered suitable for sufferers from leprosy who, according to traditional treatment, had to be kept as far removed from society as possible. It was several miles south of the town of Sukorejo and approachable only by an almost impassable road.

News of the forthcoming transfer plunged the prison into a state of gloom. Here was the Final Solution – being dumped in a remote location far from family and friends, for ever as far as we could see.

Rompis tried to persuade us that the transfer was the preliminary to release. Another of his stories was that there would be greater freedom of movement, the inmates would not be confined to cells and there would be plenty of open space.

'You'll be given a six-month training course in agricultural production so as to make you better equipped to face the outside world', he told us. Certainly no one in Bukit Duri had any intention of working in agriculture after their eventual release.

Plantungan was the women's equivalent of the Buru penal camp for men. It was pretty obvious that the guards had their own reasons for letting us in on the secret. It would be to their credit if the women looked well equipped, with mats, warm clothing and other supplies, at the time of their departure. As ever, none of these things was supplied by our captors. It was up to the women to scrape together whatever they could. As soon as we realized that a big transfer was in the offing, we all set to, sewing for dear life to make all kinds of clothing, so as to ensure that our departing sisters had a good supply of food and basic essentials; in particular, we did what we could to help those who never received any visits from relatives.

The weeks before the first transfer – for there were several – were tense and fraught with problems. Worst of all was the constant shifting round of prisoners, in and out of Block B. Some women were never sure from one day to the next whether they were coming or going. The stress of all this uncertainty sometimes became unbearable. Two women I knew well firmly believed, right up to the day before the move, that they would not be included in the transfer. The last-minute reversal for one of them apparently occurred because the Salemba Prison commander had overheard her making a remark about her husband which he regarded as 'incriminating'; he decided there and then that she should go rather than stay.

The other was a nurse, the wife of Oloan Hutapea, the PKI politbureau member who was shot dead in the operation against the Blitar base in 1968. I knew her well in pre-1965 days; we used to meet outside the school which our children attended. You could hardly have found a less politically conscious woman than Siti Suratih. She had never joined anything and had worked for years at the gynaecology department of the army hospital, RSPAD, in Jakarta, where she was respected for her excellent professional skills as a midwife. But because she was the wife of a murdered communist leader, she spent altogether more than ten years in detention. The last-minute decision to include her in the shift to Plantungan was clearly prompted by the sudden realization that her services as a nurse would come in handy. Years later, when I saw a film about Plantungan made by a Dutch television crew, I spotted her standing in the camp office, on duty as a nurse.

On the night of the transfer, when all the cell doors in Block B were unlocked at around three in the morning, the women were given strict orders to gather their belongings and leave their cells without making a sound so that the rest of us would hear nothing. They had everything packed and ready, with cylinder-shaped calico bags stuffed with slacks, blouses and jackets, vitamin pills, sugar and other things to see them through the first difficult days in their new place of detention.

Locked in our cells as we always were at night, the rest of us were not supposed to see or hear anything, but somehow a sense of what was happening penetrated the thick prison walls. Come what may, we would give them a send-off. I happened to be in a cell in Block A, on the yard side of the corridor, so one of my cell-mates scrambled up the wall and perched on another woman's shoulders to give us a whispered running commentary. We took turns going up the wall, to see for ourselves what was going on. The women in the other cells had the same idea. As it was pitch dark, we could hardly see anything, yet it made us feel good to wave them on their way.

We had no idea whether they had seen us, but years later I met one of the women who was transferred on that night; she told me that they had seen our faces through the window bars and had seen our waves of farewell. She told me they were never officially told what was about to happen. Before leaving Bukit Duri, they were subjected to body searches. She was especially struck by the fact that the women who conducted these searches wore gloves, as if to avoid contamination from physical contact with tapols. Some of the tapols got into a terrible state, thinking that they were being taken off to be killed.

After several hours of tension, they were herded into buses under military police guard. When the convoy began its journey eastward through Java at daybreak, it was escorted by motorbikes up front, at the sides and in the rear, with sirens screeching.

'We joked about being *nyonya-nyonya besar*', she told me, '"important ladies" being driven to a state event. Someone started singing. Anything to relieve the tension. But others couldn't bring themselves to open their mouths.'

The roads along which they passed had been cleared of traffic; other vehicles would not be allowed to impede the progress of this army convoy, carrying its human cargo to a secret destination. In Kendal, Central Java, they were transferred from buses to jeeps because the road up to the camp was so rocky.

Conditions in Plantungan were not as grim as those the men had to endure on Buru, but it was a forced labour camp, a concentration camp for women who had no prospects of release. Family visits were not permitted. The prisoners had to produce most of their own food and were only provided with rice. For necessities such as sugar, tea, coffee, soap and clothes, they had to rely on parcels from home, but communications were extremely difficult and mailing costs were high.

The mood in Bukit Duri after the transfer was sombre. The departure of so many friends, about 50 in the first transfer, made a deep impact on everyone, especially as we had no idea where they had been taken and what fate awaited them. We soon started worrying about whose turn it would be next. Although there was a sense of relief that we had been spared, we were at the mercy of the army who could and would do whatever they wanted. I personally had less reason to fear that I would be spirited off in the middle of the night, yet I could never be sure this wouldn't happen.

It was at times like this that we had to pull ourselves out of despair and start busying ourselves with alternative activities – choir singing, play-acting, more English lessons, anything to take our minds of things.

Ever since I was first arrested, many of my fellow-prisoners thought that the army would be unlikely to hold on to me for long, that being foreign-born meant that my release prospects were better than most, whatever the 'case' they had against me. Bud also believed this. They would often tell me they were relying on me to tell the world what I knew about the criminal system of imprisonment and all the atrocities associated with it. Everyone assumed that I would be able to return to the country of my birth and the Indonesians would be only too happy to get rid of me.

However, things did not work out like that. The weeks were dragging into months and months into years. I had now been a guest of President Suharto for close on three years and I feared that my origins were not working in my favour. Being an *orang bule* (a white-skinned person), as Indonesians would say, may have helped to keep me out of prison for the first three years after 1965. Now I was in the clutches of the army and it was becoming more and more apparent that it would take more than the colour of my skin to convince them to let me go.

During the years I had lived in Indonesia, I identified closely with Indonesian society and never lived as an expatriate. Now that I was a tapol, I felt rather uncomfortable about seeing whether being foreign-born was going to extricate me. But my fellow-prisoners had little time for such qualms. 'Get out of here as fast as you can', they would say, 'and start working for our release.' Their pleas made a strong impression on me, though I had no idea at the time how I would set about it.

There were many sides of everyday life in Bukit Duri that stick out in my mind as particularly oppressive. We had nothing that could pass for a proper medical service. I suffered from many colds while I was in Bukit

Duri and was hardly ever free of severe sinusitis which made it difficult for me to get a good night's sleep. After months of complaining about the problem, I was eventually given permission to visit the army hospital for a check-up. By this time, however, I was on the way to recovery, with the help of a remedy which I kept secret from the guards. When I was summoned to go to the hospital, I did not reveal that I was almost better. I was not going to miss the chance of having a ride through the city and seeing a bit of the outside world.

The remedy was acupuncture. One of my fellow-prisoners, Ibu L., had been given a crash course in acupuncture by a prisoner, a Chinese doctor, during the time she was at Likdam. She kept her skills rather quiet as there would have been serious repercussions if the prison authorities had found out that she was practising. I was vaguely aware of what she was doing and she hinted to me one day that she thought she could cure me. It took quite some time for me to make up my mind to accept her offer. She had no medical training or experience, so I wondered whether it would be safe to start the treatment with her. But the sinus problem was wearing me down and I eventually decided to go ahead.

The sessions were very stressful because they had to be conducted in the utmost secrecy. While I lay on my back quite still for twenty minutes or so, with needles sticking out all over my body, a special look-out system was organized with everything ready to pull out the needles and conceal them the moment a guard approached the block.

It was not just that I and others sitting with me might be punished. This was a rare source of medical treatment available in our midst and no one wanted to risk losing it. Ibu L. had gone to great lengths to smuggle the needles in when she was transferred to Bukit Duri. She had concealed them in her hair, in a bun at the back of her head. Acupuncture did wonders for my breathing and I have been a firm believer in the treatment ever since.

My only other experience of treatment was a visit to an army dentist to have one of my wisdom teeth removed. My teeth were also covered with tartar, but he did nothing to remove it and insisted that there was no need to do anything about it. When I eventually went for dental treatment in London, the dentist was horrified to see the state of my teeth. The long neglect had caused havoc for my gums.

We were not allowed access to the radio or newspapers and were kept in ignorance of everything that was happening outside. One or two women, however, managed to break the blockade. How they did it, I never discovered; my guess was that one of the guards had been bribed to bring newspapers in. We had to work out an elaborate and highly selective system of circulating clippings. It was always understood that any leak would have dire consequences for everyone. On one occasion, I had just been passed a clipping when I was suddenly ordered by a guard to go and meet a team of interrogators for questioning at Salemba Prison. I had no time to dispose of it so I stuffed it in my pocket. I spent the next few hours in great anguish until I could go to a toilet and get rid of that wretched scrap of paper.

There were periods when the atmosphere in the prison became unbearably tense, usually because of punishments, alleged infringements of the rules or external factors, and this would often lead to personal conflicts and discord. We were, after all, living almost on top of each other, often sharing cells with women of very different temperaments and from very different backgrounds. On occasions like this, some of the more politically conscious women would suggest initiatives to bolster our spirits. One very popular form of activity was drama. Planning the script, rehearsing, making the costumes and the scenery worked wonders on our spirits. Needless to say, all this required special security measures to protect our activities from being discovered.

On one occasion, we decided to perform a story from the Javanese epic drama, the *Ramayana*, not with shadow puppets but with tapols playing the roles. The preparations were very elaborate; we designed costumes and thought up things to use as make-up. I was chosen to act the part of Petruk, one of the four clowns who occupy a central role in every drama. Everyone thought I fitted the part admirably because of my long nose, a distinctive feature of the character I had to play. My 'performance' must have made a deep impression on my fellow-prisoners. Many years later, when I was completing this manuscript, I received an embroidered hanki from one of my Bukit Duri friends. The note from her said 'To my dear Carmel (Petruk)'. We had great fun during the many rehearsals and when the actual performance took place there were hoots of laughter when I appeared on the scene. We incorporated political satire in the script, commenting on the circumstances of our incarceration. Despite all our careful preparations, a guard appeared just as the performance was in full swing, so there was a rush for the cells where buckets of water had been kept in readiness to wash off the make-up. As I recollect, the incident passed off without further mishap and provided us with plenty of laughs for several days afterwards.

Having attached myself to the Protestant group of prisoners, I always attended services on Sundays and the Christian holidays. I enjoyed singing with the choir and sometimes took over as conductor. I even tried my hand at writing four-part harmony, from what I remembered of the carol singing I did when I was still at school. The services were taken by a minister, Reverend Rompas, or his wife, or sometimes a Dutch visitor, Tina Franz, who spent much of her time doing pastoral work with prisoners. I always looked forward to these occasions. The services would end with a handshake for all the prisoners, which provided us with an opportunity to whisper or receive messages. Reverend Rompas sometimes passed on messages to me about what was happening in London in the efforts to secure my release. On one occasion, some of the other women were angry with me for taking more than my fair share of time shaking hands with him, but I couldn't tell them what we had been discussing.

There were many things I learnt in prison about Javanese customs and culture that I knew nothing about when living outside. It was not considered polite, I learnt, to stand with legs akimbo and hands on your waist. You should never touch a Javanese on the head. And why, for heaven's sake, were children always rebuked when they put out their left hand to accept something from an adult? *Tangan manis, tangan manis*, they would be told. 'Use your "sweet hand".' The reason, I discovered, was that since it was assumed that everyone used the left hand to clean their bottoms after going to the lavatory, your right hand was your *tangan manis*.

These were the days too when I made up my mind never to become involved in any political activity that would not allow me to take full responsibility for my own actions. What distressed me about having worked in and with the PKI was that the leadership had taken policy decisions that had devastating repercussions for millions of people who had no idea what was going on. This was the result of democratic centralism which requires loyalty and obedience to the decisions of a centralizing body. It was not that I blamed the PKI for what happened after October 1965. Far from it. The blame rests squarely with the army and its commander, Suharto. But there was something gravely wrong with a political structure that left the members and sympathizers at a loss to understand why they were being victimized.

For the remainder of my stay in Bukit Duri, we heard nothing about conditions in Plantungan. It was while I was still in Bukit Duri, in August 1971, that a Dutch TV crew visited the labour camp. We heard nothing about this at the time but years later I was moved to tears when I saw the film in London. There they were, many of my friends, sleeping in ugly barracks, each with a space not more than two feet wide. There were shots of them toiling in the fields or working in the sewing workshop. They all looked desperately unhappy.

One scene showed a group of prisoners giving a *gamelan* performance for officers and the visiting journalists; it reminded me of the musicians required to perform for camp commanders in Hitler's concentration camps.

The camp commander, Major O. S. Prajogo, was interviewed by the Dutch journalist, Aad van den Heuvel. His words are worth repeating:

Q. What is your task?

A. *I have to make the political prisoners into Pancasila-ists, people who believe in God, by giving them religious instruction. We pump religious instruction into them. [Here, he made a pumping gesture with his hand.] And we give them work so that they have no time to have discussions with each other, by giving them cultural activity, also by giving them sport and recreation.*

Q. How do you come to be doing this work?

A. *I first got to know prisoners when I was a church official. At that time I had the task of giving them spiritual education. Some of them, so to say, were not familiar with God. So, here, we place the stress on religious education so that they can know about and believe in God.*

Q. For a number of people here, this has been going on for six years. Have you any idea how much longer they will be here before returning to society?

A. *I can't specify how much longer they will be here. But one thing is clear. Our task is to prepare them so that they are ready to return to society when there is an order to that effect from our superiors.*

Seated beside him was a woman who had been shown in an earlier scene, giving the tapols religious instruction. She had the glint of a true zealot in her eyes as she spoke in faltering English. Her words are best left unedited:

Q. What is your task?

A. *My task here: First, we have to loose their minds from the communists. Second, we have to applicate them to be real Indonesian people who based on the five principles of the Pancasila. Thirdly, we have to bring them to the society without making new problems for our Government in their lives. Fourthly, educate them to be religious people and well-educated people, and members of the society that can obey our laws, what is ordered by our Government.*

Two of the tapols interviewed were very young and both had been in detention for six years. One young woman behaved very much like a child and could hardly understand the questions she was asked. She was so small, she was probably still in her early teens. Quite a few very young women were shown carrying rocks across a bridge and planting rice in a field; none had come from Bukit Duri. This could only mean that many young girls had been taken into custody in other parts of the country as well as in Jakarta. I was never able to discover how they had got caught up in it all.

Later, the camp was visited by a medical team from the International Red Cross who interviewed a number of tapols, including Dr Sumiarsih. Meeting the team in private, she contradicted information they had been given by the camp authorities about the availability of medical implements and medicines. Other women also told the visitors things that were completely at variance with what they had been told by the officials. When this was discovered, 44 of the tapols, including Dr Sumiarsih, were transferred to a prison in Semarang as punishment. I could not track down what happened to them there, nor do I understand why removal from a labour camp to a prison was seen as a punishment. Perhaps it was easier in prison to hold them in isolation than at Plantungan.

The transfer resulted in new hardships for those left behind because they lost the services of Dr Sumiarsih. In Plantungan, the tapols and even some members of staff used to call her *doktor manjur*, the 'wonder-doctor', because of her success in curing her patients with such meagre resources.

Several hundred women prisoners were held in Plantungan for up to eight years. It was not until the late 1970s that the military regime came under such intense international pressure about the tens of thousands of untried political prisoners being held that it was compelled to reverse its policy and release them.

In 1975, I used footage from the Dutch film about Plantungan to make a documentary about the tapols. We called the film *More Than a Million Years*. By then, at least 100,000 tapols had spent ten years in detention without trial.

CHAPTER 23

Release

Since my transfer to Bukit Duri, I had been getting fragments of news suggesting that things were moving with regard to my nationality. The ever faithful John Newmann kept in close contact with Tari, Anto and the rest of the family in London throughout this period. He had few chances of meeting me and sometimes asked Par and her husband Mudjajin to pass on messages about what was happening. Sometimes, a message from John would reach me via Reverend Rompas. Throughout, John was careful never to raise my expectations because things were moving painfully slowly and could have foundered at any time.

John left Indonesia early in May 1971 and had planned to see me for the last time before leaving, to update me on the latest developments. It so happens that he asked for permission to visit me on 1 May. That was just any old day as far as he was concerned. The army, however, saw something sinister in his wanting to visit me on Labour Day and the request was turned down. John later told Tari that he was baffled, annoyed and amazed at such stupidity.

Then one day in October 1971, a prison guard came to my cell and told me he had been ordered to take my measurements but refused to say why. This was the first sign that my release was fast approaching, although at the time I found it difficult to understand what was happening. I had not foreseen that, after being released, I would be bundled onto a plane and flown out of the country within hours. I could not make the journey in the shabby clothes I wore in prison, and, anyway, I would need warm clothing for travelling in winter. It had not occurred to me that the family in London would need to send me clothes for my journey to London.

I had no idea until after I arrived in London just how much the family had done on my behalf. I knew nothing about the letters they wrote to Suharto, to Mrs Suharto and other Indonesian officials. I knew nothing about the visit my sister Miriam made to the Indonesian Embassy in London in October 1968, asking what the charges were against Bud and me and when we were likely to be tried. I knew nothing about their largely unsuccessful efforts to get publicity for me in the British press. I was totally ignorant of their extensive correspondence with several members of Parliament, some of whom showed an interest but never took the issue very far. I had no idea that, following pressure on the Foreign Office a few days after my arrest, a British diplomat in Jakarta named Peter Cormack made inquiries about me at the Jakarta military command and was told that I had been arrested because 'I had lived in Czechoslovakia for many years and had later become a member of the HSI'. Miriam and Ben, my brother, had also sought the help of cousins in the US, who started up their own campaign for my release. Friends of mine like Ingrid Palmer, who was later instrumental in persuading the World Council of Churches to bring Tari and Anto to the UK, sought the help of Dr Mervyn Jaspan, a lecturer in Indonesian studies, to get me a lectureship or fellowship at Hull University.

Being a prisoner in the hands of the Indonesian army, I was not allowed to have the slightest inkling of what was being done on my behalf. As I waded through the mass of documents and correspondence after arriving in London, I felt acutely the denial of my right to know. I saw myself back there in prison, totally oblivious of all these efforts, seeing, hearing and knowing nothing about things that were so intimately connected with my personal fate.

Immediately after my arrest in September 1968, my family in London sought high and low for advice on what to do about the legal aspects of my case. It was inconceivable to them that political prisoners were not allowed access to the law. Miriam and Ben spared no effort on my behalf. My eldest sister Lebah did what she could but she had undergone several operations for cancer and was unable to do much to help for most of the time. Even my elderly mother, who was semi-literate, having had very little schooling after her family emigrated to England from Poland, did her share of letter-writing.

Less than a month after my arrest, Miriam wrote to Indonesia's leading human rights lawyer, Yap Thiam Hien, asking him to take on the case. He willingly accepted but was not allowed to meet me, nor did I have any idea at the time that he was acting as my lawyer. In November 1968, he wrote to Miriam to say that the Jakarta military command had told him they had 'strong evidence of their [Bud's and my] involvement' and that we had both 'made confessions about our involvement with prominent PKI leaders . . . after the coup'. Nothing could have been farther from the truth.

It was not until after I was transferred to Bukit Duri in August 1970 that efforts to secure my release were focused on the question of my nationality. During my three months' 'leave of absence' from detention, I met Mr Yap, who came to see me one day at the guest house where I gave English lessons. Besides his legal practice, Mr Yap was an active member of the Indonesian Council of Churches and a friend of Andrew Sorongan. I told him I had renounced British nationality after obtaining a declaratory judgement from an Indonesian court in 1954 affirming that I had become an Indonesian citizen by virtue of my marriage to Bud in 1950. When I told him we had never registered our marriage at an Indonesian civil register office, he said this meant that the marriage had no formal standing under Indonesian law and that therefore, the declaratory judgement was null and void. The British government's decision to accept my renunciation was also invalid as it had rendered me stateless, although British nationality law was designed to prevent such a thing from happening. This would not be an easy case to argue as it would require a ruling by an Indonesian court, denouncing the 1954 declaratory judgement as flawed. It was difficult to expect an Indonesian judge to do such a thing for someone now in the hands of the military.

However, Mr Yap's advice convinced me that my nationality could be the key to a solution, so while I was still on leave of absence from detention I sent Tari a statement saying that I wanted to establish whether I could regain British nationality as I believed that my renunciation was based on a legal error. I asked her to be sure to take this matter further if I was re-arrested. What made me want to remain in Jakarta, as long as my luck held, was the thought that I was best placed there to earn loads of money teaching English so as to provide Tari and Anto with everything they needed to complete their education. There was no way the family could be expected to finance this, especially after Tari could no longer live with Lebah, who was by this time terminally ill.

In London, Amnesty International had been working on Bud's and my case since our arrest, with the help of adoption groups. After my re-arrest, Stefanie Grant, the researcher on Indonesia, reviewed the situation with Tari and decided to stop campaigning for me as an adoption case. Instead, the case was handed over to a lawyer, Sarah Leigh, to examine the question of my nationality. Sarah was at the time an articled clerk with a law firm in London and was doing voluntary work for Amnesty, helping to prepare adoption cases. It was Sarah's deft, professional and strongly committed handling of the whole affair that was crucial in reaching a satisfactory conclusion to my case.

What it boiled down to was this: was I or was I not an Indonesian national at the time I renounced British nationality in 1954? If it could be proven that I was not, my renunciation automatically became null and void. Soon after Sarah took on the case, she was informed by the Foreign

Office that the Home Office was prepared to consider revoking my renunciation if it could be proven that I was not an Indonesian citizen in 1954. For this to happen, a written statement would be required from the Indonesian Government that I 'was not and never had been a citizen of Indonesia'. The embassy in Jakarta had been asked to obtain such a statement.

At this point, Sarah decided to try to speed things up. She made what she called a 'veiled threat' to take the matter to the High Court if the British Government did not expedite proceedings and press the Indonesians for a statement. The statement, issued by the Indonesian Department of Justice, was not long in coming. It simply said that I had become an Indonesian citizen in 1959 following the enactment of a new nationality law in Indonesia in 1958, which stipulated that foreign women married to Indonesians would assume the nationality of their husbands within a year. There was no mention of my nationality status in 1954, though the implication was obvious. Even so, the British Government told Sarah that my renunciation would not be revoked unless the Indonesian Government could be prevailed upon to make a further statement to the effect that I was not an Indonesian national in 1954. Sarah argued that this was unreasonable; it would be virtually impossible to get the Indonesians to say any more than they had already said about someone in such a vulnerable position as me.

It was therefore decided to instruct counsel, Anthony Lester (now Lord Lester), to advise on the best solution to this problem. His advice was to take proceedings against the Government for a declaration that I was still a British national, because my renunciation of citizenship had not been valid in English law. This was very risky as it meant incurring enormous costs if we lost; we would have to pay the Government's costs as well as our own. An application for legal aid received short shrift from the Law Society on political grounds. They argued that I had been 'content to remain an Indonesian citizen during the time when Indonesia was in effect at war with Malaysia and when British soldiers had been killed in Malaysia', which meant that I was 'not a proper person for the Legal Aid Fund to support'. They were referring here to Sukarno's strategy of confrontation with Malaysia and Britain from 1963 to 1965.

Despite the lack of financial support and uncertainty about where the money would come from if the case were unsuccessful in court, Sarah decided to press on. There was a tense period while the family waited to hear whether the Government would concede or defend the claim within the time given for them to respond. It was a nail-biting finish. The Government finally wrote a short letter conceding that I was still a UK citizen. They also agreed to pay Sarah's costs.

Now that my British credentials had been restored, it was unclear whether the British Government would seek to persuade the Indonesians to set me free. No one seemed sure whether I now had dual nationality; under Indonesian law, dual nationality was not recognized. Even so, the British Government argued that if I was still an Indonesian national, they had no standing against the Government of my other nationality while I was in their territory. What happened next is not entirely clear. I later heard that the British Ambassador in Jakarta met Foreign Minister Adam Malik informally at a social event and suggested that it might help matters if I were released. Malik was keen to make a good impression since Indonesia was occupying the presidency of the UN General Assembly. He therefore decided to talk to the military about releasing me. This was apparently enough to swing the argument in my favour. By July, five months before my release, it had been decided that I would be coming home. As ever, I was the last person to know.

In London, Tari and Anto were now living in Miriam's flat in Central London, not the most suitable of arrangements for a number of reasons, especially as it meant travelling so far to school. Tari had also become engaged to Roger, a schoolteacher whom she got to know in a youth drama group, and they planned to get married on 7 August. In July, Mudjajin passed me a message, asking whether they should go ahead with the wedding or wait for my release. I had no idea what my release prospects were, so I urged them to go ahead. In the event, I missed the wedding by three months; Bud missed it by eight years.

It was not long after I had been measured for my travelling gear in October 1971 that two officers came to my cell in Bukit Duri and asked me to accompany them. It was the first Friday in November 1971. As usual, they wouldn't say where we were going. I was not to take any of my belongings, they said. We drove to Salemba Prison and they took me into a small out-house near the main gate. We sat round a table on comfortable chairs; clearly this was not going to be yet another interrogation. One of the officers took out a document from his briefcase and said that arrangements had been made for me to leave prison and go home to England. I was stunned and thrilled at the news. But before anything could happen, he said, I would be required to give an under-taking that I would sign a statement which he invited me to read. It said that, on my release, I would leave the country and never come back. My heart was thumping and I was shaking like a leaf at the suddenness of it all. After reading the statement over and over again, I said I wanted to consult with Bud before giving any such undertaking.

'I'm sorry, that won't be possible. You can see your husband before you leave but we cannot allow you to do so until you have told us whether you will sign. Everything that happens from now on depends on that.'

'But you are being unreasonable', I replied. 'He's right here, behind these walls. Why can't I consult him before taking such a momentous decision? I'll be leaving him here in prison and you want me to promise to sign a document pledging never to return to Indonesia. Can't you understand that I should speak to him first?'

'Sorry, but those are our orders, Ibu Carmel.'

Try as I might, they would not budge, so I decided to give them the undertaking they sought. Now, I asked, when will I be allowed to meet my husband. All in good time, was all they would say.

Then I began to think of the women I had left so abruptly. 'Can you please take me back to Bukit Duri to say goodbye to all my friends?' I asked.

'That's not allowed either', they said. 'We'll send someone there to pick up your belongings.' Again I pleaded with them but they were adamant. Couldn't they realize how cruel and unreasonable they were being?

Nor was I allowed to make contact with Par and Mudjajin to say goodbye. As far as I knew, they had no idea what was happening to me.

The officers in charge of the arrangements for my release and departure told me that I would be leaving the following Tuesday as the formalities would take several days, including jabs for immunization. The small room where we were sitting, plus a bedroom and bathroom behind, would be put at my disposal. This was a small apartment near the entrance to the prison that was used by the prison commander whenever he needed to stay on the premises overnight. So here I was, the 'house guest' of my old adversary, Sani Gondjo.

I did not meet Bud until Saturday afternoon, but this time, at least, the prison officers allowed us to meet in private. He was overjoyed at the news. My emotions were a mixture of sadness at having to leave him like this, not knowing when we might meet again, and joy at the realization that I would soon be with Tari and Anto again. We talked about whether my release might help to speed up his own release. As it turns out, my efforts were of no avail; he was to spend another seven years in detention.

I was taken to a clinic for the immunization jabs; for the rest of the time, I remained all alone in the apartment. The officers had warned me to make no attempt to attract the attention of visiting relatives when they congregated outside the prison on Saturday morning, bringing food for their men-folk. When they began to arrive, I sat by the window watching the familiar scene, hoping that someone would catch a glimpse of me. If anyone did, they made no sign.

My accommodation was rather grand by comparison with what I had had to put up with but I desperately missed the companionship of my fellow prisoners in Bukit Duri. During those last four days, my emotions were pulled in all directions. Hardly able to imagine the forthcoming meeting with my family in London, I spent most of the time thinking about the people I had grown to love – the tapols, and the families doing what they could to help. They were all so near, yet I was surrounded by a curtain of silence. My only visitors now were soldiers, bringing me food, telling me what would happen next, or just wanting to have a chat for a few minutes with 'Ibu Carmel'.

There was one visitor that I could have gladly done without. That was Sani Gondjo, the commander of Salemba Prison. He swaggered in, sat down and began to tell me what he thought of my impending release.

'It's nothing to do with me', he said. 'Why should we trust you to stick to the terms of your statement? I've told my superiors that I don't believe that you will not start criticizing the Government as soon as you get back to England. I've told them not to let you go.'

'But if I sign something, I will keep my word', I said, not very convincingly.

'I don't believe a word of it', he said, as he got up to leave.

At that point I hadn't even started to think about what I would do, but I knew that he was right.

The day of my release, Tuesday, 9 November, arrived and I was up very early, thrilled at the thought that I would soon be on my way home to England. I had to wait several hours before they came to pick me up. I was driven from Salemba Prison to army headquarters in Jakarta. There, waiting for me, were two diplomats from the British Embassy, a Mr Preston, the Consul-General, and Cindy Shepherd, a consular official. I had met Miss Shepherd before, though I couldn't remember where. We were led into a room where several army officers and government officials were seated round a large table; I was invited to sit down, in between the two diplomats. This was quite a gathering, all for me; I should have felt honoured. The Indonesians were not going to let me get away without a 'handing-over' ceremony. It was a huge farce, one of those ceremonials so beloved of Indonesian officialdom.

A Foreign Ministry official named Suparman presided over the proceedings and made a short address. He spoke about the generosity of the Indonesian authorities in deciding to release me and allowing me to leave the country; he hoped that I would respond by sticking to the terms of the statement I was about to sign. I nodded solemnly, though I was not given the chance to say anything. Mr Preston made a few polite remarks, thanking the Indonesians for their help in resolving this question.

Then the statement that I had already been shown was placed on the table for me to sign. The Foreign Ministry official and Mr Preston signed as co-witnesses. The statement reads, word for word as it appears in the original:

I, the undersigned,

Mrs CARMEL BUDIARDJO, Dra, née Brickman, born in London on June 18, 1925, Christian Protestant, Indonesian citizen of British origin, ex-official of the Department of Foreign Affairs of the Republic of Indonesia, latest address Djl Persatuan III/21 Jakarta, do sincerely declare the following:

1. I am prepared to renounce my Indonesian citizenship and to adopt again my former British nationality;

2. I am prepared to leave Indonesia for the United Kingdom as soon as possible under the supervision of the British Embassy in Jakarta, and not come back against in Indonesia;

3. I promise not to embark by whatever means and in Whatever way in political activities or in any other activities that might be hostile to or against the Government of the Republic of Indonesia;

4. I hereby express my gratitude for the pardon granted and the policy followed by the Indonesian Government is settling the case in which I have been involved, and I shall not undertake to sue nor bring any charges against the Government of the Republic of Indonesia.

Such is the statement I made truthfully and voluntarily, and without any pressure or coercion from the other party, before the functionaries of both the Republic of Indonesia and the British Embassy in Jakarta.

I well remember that at some point during the proceedings, Mr Preston made it clear that he was only there to witness my signature; the Embassy took no responsibility for the statement I had been required to sign. This was hardly surprising. How on earth could I be granted a pardon when I had never been convicted for anything? Nor did it make sense to say that 'there was no coercion from the other party'. My choice had been pretty stark: sign or else go back to prison.

It was evident from the language that no one at the embassy had helped to draft it. The copy I have bears no date, only the stamp of the Indonesian Foreign Ministry; some words have been corrected by hand and others are almost illegible.

After the formalities were over and done with, I was led away to a room with Miss Shepherd where she gave me a parcel of clothes. Everything fitted me fine, though I had trouble getting into the tights. From then on, I was in her charge. We left the building as quickly as possible and she hustled me into her car. We sped through the streets to her residence where she settled me down in her lounge, gave me a cup of tea and handed me my passport, adorned with a photo that had been taken from prison files, and my air ticket. She was clearly delighted to have got me out of the 'clutches of those awful people' and pleased to have completed her assignment. Cindy Shepherd had been in charge of my affairs for a long time and was very excited that things had turned out so well for me, at last. She didn't stop chattering. There was little I could say, as I found it very difficult to adjust to this sudden shift into surroundings that were so different from those I had just left.

As she drove me to the airport, I remember her telling me not to worry about my clothes being unfashionable.

'It's wonderful back home these days. Anything goes – mini skirts, knee-length, ankle-length. You can wear what you like', she told me enthusiastically. I hardly knew what she was talking about. Fashion was the last thing on my mind.

One thing had really annoyed her; after the ceremony, two army officers told her they would be at the airport to make sure I left on schedule.

'I told them not to bother. What do they think I'm going to do, spirit you away somewhere?' she said. When we arrived at the airport, there they were to 'see me off'. I was whisked through the VIP lounge; within minutes I was sitting on a plane, en route for London.

I can remember nothing about the flight except that I stared out of the window for most of the time and found it very difficult to sleep, trying yet again to adjust to strange surroundings.

When I arrived in London, it was bitterly cold, the first real winter's day of the year. I felt rather self-conscious arriving at Heathrow carrying a tiny bundle of belongings and dressed only in a jumper, skirt and jacket. It had been agreed that the family would give me a warm overcoat on my arrival. As I walked through the barrier, I saw Tari, Anto and Roger, the son-in-law about whom I knew so little. As we hugged and embraced each other, the tears flowing with joy, I felt as if I was in a dream. Just behind were Miriam, Ben and my mother, too full of emotions to say anything.

We drove in two cars to Tari and Roger's new home where Anto was also living. I sat in the back, next to Anto, hardly knowing what to say. Within minutes of leaving Heathrow, Roger stopped the car near a phone box and Tari got out to phone Sarah – I had no idea who she was – saying that she had insisted on being informed, the moment I arrived.

As we continued the journey into London, I suddenly realized that someone was missing.

'Where's Lebah?' I asked. In all the excitement I hadn't even noticed her absence. Tari turned round to look at me and began to sob. I knew then that she had died and that the family had decided not to tell me for fear of casting a shadow over this happy reunion.

Postscript

After arriving back in London, I soon realized that it would not be possible to plunge immediately into a campaign for the release of Indonesia's many tens of thousands of political prisoners. Everyone in the family agreed that my first responsibility was to press the Indonesian authorities to release Bud. If I had started campaigning publicly straight away, I would have given Jakarta a pretext to reject our pleas on his behalf. Although the statement I had been required to sign as the condition for my release was not worth the paper it was written on, it seemed advisable at the time to stand by the pledge I had given for at least a year so as not to give the military grounds to accuse me of acting in bad faith. But, as we might have known, the authorities were not interested in these subtleties. As we soon discovered, for them, it made no difference how I behaved.

None of the officials we wrote to, from Suharto down, even bothered to acknowledge our letters. Their decision to release me was not going to make things any easier for Bud. His fate was bound up with that of all the prisoners. During the early 1970s, there were no signs of any shift in the position of the military on the question of political imprisonment. On the contrary, when we began to hear about the scandalous conditions at the Buru forced labour camp, the need for an international campaign became extremely pressing.

Soon after my arrival in London, I familiarized myself with the work of Amnesty International and provided the secretariat in London with a great deal of information about the tapols whom I had got to know intimately. There was much I had to share with Amnesty about treatment, conditions in the prisons and, particularly, the practices of the army torturers; I was frequently invited to address Amnesty groups in the UK and elsewhere.

It soon became apparent to many of us in London, however, that the work of Amnesty was not enough, that we needed an organization devoted specifically to Indonesia. Thus, TAPOL, the British Campaign for the Release of Indonesian Political Prisoners, was born. At the time of its birth in August 1973, the only other group working for similar objectives anywhere in the world was in Holland. It seemed extra-ordinary to me that country-specific groups were working in many parts of the world for Greece under the colonels, Chile under Pinochet and the Philippines under Marcos. Yet Indonesia, the worst violator of them all, was largely ignored.

In its early beginnings, TAPOL owed much of its success to the activities of various members of the family and the support of friends. My sister Miriam, a casting director in films, knew many famous film stars who were only too willing to join us in demonstrations. When Queen Elizabeth visited Indonesia, our demonstration consisted mainly of relatives, demanding Bud's release. One of our most successful activities was the production of a play in a London theatre about Buru, written by Tari's husband Roger and directed by the leading British film director Lindsay Anderson.

During the 1970s, other groups in Indonesia became the target of the repressive machinery that had been initially created to crush the left-wing movement. The invasion of East Timor in 1975 added a new dimension to the work of TAPOL. We also began to get information about atrocities in West Papua, occupied by Indonesia since 1963. As the focus of our campaigning broadened and our activities began to extend well beyond the borders of Britain, we changed the sub-title of the organization to the 'Indonesia Human Rights Campaign'. The regime constantly vilified us as an offshoot of the PKI and accused me personally of being engaged in a hate campaign against Indonesia. Far from damaging our links with many groups that were on the front line in the struggle for democracy and against human rights abuses, this malicious campaign only enhanced them.

During the early years of TAPOL's existence, I had to earn my keep by taking on a job, which meant running the organization on a part-time basis. I had no home of my own and lived at the time with Miriam and my mother, doing all the organizational work on the kitchen table. Without Miriam's support, it would have been impossible to get through those first difficult years.

The big breakthrough financially came with an anonymous donation of $15,000, from the legacy of a well-wisher in the US whose identity we never discovered. From that time on, TAPOL became financially viable and I was able to work full time, thanks to regular support from a variety of sources outside the UK. Unfortunately, the strictures imposed within Britain on funding activities seen as 'political' by the Charities

Commission have forced us to turn for help to funding agencies in other countries.

As for the family, it came as a shock to me to learn that Lebah had died more than a year before my release from prison. I only felt the full force of her loss after hearing about her long and painful illness from her daughters Nina and Karen. From my brother Ben, I learned about the pleasures of walking in the countryside, a favourite English recreation that I missed out on in my youth.

As for Miriam, she became my dearest friend. I had spent so many years of my life away from home, first in Prague and later in Indonesia, that it was not until I returned to London in 1971 that I became very close to her. Unmarried to the end of her life, she was devoted to her many nephews and nieces, including Tari and Anto. It was not until after she died in 1977 and left a small legacy that I was able to buy a home of my own, a tiny flat in a London suburb which became the hub of TAPOL campaigning.

Normally, with age and as children grow up, people move from bigger homes to smaller ones but, in my case, I moved in the opposite direction. I quickly outgrew the accommodation I had and was forced to find myself a three-bedroom house and turn two of the upstairs rooms into offices. It sometimes comes as a surprise to visitors to realise that TAPOL functions in such modest surroundings.

Bud was released from prison in 1978, having by then spent twelve years in detention without charge or trial. Some months later, he left Indonesia to settle down in London, where he has been able to make a home of his own, after we decided to separate. I am in the fortunate position of living close enough to Tari and Anto to enjoy the pleasure of having grandchildren.

As long as the Suharto military dictatorship remains in power, there will be work for TAPOL to do, and possibly after he falls from power as well. Although his position still seems impregnable, the military grip on the country is definitely in decline. My only hope is that I live long enough to celebrate his downfall and demise, and to see the creation of a democratic Indonesia.

Chronology

1965

October 1 The Untung Group of army officers stages a coup attempt by kidnapping and murdering six top-ranking army generals. The attempt is crushed on the same day by troops under the command of Major-General Suharto, signalling the start of the Suharto Coup.

October 10 Using powers conferred on him by President Sukarno, Suharto sets up Kopkamtib, the Operational Command for the Restoration of Security and Order, the army security agency which he uses to outlaw left-wing organizations and round up hundreds of thousands of people.

Mid-October Army units, spearheaded by the élite corps, RPKAD, start the massacre of alleged communist suspects in the countryside in Central Java. The massacres spread to East Java, Bali, North Sumatra and other parts of the country, killing an estimated one million people within a six-month period.

October Anti-communist mobs attack communist and left-wing offices and the homes of communist suspects in Jakarta and other cities.

Mid-October Budiardjo, my husband, is arrested for the first time.

Late October Our house is ransacked by anti-communist mobs.

Late October I am arrested, but released several hours later.

November 22 D. N. Aidit, Chairman of the Indonesian Communist Party, is captured in Central Java by an army unit led by Colonel Yasir Hadibroto and shot dead a few hours later.

December Sukarno dispatches an investigation team to assess the magnitude of the killings that have been sweeping the country since October. The team concludes that 78,000 people have been killed, though members admit that the actual figure is probably ten times that amount.

1966

January/February Army-backed student demonstrations call for the crushing of the PKI and press for action against President Sukarno and members of his cabinet. The political and economic crisis created by the events of 1 October, the massacres and the constant undermining of the Sukarno government are nearing a climax.

March 11 A meeting of the cabinet in Jakarta, chaired by President Sukarno, is surrounded by troops and Sukarno is forced to flee to his palace in Bogor.

Under pressure from three generals acting at the behest of Suharto, Sukarno signs over powers to Suharto 'to take all necessary steps to guarantee security and calm and the stability of the running of the Government'. Suharto uses these limited powers to take over the reins of government.

March 13 Thirteen members of Sukarno's cabinet are arrested on the orders of Suharto.

Mid-March Bud is released.

Mid-March Suharto convenes a meeting of the heavily purged Supreme Consultative Assembly, the MPRS, to confirm the 11 March Order as a state decree.

Late March Bud is rearrested.

1967

March Suharto convenes a second meeting of the Supreme Consultative Assembly which strips Sukarno of his designation as President-for-Life and appoints Suharto Acting President.

December After months of trying, I secure the release of Bud by General Sumitro who had ordered his arrest 21 months earlier.

1968

March Suharto convenes a third meeting of the MPRS at which he is appointed President.

July The army launches Operation Trisula to smash a base set up in South Blitar, East Java, by communists and others in an attempt to restore the Party. Several leaders are shot dead and hundreds are arrested.

September 3 Bud and I are arrested. We are held for several weeks in a new interrogation centre, Satgas-Pusat on the outskirts of Jakarta.

End September Bud and I are transferred to Likdam detention camp in central Jakarta.

November Bud is transferred to Salemba Prison.

1969

February Human rights activist J. C. Princen exposes the massacre, torture and maltreatment of several thousand communist suspects in Purwodadi, Central Java. Several newspapers cover the issue for a few weeks until the story is killed by army censors.

June Tari and Anto leave for London with the assistance of the representative in Jakarta of the World Council of Churches.

August The Buru hard labour penal camp is set up in Maluku. More than 13,000 male tapols are sent there and remain there till the late 1970s.

December I am transferred to my third detention camp, Satgas-Jaya.

1970

May I am allowed to leave Satgas-Jaya, but remain under the supervision of officers from the unit.

June 20 Sukarno, Indonesia's first President, held since 1966 under house arrest, dies.

August I am rearrested and taken to Bukit Duri Prison.

1971

April A labour camp for women tapols is opened in Plantungan, Central Java, a former leper colony. A group of women are transferred to the camp from Bukit Duri Prison, followed by several other groups later in the year.

July After months of pressure on the British Government by an English lawyer, the Government finally concedes that I continue to be a British subject because my renunciation of British citizenship in 1954 was legally flawed.

November 9 I am released and fly to London to be reunited with Tari and Anto.

Glossary

CPM   Corps Polisi Militer, Military Police Corps.

DEKON   Deklarasi Ekonomi, the Economic Declaration.

G30S   Gerakan 30 September, the 30 September Movement initiated by three middle-ranking army officers led by Lieutenant-Colonel Untung.

Gerwani   Gerakan Wanita Indonesia, the Indonesian Women's Movement, banned in October 1965.

HSI   Himpunan Sarjana Indonesia, Indonesian Association of Scholars, banned in October 1965.

IPPI   Ikatan Pemuda Pelajar Indonesia, Indonesian school-pupils association.

Kalong   Operation of the Bats, torture centre of the Jakarta Military Command.

Kopkamtib   Komando Pemulihan Keamanan dan Ketertiban, Operational Command for the Restoration of Security and Order set up by Major-General Suharto on 10 October 1965.

Kostrad   Komando Strategis Angkatan Darat, the Army Strategic Command.

Likdam   Jakarta Military Command's centre of investigation, also known as Lidikus.

Pancasila   The ideological doctrine of the Indonesian State, consisting of five principles: belief in one God, nationalism, humanitarianism, consensus through consultation, and social justice.

PKI   Partai Komunis Indonesia, the Communist Party of Indonesia.

PNI   Partai Nasional Indonesia, the Indonesian National Party.

Satgas-Jaya   The army's Special Task-Force in Jakarta.

Satgas-Pusat   The army's Central Special Task-Force.

SOBSI   Sentral Organisasi Buruh Selruh Indonesia, All Indonesian Trade Union Organization.